T0327589

RESEARCH IN MARITIME HISTORY
NO. 37

INTERNATIONAL MERCHANT SHIPPING IN THE NINETEENTH AND TWENTIETH CENTURIES: THE COMPARATIVE DIMENSION

Edited by
Lewis R. Fischer and Even Lange

International Maritime Economic History Association

St. John's, Newfoundland
2008

ISSN 1188-3928
ISBN 978-0-9738934-7-2

Research in Maritime History is available free of charge to members of the International Maritime Economic History Association. The price to others is US $25 per copy, plus US $5 postage and handling.

Back issues of *Research in Maritime History* are available:

No. 1 (1991)   David M. Williams and Andrew P. White (comps.), *A Select Bibliography of British and Irish University Theses about Maritime History, 1792-1990*

No. 2 (1992)   Lewis R. Fischer (ed.), *From Wheel House to Counting House: Essays in Maritime Business History in Honour of Professor Peter Neville Davies*

No. 3 (1992)   Lewis R. Fischer and Walter Minchinton (eds.), *People of the Northern Seas*

No. 4 (1993)   Simon Ville (ed.), *Shipbuilding in the United Kingdom in the Nineteenth Century: A Regional Approach*

No. 5 (1993)   Peter N. Davies (ed.), *The Diary of John Holt*

No. 6 (1994)   Simon P. Ville and David M. Williams (eds.), *Management, Finance and Industrial Relations in Maritime Industries: Essays in International Maritime and Business History*

No. 7 (1994)   Lewis R. Fischer (ed.), *The Market for Seamen in the Age of Sail*

No. 8 (1995)   Gordon Read and Michael Stammers (comps.), *Guide to the Records of Merseyside Maritime Museum, Volume 1*

No. 9 (1995)   Frank Broeze (ed.), *Maritime History at the Crossroads: A Critical Review of Recent Historiography*

No. 10 (1996)   Nancy Redmayne Ross (ed.), *The Diary of a Maritimer, 1816-1901: The Life and Times of Joseph Salter*

No. 11 (1997)   Faye Margaret Kert, *Prize and Prejudice: Privateering and Naval Prize in Atlantic Canada in the War of 1812*

No. 12 (1997)   Malcolm Tull, *A Community Enterprise: The History of the Port of Fremantle, 1897 to 1997*

No. 13 (1997)   Paul C. van Royen, Jaap R. Bruijn and Jan Lucassen, *'Those Emblems of Hell'? European Sailors and the Maritime Labour Market, 1570-1870*

No. 14 (1998)   David J. Starkey and Gelina Harlaftis (eds.), *Global Markets: The Internationalization of The Sea Transport Industries Since 1850*

No. 15 (1998)   Olaf Uwe Janzen (ed.), *Merchant Organization and Maritime Trade in the North Atlantic, 1660-1815*

No. 16 (1999)   Lewis R. Fischer and Adrian Jarvis (eds.), *Harbours and Havens: Essays in Port History in Honour of Gordon Jackson*

No. 17 (1999)   Dawn Littler, *Guide to the Records of Merseyside Maritime Museum, Volume 2*

No. 18 (2000)   Lars U. Scholl (comp.), *Merchants and Mariners: Selected Maritime Writings of David M. Williams*

No. 19 (2000)   Peter N. Davies, *The Trade Makers: Elder Dempster in West Africa, 1852-1972, 1973-1989*

No. 20 (2001)   Anthony B. Dickinson and Chesley W. Sanger, *Norwegian Whaling in Newfoundland: The Aquaforte Station and the Ellefsen Family, 1902-1908*

No. 21 (2001)   Poul Holm, Tim D. Smith and David J. Starkey (eds.), *The Exploited Seas: New Directions for Marine Environmental History*

No. 22 (2002)   Gordon Boyce and Richard Gorski (eds.), *Resources and Infrastructures in the Maritime Economy, 1500-2000*

No. 23 (2002)   Frank Broeze, *The Globalisation of the Oceans: Containerisation from the 1950s to the Present*

No. 24 (2003)   Robin Craig, *British Tramp Shipping, 1750-1914*

No. 25 (2003)   James Reveley, *Registering Interest: Waterfront Labour Relations in New Zealand, 1953 to 2000*

No. 26 (2003)   Adrian Jarvis, *In Troubled Times: The Port of Liverpool, 1905-1938*

No. 27 (2004)   Lars U. Scholl and Merja-Liisa Hinkkanen (comps.), *Sail and Steam: Selected Maritime Writings of Yrjö Kaukiainen*

No. 28 (2004)   Gelina Harlaftis and Carmel Vassallo (eds.), *New Directions in Mediterranean Maritime History*

No. 29 (2005)   Gordon Jackson, *The British Whaling Trade*

No. 30 (2005)   Lewis Johnman and Hugh Murphy, *Scott Lithgow: Déjà vu All Over Again! The Rise and Fall of a Shipbuilding Company*

No. 31 (2006)   David Gleicher, *The Rescue of the Third Class on the Titanic: A Revisionist History*

No. 32 (2006)   Stig Tenold, *Tankers in Trouble: Norwegian Shipping and the Crisis of the 1970s and 1980s*

No. 33 (2007)   Torsten Feys, Lewis R. Fischer, Stéphane Hoste and Stephan Vanfraechem, *Maritime Transport and Migration: The Connections between Maritime and Migration Networks*

No. 34 (2007)   A.B. Dickinson, *Seal Fisheries of the Falkland Islands and Dependencies: An Historical Review*

No. 35 (2007)   Tapio Bergholm, Lewis R. Fischer and M. Elisabetta Tonizzi (eds.), *Making Global and Local Connections: Historical Perspectives on Ports*

No. 36 (2008)   Mark C. Hunter, *Policing the Seas: Anglo-American Relations and the Equatorial Atlantic, 1819-1865*

Research in Maritime History would like to thank Memorial University of Newfoundland for its generous financial assistance in support of this volume.

Table of Contents

Contributors' Notes / iii

Introduction / vii

Yrjö Kaukiainen, "Growth, Diversification and Globalization: Main Trends in International Shipping since 1850" / 1

Stig Tenold, "Norwegian Shipping in the Twentieth Century" / 57

Gelina Harlaftis, "The Greek Shipping Sector, c. 1850-2000" / 79

Peter N. Davies, "A Guide to the Emergence of Japan's Modern Shipping Industries" / 105

Sarah Palmer, "British Shipping from the Late Nineteenth Century to the Present" / 125

Graeme J. Milne, "North of England Shipowners and Their Business Connections in the Nineteenth Century" / 143

Gordon Boyce, "Network Structures, Processes and Dynamics: Inter-firm Cooperative Frameworks in the Shipping Industry" / 165

ABOUT THE EDITORS

LEWIS R. FISCHER < lfischer@mun.ca > is Professor of History at Memorial University of Newfoundland, Editor-in-Chief of the *International Journal of Maritime History* and Series Editor of *Research in Maritime History*. A former Secretary-General of the International Commission for Maritime History and Secretary of the Canadian Nautical Research Society, Professor Fischer has served on numerous committees and editorial boards around the world and has been a Visiting Professor at universities in Australia, Germany, Norway and the United Kingdom. A specialist in nineteenth- and twentieth-century maritime economic history, his recent publications include *Maritime Transport and Migration: The Connections between Maritime and Migration Networks* (St. John's, 2007, *Research in Maritime History* No. 33, edited with Torsten Feys, Stéphane Hoste and Stephan Vanfraechem) and *Making Global and Local Connections: Historical Perspectives on Ports* (St. John's, 2007, *Research in Maritime History* No. 35, edited with Tapio Bergholm and M. Elisabetta Tonizzi).

EVEN LANGE < even.lange@iakh.uio.no > is Professor of History at the University of Oslo, Senior Researcher at the Institute for Social Research and Co-chair of the Forum for Contemporary History at the University. He was also the founder and Director of the Centre for Business History at the Norwegian School of Management between 1989 and 2000 and President of the Organizing Committee of the Nineteenth International Congress of Historical Sciences, held in Oslo in 2000. He has been a Visiting Professor at the University of Aix-en-Provence, the University of Wisconsin, the University of Toulouse-le-Mirail and the University of Oxford, as well as a former Vice President of the European Business History Association and a member of the academic advisory board of the European Association for Banking History. He is the author of many books and articles on industrial development, banking and economic policy in the nineteenth and twentieth centuries, including serving as co-editor of the most recent multi-volume History of Norway, where he also authored the volume covering the period 1935-1970.

CONTRIBUTORS

GORDON BOYCE < Gordon.Boyce@newcastle.edu.au > is Head of the School
of Business and Management and Director of the Centre of Institutional
and Organisational Performance at the University of Newcastle,
Australia. He serves on several editorial boards and academic societies
and has been a Visiting Fellow at the Australian National University,
Duke University and the Centre for Business History. He is the author of
six books and numerous journal articles, book chapters and reviews. His
recent publications include *How Organisations Connect: Investing in
Communication* (Carlton, VIC, 2006, edited with Simon Ville and
Stuart MacIntyre); Over *Half a Million Careful Owners: A 75-Year
History of PSIS, 1928-2003* (Wellington, NZ, 2005); and *Co-operative
Structures in Global Business: A New Approach to Networks, Technology
Transfer Agreements, Strategic Alliances and Agency Relationships*
(London, 2000). He has been the recipient of the Cass Prize, a Caird
Fellowship and a British Commission for Transport History Prize.

PETER N. DAVIES < peterndavies@btinternet.com > is Professor Emeritus of
Economic History at the University of Liverpool. A former President of
both the International Commission for Maritime History and the
International Maritime Economic History Association, he has served as
Visiting Professor at Musashi University in Tokyo and at Shudo
University in Hiroshima. His published works include studies of major
Liverpool shipping companies and (with Tomohei Chida) of the Japanese
shipping and shipbuilding industries.

GELINA HARLAFTIS < gelina@ionio.gr > has taught maritime history at the
University of Piraeus (1991-2002) and since 2003 has been at the
Department of History of the Ionian University in Corfu. A former
President of the International Maritime Economic History Association
(2004-2008), she has been a Visiting Professor at universities in Canada,
the United States and the United Kingdom. Her most recent book,
*Leadership in World Shipping: Greek Family Firms in International
Business*, co-authored with Ioannis Theotokas, will be published shortly
by Palgrave/Macmillan in London.

YRJÖ KAUKIAINEN <yrjo.kaukiainen@helsinki.fi> is Emeritus Professor of European History in the Department of History at the University of Helsinki and a former President of the International Maritime Economic History Association. His research has focussed in particular on the history of shipping in the eighteenth, nineteenth and twentieth centuries, as well as on the history of information transmission in the nineteenth century. His publications include *Sailing into Twilight: Finnish Shipping in an Age of Transport Revolution, 1860–1914* (Jyväskylä, 1991); and *A History of Finnish Shipping* (London, 1993). A selection of his articles was published as Lars U. Scholl and Merje-Liisa Hinkkanen (comps.), *Sail and Steam: Selected Maritime Writings of Yrjö Kaukiainen* (St. John's, Researh in Maritime History No. 27, 2004).

GRAEME J. MILNE <G.J.Milne@liv.ac.uk> is Research Editor with the AHRC Liverpool in Print Project at the School of History in the University of Liverpool. His publications include "British Business and the Telephone, 1878-1911," *Business History,* XLIX, No. 2 (2007), 163-185; "Maritime Liverpool," in John Belchem (ed.), *Liverpool 800: Culture, Character, History* (Liverpool, 2006), 257-309; and *North East England, 1850-1914: The Dynamics of a Maritime-Industrial Region* (Woodbridge, 2006).

SARAH PALMER <S.R.Palmer@greenwich.ac.uk> is Professor of Maritime History and Director of the Greenwich Maritime Institute at the University of Greenwich. An economic historian, her research and teaching interests focus particularly on commercial shipping, port development and maritime policy from the nineteenth century to the present. She chairs the British Commission for Maritime History and has been a Trustee of National Museums Liverpool since 2000.

STIG TENOLD <Stig.Tenold@nhh.no> is Associate Professor of Economic History in the Department of Economics at the Norwegian School of Economics and Business Administration. He has published primarily on modern maritime history, including *Tankers in Trouble: Norwegian Shipping and the Crisis of the 1970s and 1980s (Research in Maritime History* No. 32, St. Johns, 2006). Among his recent articles are "Strategies, Market Concentration and Hegemony in Chemical Parcel Tanker Shipping, 1960-1985," *Business History*, C, No. 3, (2008), 291-309 (with Hugh Murphy); and "Norway's Interwar Tanker Expansion: A Reappraisal," *Scandinavian Economic History Review*, CV, No.3 (2007), 244-261.

Introduction

Lewis R. Fischer and Even Lange

Almost five centuries ago, the great Italian political philosopher Niccolò Machiavelli observed that "one change always leaves the way prepared for the introduction of another."[1] Machiavelli, of course, was writing about political transformations, and there is no evidence in any of his works that he ever turned his inquisitive mind to the topic of waterborne transport. Nonetheless, his insight that one shift leads ineluctably to even greater changes certainly is an apt way to think about the evolution of merchant shipping since the mid-nineteenth century.

Few observers of the marine transportation sector in the middle of the nineteenth century could possibly have been prepared for the exponential growth in the rate of change that reconfigured merchant shipping over the next 150 years. The repeal of the British Navigation Acts – a reflection of the replacement of the doctrine of mercantilism by a movement toward free trade – combined with a surge of technological innovation to lay the groundwork for a total transformation of the world economy and international trade. The merchant marine was at the heart of this process of globalization.[2]

Between 1850 and 2000 virtually everything about the shipping sector was altered beyond virtually beyond recognition. In the middle of the nineteenth century the vast bulk of deep-sea trade was carried in wooden vessels propelled by the wind. Although ships and shipping had changed a great deal since the beginnings of the industrial revolution, the demand for reliable carrying capacity after 1850 spurred a veritable revolution. Wood was soon superseded by iron and steel, and improvements in boiler and engine technology led first to the dominance of steam by the 1880s and by the Second World War to the triumph of turbines and motor ships. Vessels became ever larger, more specialized and, for a time at least, faster. Cargo-handling was improved through the increasing use of mechanical devices both on ships and in ports, and the time required to load and

---

[1]Niccolò Machiavelli, *The Prince* (1532; reprint, New York, 2004), 17.

[2]The most provocative study of the historical process of globalization is Kevin H. O'Rourke and Jeffrey G. Williamson, *Globalization and History: The Evolution of a Nineteenth-Century Atlantic Economy* (Cambridge, MA, 1999). O'Rourke and Williamson downplay the role of technology in bring this about, preferring instead to emphasize the role of factor flows, especially trade. The most rapidly growing form of trade, especially in the period 1850-1950, was of course carried by sea.

discharge goods plummeted. After 1945 the introduction of giant tankers and a drive towards intermodalism culminated in the modern container vessel and a new emphasis on logistics which totally transformed the maritime sector. All of this was abetted by significant innovations in communications: first the telegraph, then the wireless and finally satellite-based systems that made it possible for and managers to control the global deployment of vessels with a precision that would have baffled their nineteenth-century counterparts. This was all accompanied by a revolution in ownership. Aside from the great chartered trading companies, in the first half of the nineteenth century most of the men (and the occasional woman) who invested in shipping were merchants who used their vessels to carry their own goods; other people's consignments were loaded only when there was sufficient space. But soon a new breed of investor emerged who thought of themselves as shipowners, and the increasing need for capital also led to a search for new forms of business organization, including single-ship and limited-liabilities companies. This latter point also reminds us of the shifting role of government in stimulating (or hindering) the development of and industry like shipping. Almost everywhere, the impact of political decisions played a significant role in the shifting fortunes of national fleets in the nineteenth and twentieth centuries.

In short, the century and a half after 1850 was a period of unprecedented change both on land and at sea. This fact is the underlying theme that links the seven essays that comprise this book. The volume begins with a lengthy essay by Professor Yrjö Kaukiainen of the University of Helsinki which analyzes the myriad changes that swept through the shipping industry in the wake of the growth of the international economy and increasing globalization from the mid-nineteenth century to the present. He weaves together a vast amount of data to provide the context for the chapters that follow. In particular, he concentrates on the inextricable relationship between the growth of trade and the provision of shipping tonnage and demonstrates that ocean transport costs today are in real terms on average only about one-fifth of the prevailing levels in 1850.

Professor Kaukiainen's essay is followed by four articles on some of the major fleets that contested for global supremacy over the past century and a half. Dr. Stig Tenold of the Norwegian School of Economics and Business Administration analyzes the success of the Norwegian fleet in the twentieth century. He shows how Norwegian shipowners built upon the "traditions and experience" of their forbears, adapted extremely well to changing conditions and took advantage of domestic policy changes, especially the introduction of the Norwegian International Shipping Register in 1987, to maintain and enhance the country's role in international shipping. This was always largely a tramp fleet, and despite some attempts to shift the balance, Norway was never a major player in international liner shipping.

Norway is an excellent example of a nation whose share of international shipping has far outstripped its shares of both world population and international trade. This observation is equally true of Greece, as Professor Gelina Harlaftis of the Ionian University shows in her essay on Greek shipping since 1850. She demonstrates that through the development of unique business networks and a skilful use of the opportunities presented by flags of convenience, Greek shipowners were able to amass and operate the world's largest fleet in the post-World War II era. No other major shipping nation constructed business networks in quite the same way as did Greece, and her insightful discussion of how these webs functioned shows that how important they were to Greek success. Like Norway, Greek shipowners always concentrated on the tramp sector.

Japan, on the other hand, followed a very different path in developing what was by 2000 the second largest fleet in the world, as Professor Peter Davies of the University of Liverpool shows. Perhaps more than in any of the other major shipping countries, the Japanese experience has been marked historically by the close relationship between government and shipowners. Professor Davies shows how these close ties developed and the way in which government policy created a heightened comparative advantage for Japanese ship- owning companies. He also stresses the close links between the shipbuilding and shipowning sectors in enhancing these benefits and shows how, unlike either their Norwegian or Greek competitors, the major Japanese shipping firms concentrated on liner shipping.

If the close ties between shipowning and shipbuilding and sympathetic government policy have assisted the Japanese in maintaining their position in international merchant shipping, the increasing separation of these sectors are one reason for the less successful experience of the United Kingdom in the twentieth century. As Professor Sarah Palmer of the University of Greenwich reminds us, at the beginning of the twentieth century over forty percent of the world's merchant tonnage flew the Union Jack, a figure that had been remarkably stable since the middle of the nineteenth century. But British hegemony began to shrink in the interwar years, and after 1945 the story has largely been one of both absolute and relative decline, to the point where in 2007 the UK's share of world tonnage was less than three percent. As Professor Palmer shows, if part of British success in the nineteenth century can be attributed to the close ties between shipowners and shipbuilders, the period of decline was marked by an increasing separation between the two. It was also characterized by a precipitous decline in the country's role in liner shipping and, perhaps, less of a willingness to innovate. The role of government, in sharp contrast to the experience of Japan, also shifted. In the nineteenth century government subsidies had played a major role in stimulating British success, but halting and inconsistent policies in the twentieth century did little to assist in the preservation of traditional British dominance in merchant shipping.

The final two essays in this collection focus more on shipowners than on the experience of national fleets. Dr. Graeme Milne of the University of Liverpool provides a careful analysis of business networks in the North of England in the nineteenth century. He places shipowners within the wider regional and national economies in which they operated and stresses the importance of understanding not only the relationships among shipowners but also those between shipowners, merchants and other economic actors. Perhaps his principal finding is to underscore the importance of the pathbreaking work of Mark Casson and others on the need to understand business culture and the way in which it affected commercial decisions.[3] Shipowners were part of this commercial milieu, and the way in which they conceptualized it played a decisive role in the way in which they made decisions.

The final essay in this book is by Professor Gordon Boyce of the University of Newcastle in Australia. His article addresses a topic which has become the focus of debate in recent years: the role of theory in understanding the decisions of shipowners.[4] In a powerful essay, Professor Boyce argues that network theory, in particular, can generate a series of important questions and insights that maritime historians can utilize to better comprehend the industry. His examples, drawn principally from his ongoing studies of British shipowning, make a compelling case for the utility of the judicious use of theory in maritime history.

This volume grows out of a major project on the history of the Norwegian deep-sea merchant marine in the nineteenth and twentieth centuries sponsored by the Norwegian Shipowners' Association. Centred at the University of Oslo, it aims not only to comprehend the development of the Norwegian ocean-going fleet but also to place it in the broadest possible international context. These essays reflect the thrust of this endeavour.

---

[3]See especially Mark C. Casson, *Information and Organization: A New Perspective on the Theory of the Firm* (Oxford, 1997).

[4]For an opposing perspective, see Lewis Johnman and Hugh Murphy, "Maritime and Business History in Britain: Past, Present and Future?" *International Journal of Maritime History*, XIX, No. 1 (2007), 239-270.

Growth, Diversification and Globalization: Main Trends in International Shipping since 1850

Yrjö Kaukiainen

Introduction: Shipping and International Trade

For almost five decades the history of long-term trends in global ocean transport has attracted the interest mainly of economists and economic historians rather than maritime historians.[1] Maritime historians, on the other hand, have concentrated on topics which have been more limited in chronological or geographical scope or with special aspects of shipping history. This paradox likely reflects the different traditions of the various specialties. Maritime historians typically have been empirically oriented scholars who know all too well the gaps in our understanding of many of the most important trends of international shipping, even for a period as recent as

---

[1]The pioneer in an empirical sense was the British statistician, L. Isserlis, especially his "Tramp Shipping Cargoes, and Freights," *Journal of the Royal Statistical Society*, CI, No. 1 (1938), 53-146. For more recent research see, in particular, Douglass C. North, "Ocean Freight Rates and Economic Development, 1750-1913," *Journal of Economic History*, XVIII, No. 4 (1958), 537-555; North, "Sources of Productivity Change in Ocean Shipping, 1600-1850," *Journal of Political Economy*, LXXVI, No. 5 (1968), 953-970; C. Knick Harley, "Ocean Freight Rates and Productivity, 1740-1913: The Primacy of Mechanical Invention Reaffirmed," *Journal of Economic History*, XLVIII, No. 4 (1988), 851-876; Harley, "Late Nineteenth Century Transportation, Trade and Settlement," in Wolfram Fischer, R. Marvin McInnis and Jürgen Schneider (eds.), *The Emergence of a World Economy, 1500-1914* (2 vols., Wiesbaden, 1986), II, 539-617; Gary C. Hufbauer, "World Economic Integration: The Long View," *International Economic Insights*, II, No. 3 (1991), 26-27; David Hummels, "Have International Transportation Costs Declined?" (Unpublished paper, 1999, available at http://www.mgmt.purdue.edu/faculty/hummelsd/); Antoni Estevadeordal, Brian Frantz and Alan M. Taylor, "The Rise and Fall of World Trade, 1870-1939," *Quarterly Journal of Economics*, CXVIII, No. 2 (2003), 359-407; Kevin H. O'Rourke and Jeffrey G. Williamson, *Globalization and History: The Evolution of a Nineteenth-Century Atlantic Economy* (Cambridge, MA, 1999), 30–41; and Saif I. Shah Mohammed and Jeffrey G. Williamson, "Freight Rates and Productivity Gains in British Tramp Shipping, 1869-1950," *Explorations in Economic History*, XLI, No. 2 (2004), 172-203.

the last century and a half. Rather than attempting far-reaching speculations, they prefer to collect reliable data from smaller parts of the universe which can be adequately mapped with available resources and to produce analyses solidly founded on such material. Economists, on the other hand – at least compared with historians – depend more on theoretical approaches and logical deductions than empirical analyses and are primarily interested in general rules of economic behaviour and development. Their interest in shipping history is explained by a concern with the growth of international trade, especially after 1850, since it is generally believed that this – in addition to factors like tariff policies and exchange systems – was triggered by a decline in transport costs. As a result, ocean shipping became one of the major exogenous variables to explain the rapid economic growth.

Since the demand for shipping services is closely connected to the volume of goods exchanged, the growth of international trade is undoubtedly a meaningful context within which to study the fundamental trends and crucial developments of maritime transport. Yet the doubts of the empiricists are far from irrelevant: the availability of quantitative (or quantifiable) data, in particular on the aggregate level, is tightly bound to *anno domini*: while there is a fairly satisfactory supply of statistics on global shipping, merchant tonnage and freight development for the 1980s and 1990s, the dearth of material places serious constraints on the study of the late nineteenth and early twentieth centuries. Considering this asymmetrical distribution of data, it is surprising that much more research has been conducted on the late nineteenth than on the late twentieth century.

There is always a risk that poor and seemingly random data may have affected the theoretical and methodological approaches which have been applied in the study of shipping and trade. In any case, there has been a long tradition of regarding transport costs as an exogenous factor and thus of seeing the causal relationship as operating in only one direction, from ocean shipping to international trade. And it has been equally common to explain the decline of transport costs primarily in terms of technological developments which resulted in more efficient and economical ships. Yet it must also be remembered that the demand for shipping services depends primarily on the volume of trade, which means that the price of these services will in the short run be determined by the respective levels of demand and supply. This, however, did not only result in short-term market imbalances and sudden fluctuations in freight rates. Since shipping is a capital-intensive industry and the life expectancy of vessels is fairly long, the supply of tonnage changes only slowly, and market imbalances – typically tonnage surpluses – can be sufficiently persistent to produce a distinct longer-term cycle in the pattern of ocean freights. On the other hand, a long-term growth in international trade (demand) is of importance irrespective of the actual balance between it and the supply of vessels. Growing volumes of cargo can induce favourable economies of scale which may substantially lower the unit costs of shipping.

The relationship between international trade and ocean transport is further complicated by the fact that there is not, and hardly ever has been, a single homogeneous, competitive and continuous freight market for the carriage of all commodities. While it is true that local freight markets began to be integrated into an international system before the middle of the nineteenth century, there was also an increasing specialization and diversification of shipping which has continued since that time. As new types of vessels, such as tankers, passenger and cargo liners, bulk carriers and container ships, were developed to carry different cargoes at optimal efficiency, the freight market was fragmented into corresponding spheres. Such sub-markets not only differed from each other in terms of ships and cargoes but also in terms of market mechanisms and price-setting. Thus, there was not a single balance (or imbalance) between demand and supply but several.[2]

The development of both trade and maritime transport also reflected regional or national differences in terms of so-called "comparative advantages," above all the prices of capital and labour. It is particularly significant that various sectors of shipping presented quite different combinations of factors of production: the "quality end" (big liners) has often thrived in a capital-intensive, "high-cost" environment, while technically less efficient shipping (such as sailing vessels in the late nineteenth century) were associated with "low-cost" countries. In addition to general economic development, such differences could also depend on the intervention of state authorities or trade unions, as exemplified by various subventions to shipping and shipbuilding and other discriminatory measures or restrictions on the use of a non-national labour force and "featherbedding" wage policies. Against such a background, the recent universal move to "flag-of-convenience" registers and the influx of cheap labour from the less developed world have led to a major revolution in international shipping.

One other extremely important element which directly affects shipping and to some degree even international trade must be mentioned. Ports are not only an integral part of maritime transport but also represent a major source of costs. On medium-to-long (c. 5000 nautical miles) ocean voyages, the share of terminal (port) costs today can often comprise more than half of the total expense. At least on the level of cash flows, ports can be regarded as an important exogenous factor for shipping and, on a smaller scale, even to commodity trade. Thus, the decline of transport costs cannot be satisfactorily

---

[2]See Stig Tenold, "The Shipping Crisis of the 1970s: Causes, Effects and Implications for Norwegian Shipping" (Unpublished PhD thesis, Norwegian School of Economics and Business Administration, 2001), 27-31. A revised version of the thesis has been published as *Tankers in Trouble: Norwegian Shipping and the Crisis of the 1970s and 1980s* (St. John's, 2006).

understood unless ports are included in the analysis. Unfortunately, representative long-term data on port costs is extremely scarce.[3]

The title of this essay suggests that the main long-term trends in international shipping can be summarized in three catchwords. As far as the first of them – the growth of tonnage and transport – is concerned, the period 1850-2000 can be divided into four phases: rapid growth before the First World War, stagnation in the interwar period, a new rapid growth from the late 1940s to the early 1970s and stagnation followed by slower growth during the last quarter of the twentieth century. Diversification of the freight market, on the other hand, has been fairly continuous (albeit with some counter-currents) and obviously has been connected to structural changes in transport demand and technical innovations in shipping. Finally, globalization, or the lowering of national boundaries, in particular as far as the transfer of production factors is concerned, advanced before the First World War, halted during the second and third quarters of the twentieth century and gained a new momentum after the 1970s. After looking more closely at these trends, this essay will conclude with an attempt to estimate the long-term development of ocean transport costs – or at least some sections of them – and their possible connections to growth, diversification, globalization and technological change.

Growth of World Merchant Tonnage and Maritime Transport

The only primary data on the growth of shipping which covers the entire period 1850-2000 are tonnage statistics. In most maritime nations these were published before the middle of the nineteenth century. Later, classification societies, above all Lloyd's Register of Shipping, started to publish estimates of aggregate world tonnage. These seem quite reliable from the early 1920s and remain today the principal data cited in various statistical yearbooks of shipping (*Shipping Statistics Yearbook* published by the Institute of Shipping Economics and Logistics [ISL]; *Review of Maritime Transport* by the United Nations Conference on Trade and Development [UNCTAD]; *Fearnleys Review*, etc.).[4]

---

[3]Yrjö Kaukiainen, "Journey Costs, Terminal Costs and Ocean Tramp Freights: How the Price of Distance Declined from the 1870s to 2000," *International Journal of Maritime History*, XVIII, No. 2 (2006), 21-22 and 32. The examples concerned the grain and coal trades.

[4]The original Lloyd's tonnage statistics also included fishing and other non-trading vessels, such as research ships, icebreakers, service vessels and tugs which only operate in ports; on the other hand, they excluded sailing vessels after 1950. Various publications therefore have prepared different statistics excluding non-merchant tonnage; a common pattern is to include only tanker and dry-cargo tonnage (in the strictest sense of the words), thus excluding, for example, passenger tonnage. A rather

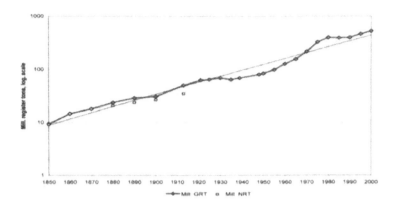

Figure 1: Growth of World Merchant Tonnage, 1850–2000

Note: The principal series refer to gross registered tons (grt) and from the 1990s to gross tons of the 1969 London rule. From 1870 to 1913, aggregate net tonnages are indicated (note that before 1867 there was no net ton).

Sources: 1850-1890: Lewis R. Fischer and Helge W. Nordvik, "Maritime Transport and the Integration of the North Atlantic Economy, 1850-1914," in Wolfram Fischer, R. Marvin McInnis and Jürgen Schneider (eds.), *The Emergence of a World Economy, 1500-1914* (2 vols., Wiesbaden, 1986), II, 526. 1900-2000: Lloyd's Register, *Statistical Tables* (later, *World Fleet Statistics*); before 1921 sailing vessel tonnages according to *Die Norske Veritas*, whose statistics are much more comprehensive in this respect; tanker tonnage, 1900-1923: Robert S. Nielsen, *Oil Tanker Economics* (Bremen, 1959), 12. Since Lloyd's statistics (with the exception of sailing vessels before 1921) record fleet sizes in grt, the net tonnage figures in Fischer and Nordvik have been converted to grt by multiplying sailing vessel tonnages by 1.08 for 1880 and 1.1 for 1890, and steamship tonnages by 1.62 (see L. Isserlis, "Tramp Shipping Cargoes, and Freights," *Journal of the Royal Statistical Society*, CI, No. 1 [1938], 63, table D). From 1925, fishing craft and non-trading vessels have been deducted from overall tonnages. For 1955, 1960 and 1965 fishing vessel tonnages were not specified in Lloyd's statistics, but such data fortunately exists for 1965 and 1967 in ISL, *Shipping Statistics* (Bremen, 1966), 33; and (Bremen, 1968), 24. Using the 1965 data, a linear estimate of the world fishing fleet was produced for 1955 and 1960.

---

peculiar principle has been followed in recent editions of Institute of Shipping Economics and Logistics (ISL), *Shipping Statistics Yearbooks*. Its table of total merchant fleet development from 1921 onwards includes "fishing types and non-trading vessels" but not sailing vessels (although this is not indicated).

The growth of world merchant fleets is depicted in figure 1. Overall, global shipping capacity has grown about sixty-fold in 150 years, which implies an average rate of growth of 2.8 percent per annum. The rate was clearly above average both in 1850-1870 (c. four percent a year) and 1950-1975 (5.7 percent a year), the latter being the all-time high. Periods of slow growth and even contraction occurred in the interwar period and the 1980s, while the rest of the century and a half represented more-or-less average development. But there is one discontinuity in the data that must be considered in order to interpret smaller deviations from the trend: from about 1910 to the 1980s ships designed to carry light and valuable goods (such as shelter-deck liners and roll-on roll-off [ro-ro] ships) were able to exploit loopholes in the measurement rules to be credited with disproportionately low gross and net tonnages compared to their actual carrying capacities; accordingly, the official tonnages suggest growth that was fractionally too slow. This anomaly was corrected with the new 1969 measurement rules, and consequently the growth of measured gross volumes was slightly faster than that of real capacity from 1982 to 1994, a period of transition from the old to the new system.[5]

Estimates of the physical volume of world trade can be regarded as secondary: they are derived from national databases of foreign trade and shipping statistics which were first collected by the Economic Intelligence Service of the League of Nations and subsequently by the Statistical Division of the United Nation's Secretariat. The first actual global estimates of maritime transport were published by the latter in 1950-1951.[6] Because the standards and coverage of the original statistics were far from perfect, the compilation of aggregate figures involved a good deal of extrapolation and approximation, and the margin of error was originally estimated at eight percent for the years 1929-1933 and six percent for more recent data. Subsequently, the UN's estimates have also been published in slightly different versions by the Organisation for Economic Co-operation and Development (OECD), UNCTAD and a few research institutes. While these series usually agree quite well, there are deviations which demonstrate the problems of aggregation. For example, a special survey by the UN Statistical Office in 1980 estimated the overall volume of world maritime transport at 3507 million metric tons, while UNCTAD's *Review of Maritime Transport* and OECD's *Maritime Transport* set the figure at 3704 million tons; ISL's *Shipping Statistics Yearbook* (which

---

[5]Yrjö Kaukiainen, "Tons and Tonnages: Ship Measurement and Shipping Statistics," *International Journal of Maritime History*, VII, No. 1 (1995), 183-186.

[6]In March 1950 the United Nations (UN) *Monthly Bulletin of Statistics* published an estimate based upon entrances and clearances (in net tons), but subsequently also published a parallel estimate on loaded and unloaded freight (in metric tons); cf. the *1950 Supplement to the Monthly Bulletin of Statistics* and *Monthly Bulletin of Statistics*, March and December 1952.

relies on *Fearnleys Review*) presented a figure which fell between these two at 3606 million tons.[7] But since the difference between the highest and lowest estimates is less than six percent, any of these sources should be adequate to present a realistic picture of the most important trends, at least since 1950. On the other hand, in terms of major cargo categories, such as tanker and dry cargo, the various estimates are far more diverse, in particular for the 1960s and 1970s; typically, the OECD presents figures that are twelve to fifteen percent higher for tanker cargoes than those in *Fearnleys Review*.[8] Figure 2 presents the existing series from 1929 onwards and also includes two simple extrapolations for 1913 and 1975 which should be treated with some caution.

In any case, the growth pattern of world maritime transport agrees quite well with the development of merchant tonnage, with practically identical periods of faster and slower growth. The most important feature is, of course, that transport has systematically grown faster than tonnage, increasing on average by 3.3 percent per annum from 1875 to 2000, while annual tonnage growth over the same period amounted to 2.6 percent per year. This suggests that the efficiency of shipping improved more or less systematically. If we divide the estimated aggregate transport by the respective tonnage – thus producing a figure which is roughly proportional (but not equal) to the average number of voyages by one ship – we can see an increase from four or five in the 1870s to about seven by 1910 and ten in 2000.[9] The development, however, was not straightforward: the 1950 figure was lower than 1910, and eleven was already exceeded around 1970. Indeed, this comparison must not be given too much weight because the actual demand for tonnage depends, in

---

[7]UN, Commodity Trade (By Sea) Statistics, 1980 *Maritime Transport Study (Statistical Papers*, ser. D, XXVII–XXX, No. 2, [New York, 1983]); and United Nations Conference on Trade and Development (UNCTAD), *Review of Maritime Transport*, various years; Organisation for Economic Co-operation and Development (OECD), *Maritime Transport*, various years; and ISL, *Shipping Statistics Yearbook*, various years.

[8]In addition to errors of estimation, there are systematic differences between these series. First, OECD figures referred to cargo loaded, which tends to be larger than unloaded volumes. This not only is caused by a small fraction of ships being lost at sea but may also reflect the fact that higher customs and other dues are paid on imports than on exports. Some marginal differences also depend upon natural factors: oil cargoes may diminish slightly because of spillage and evaporation, while some dry cargoes may actually increase in weight because they absorb water. A more important factor, however, seems to be that tanker cargo is defined differently in the various estimates. For example, *Fearnleys Review* only includes crude oil and oil products but not chemicals or liquid gas carried in specialized tankers.

[9]Gross tonnage includes all spaces inside a vessel; the measurement unit traditionally was 100 cubic feet, while transport output is estimated in tons.

addition to the volume of trade and business cycles, on the average length of haul; unfortunately, systematic data for this variable are only available from the early 1960s onwards. During this period, the major change was the sudden lengthening of crude-oil transports from about 4500 to 7000 miles because the Suez Canal was closed from 1966 to 1975, thus increasing the demand for tanker tonnage in proportion. A distinct but more gradual increase also took place in ore and coal transports during the 1960s. On the other hand, the average hauls remained fairly stable in all major trades after 1980, and the ratio of ton-miles to grt increased by roughly one-quarter until 2000.[10]

Unfortunately, even the modern ton-mile series do not supply a precise basis for describing improvements in efficiency. First, they do not measure the work involved in loading and unloading, which is a major element in the overall transport effort. Moreover, the "ton" is a less-than-perfect gauge for various cargoes. It is a good measure only when dealing with goods with specific gravities equal to or higher than sea water. For lighter goods, such as timber, cotton, cars or containers filled with merchandise, volume is the main stowage constraint while weight has much less to do with the quantities that can be loaded. Recently, the average net weight of goods in containers has been around nine tons per Twenty-foot Equivalent Unit (TEU). Such a box, however, has a volume of about thirty-three cubic metres, which means that it occupies a space in which about twenty-five tons of heavy grain or thirty-three tons of hard coal or iron ore could be loaded (note that the stowage of the latter two items depends on the deadweight capacity of the ship, not on its cargo-hold volume).[11] Accordingly, average containers, as well as other light commodities, are grossly underrated in transport statistics which only refer to the weight of cargo. As a result, the efficiency of vessels designed to carry light cargo will be underrated compared with tankers or dry-bulk carriers.

Finally, it must be noted that the available estimates of maritime transport only concern commodity trades; passengers have never been included. This is obviously because the ton would be an even more irrational gauge for them than for light-volume goods.[12] Since certain "bulk passenger trades," as David Williams has termed them, moved millions of people from

---

[10]Series on maritime trade in ton-miles can be found in *Fearnleys Review*; see also Martin Stopford, *Maritime Economics* (London, 1988; 2nd ed., London, 1997), 125.

[11]For containers and stowage ratios, see Stopford, *Maritime Economics*, 362, 386 and 394.

[12]Even on nineteenth-century emigrant sailing vessels, one passenger was allowed a space of 100 cubic feet (or one register ton), a space into which almost two tons of cargo could have been loaded rather than a human being of less than one hundred kilograms. On modern cruising vessels, the ratio of course is much higher.

Europe to other continents, we lack some quite important production figures for the period before modern air travel. As well, the recent rapid growth of short-sea travel on car ferries and cruise ships cannot be accounted for.

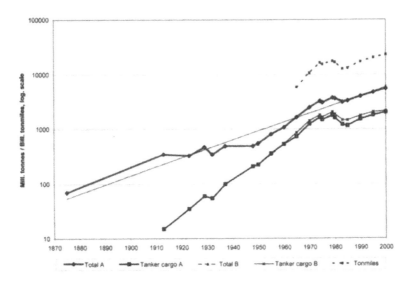

Figure 2: Growth of Maritime Transport, 1875–2000

Note: From 1950 onwards two parallel series are depicted; A is based upon ISL/Fearnley data and B upon OECD (1954-1997) and UNCTAD (1998-) estimates.

Sources: United Nations, *Monthly Bulletin of Statistics*; OECD, *Maritime Transport*; UNCTAD, *Review of Maritime Transport*; *Fearnleys Review*; and ISL, *Shipping Statistics/Shipping Statistics Yearbook* (various years). The figure for 1913 is an estimate based upon the volume of world trade in 1929 and 1913 published in Tomohei Chida and Peter N. Davies, *The Japanese Shipping and Shipbuilding Industries: A History of Their Modern Growth* (London, 1990), 204, table G. The 1875 estimate is based upon the growth of world tonnage from 1875 to 1913 in terms of the so-called "sail tons" (one steam ton = three sail tons). The estimate for 1923 is based upon S.G. Sturmey, *British Shipping and World Competition* (London, 1962), 65. The figures for 1928-1950 come from the original UN estimates, but those for tanker transport are based upon Stig Tenold, "Crisis? What Crisis? – The Expansion of Norwegian Shipping in the Interwar Period" (Discussion Paper 29/05: Norwegian School of Economics and Business Administration, http://bora.nhh.no/handle/ 2330/557), 12, chart 7.

Structural Development of Markets and Trends in Diversification

During the "golden age of sail" there was already some specialization, not only between coastal and ocean-going vessels but also between fast ships carrying valuable goods and slower ones designed to load large quantities of bulk goods which did not require rapid delivery. The advent of steam created a new, specialized market because early steamers were suitable only for the transport of passengers, mail and other light and valuable cargoes; indeed, they inaugurated a direct genetic line to different types of passenger and cargo liners. The development of economical steam "tramps" linked the markets for sail and steam, but at the same time cargo steamers began to specialize according to commodities and routes. By the 1870s the first tankers in the modern sense were launched, and shortly thereafter the first refrigerated compartments for meat and fruit were built in a cargo liner. Specialized ore carriers (such as the so-called "turret-deckers") appeared in the 1890s.[13] In more recent times, the technical diversification of ships has proceeded much further, and today's ships differ not only in terms of the design of their cargo holds and weight-carrying ability but also in their loading and unloading systems. Therefore, not all ships can operate in every freight market. The trends and fluctuations of maritime transport and merchant tonnages should thus be examined primarily through the development of various sub-markets.

Until the 1960s there are only limited data on tonnage by ship type. In fact, the only trends which can be described with some accuracy are the proportions of sailing vessels to steam and later motorships, and since 1900 the growth of tanker tonnage (see figure 3). Around the middle of the nineteenth century, sail still ruled the waves. Steam equalled sail in terms of nominal tonnage in the 1890s, but in actual carrying capacity this occurred a decade earlier. The dominance of steam subsequently increased rapidly: by 1900, sailing-ship tonnage only comprised one-fifth of the total (or less than one-tenth of carrying capacity) and dwindled to insignificance after 1930.[14] Tanker tonnage grew more quickly than total tonnage, at about nine percent per annum between 1900 and 1939, but before World War I it was such a small factor that its influence on overall development was negligible. In the 1920s and 1930s, however, it was beginning to matter; if we subtract tankers from total tonnage

---

[13]Cf., for example, the articles on passenger vessels, cargo ships and bulk cargo carriers in Robert Gardiner (ed.), *The Golden Age of Shipping: The Classic Merchant Ship 1900–1960* (London, 1994). *Gluckauf* (1886) is usually mentioned as the first tanker, but Ludvig Nobel's *Zoroaster* (1877) was the first actually to carry oil in bulk, albeit only in the Caspian Sea.

[14]According to Lloyd's, sail accounted for sixteen percent in 1900; according to Veritas (which also included coastal sail), the ratio was twenty-one percent. In 1930 Lloyd's claimed that the proportion was only two percent.

we can see that the vast majority of vessels only experienced an average growth of 0.1 percent per year between 1920 and 1939.

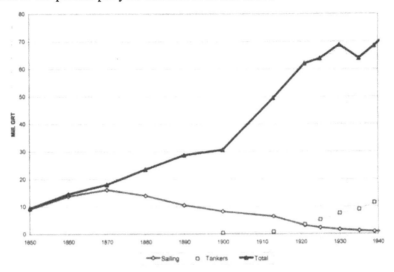

Figure 3: World Merchant Tonnage, 1900–1940: Structural Changes (grt)

Sources: See figure 1.

Oil transport can be regarded a separate market because until the Second World War petroleum products and crude oil were only carried in dedicated tankers, and about sixty percent of the tonnage was owned by big oil companies or governments.[15] The lack of further classification by type of ship in the early tonnage statistics may perhaps suggest that the technical specialization of other cargo ships had not yet proceeded as far as in the latter half of the twentieth century. But market diversification did take place due to the way vessels were operated. For a long time the most important division in shipping was between liner and tramp trades. Liners not only sailed on fixed schedules but also combined a large number of smaller consignments on a single ship, and these were charged according to fixed tariffs announced in advance. Thus, there was no freight bargaining comparable with that on the tramp market. Moreover, since liner companies operating on the same routes formed cartels (the so-called "conferences"), the market was neither

---

[15]Although the first combination ore/oil carrier was constructed in 1921, this concept only became popular after the Second World War; see P.B. Watson, "Bulk Cargo Carriers," in Gardiner (ed.), *Golden Age of Shipping*, 78. On the other hand, carrying case oil in ordinary dry-bulk carriers became an exception after the last decade of the nineteenth century. On tanker ownership see, for example, Robert S. Nielsen, *Oil Tanker Economics* (Bremen, 1959), 16.

competitive in the normal sense nor necessarily continuous because tariffs on different routes could differ significantly.

The separation of liner and tramp markets was even reflected in some degree of technical specialization. This was particularly conspicuous on routes, such as the North Atlantic, where the increasing number of passengers resulted in the development of large, luxurious passenger liners. Even on routes where such demand was low, the special requirements of "general cargo" accounted for the evolution of a fairly standard type of liner, the so-called "open shelter-decker," which prevailed from the beginning of the twentieth century to the 1960s. Such ships had two decks, several hatches and efficient cargo-handling gear; because they carried fairly light cargoes, their deadweight tonnage (dwt) was relatively low compared with the volume of cargo that could be carried. In addition, because of certain peculiarities of the pre-1969 measurement rules, their upper holds (the so-called "tweendecks") were exempted from both gross and net tonnages, which was a substantial advantage in terms of port charges.

In practice, however, it is difficult to draw any clear dividing line between cargo liners and tramps. This observation was borne out in Britain after Parliament passed an act in 1935 to provide subsidies for the latter; the drafters of the bill could not make a clear distinction according to ships but only by the type of voyage.[16] Thus, it is not surprising that meaningful estimates of the size of liner fleets can only be found in a limited number of countries and periods. For example, it has been estimated that liners comprised some fifty-five percent of Danish steam tonnage in 1890; in Britain, just before the First World War their share seems to have been about one-half. It must have been higher in Germany since the two biggest liner companies, the Hamburg-America Line (HAPAG) and Norddeutscher Lloyd (NDL), between them owned no less than forty percent of all German tonnage. Later, the Royal Institute of International Affairs estimated that in 1914 the global tramp fleets amounted to 22.7 million gross tons, which suggests that the proportion of liner tonnage was about forty-five percent of total steam and motor tonnage.[17] Such high proportions are not surprising considering the dominance of liners in

---

[16]Isserlis, "Tramp Shipping," 60.

[17]Anders Monrad Möller, Henrik Dethlefsen and Hans Chr. Johansen, *Dansk söfarts historia 5: 1870-1920, Sejl og damp* (Århus, 1998), 86; Peter N. Davies, "The Development of the Liner Trades," in Keith Matthews and Gerald Panting (eds.), *Ships and Shipbuilding in the North Atlantic Region* (St. John's, 1978), 193; Ronald Hope, *A New History of British Shipping* (London, 1990), 338; and W.S. Woytinsky and E.S. Woytinsky, *World Commerce and Government: Trends and Outlooks* (Baltimore, 1955), 456. In the last volume, the proportion of tramp tonnage is given at forty-three percent, but then the tonnage is compared to the total, which also includes sailing vessels. If tankers were excluded, liners would represent about forty-six percent of dry-cargo tonnage.

early steam shipping – moreover, it seems that liner companies not only represented the quality end of shipping but also were more profitable in the long run.

In 1935, thirty-two percent of all British grt was classified as tramps, while tankers already comprised twelve percent. Accordingly, fifty-six percent consisted of liners, of which more than half (thirty percent of the total) carried only cargo. In Germany, the share accounted for by liners was greater than sixty percent.[18] On the other hand, there were a number of important national fleets, above all the Greek and Norwegian, in which tramps, including tankers, comprised an overwhelming majority. Even in Denmark liner shipping seems to have lost its dominant position after the First World War. Still, the British research mentioned above estimated that the total tonnage of tramps had sunk to 21.3 million gross tons in 1933, which would imply that the share accounted for by liners may have been about fifty-six percent of steam and motor tonnage (or sixty-four percent of dry-cargo tonnage). This seems high, but it certainly agrees with contemporary observations that liner shipping was expanding in the 1920s and 1930s.[19]

Liner trades have traditionally been associated with the carriage of finished, relatively valuable goods and small parcels. In reality, however, they

---

[18]Isserlis, "Tramp Shipping," 62–63; Davies, "Liner Trades," 193–194; and Lars U. Scholl, "The German Merchant Marine in the Inter-War Period," in Lewis R. Fischer and Helge W. Nordvik (eds.), *Shipping and Trade, 1750–1950: Essays in International Maritime Economic History* (Pontefract, 1990), 204-205. The data for Germany are for the years 1926-1927, when seven liner companies owned over two million gross registered tons (grt) of the total of about 3.3 million grt. According to Davies, "Liner Trades," 193, the German ratio in the 1930s was eighty percent.

[19]Gelina Harlaftis, *A History of Greek-Owned Shipping: The Making of an International Tramp Fleet, 1830 to the Present Day* (London, 1996), 369, appendix 6.7, has published a time series of national dry-cargo tramp tonnage from 1938, according to which about eighty-three percent of Greek tonnage consisted of tramps. These statistics, however, only included ships of over 2500 grt, and the figure for Britain is about one million grt smaller than the one referred to above. This probably explains at least in part why the figure for Norway is less than twenty percent. Norwegian research, however, indicates that the proportion of liner tonnage was only eight percent in 1914, twenty-five to thirty percent around 1930 and fifteen percent in the early 1960s; Tenold, "Shipping Crisis," 29. On the other hand, Norway already owned a substantial fleet of tankers around 1930, and this was also the case in Greek shipping after the Second World War. For Denmark, see Frank A. Rasmussen, Bent Vedsted Rönne and Hans Chr. Johansen, *Dansk söfarts historie 6: 1920–1960, Damp og diesel* (Århus, 2000), 81, which shows that in 1930 about forty percent of total shipping income derived from the liner trades. In Sweden and Finland, liner shipping was more important than in Norway. For a 1933 estimate, see Woytinsky and Woytinsky, *World Commerce*, 456-457, which claims that the proportion of tramps was one-third of total merchant tonnage.

also carried bulk goods, such as grain, wood products and other commodities, which typically provided cargoes for tramps and bulk carriers. Indeed, it was common for liners to be unable to find full loads of general cargo, in particular on low-demand legs of voyages, and their owners were quite happy to earn marginal income by carrying low-value, bulk goods. For example, Atlantic emigrant liners stowed grain on their 'tweendecks when returning to Europe, and Scandinavian liners operating to East Asia carried timber products to South Africa and pig iron to Japan.[20] In such cases, liner companies operating in the bulk (spot) market behaved similarly to full-time tramps, negotiating charters at similar or even lower freight rates. On the other hand, it was less common for tramps to carry "liner goods" because a full loading would have required the time-consuming collection of a variety of different "general" goods. Instead, it was more typical for tramps to be chartered by liner companies in times of high demand. In any case, it is important to remember that liner and tramp trades were not fully separate, even if the amorphous border was traversed more regularly by the former than the latter.

In principle, the tramp (or dry-bulk) market was global because there were no cartels to limit competition. Moreover, its was fairly unified: before the Second World War the majority of tramps were engaged in some form of "joint production," alternating between different bulk cargoes on their voyages outward and homeward. Typically, imports to Western Europe, such as grain, ore, phosphates, jute or timber, required more cargo space than exports, but British coal exports offered freight opportunities for most of the ships on their outward legs to destinations other than North America. Such combinations of cargo effectively diminished the proportion of passages in ballast, although coal on low-demand legs was often carried at lower freight rates than those on high-demand passages. This also discouraged any trend toward specialized ships designed to carry a single commodity.

The relative as well as absolute decline of tramp tonnage strongly suggests that these trades fared worse in the 1920s and 1930s than before the First World War. This seems to be connected with declining demand; existing estimates suggest that dry-cargo transports (total cargo minus oil cargo) actually declined in the 1930s due mainly to a dramatic fall in outward coal cargoes from Western Europe (see figure 4).[21] In the 1910s, for example,

---

[20]See, for example, C. Knick Harley, "North Atlantic Shipping in the Late Nineteenth Century," in Fischer and Nordvik (eds.), *Shipping and Trade, 1750–1950*, 149-151; and Berit Larsson, *Svenska varor på svenska kölar: Staten, industrialiseringen och linjesjöfartens framväxt i Sverige, 1890-1925* (Göteborg, 2000), 122 and 185.

[21]A similar and more detailed picture is presented by Stig Tenold, "Crisis? What Crisis? – The Expansion of Norwegian Shipping in the Interwar Period" (Discussion Paper 29/05, Norwegian School of Economics and Business Administration, http://bora.nhh.no/handle/2330/557), 12, chart 7.

British coal exports peaked at almost ninety million tons a year, but by 1935 the volume had plummeted to only about forty million.[22] In addition to the problems of the British coal industry, this trend obviously reflected the increasing role of oil as fuel for ships and other transport. Given the central role of British coal in joint-production arrangements, such a drop must have affected a substantial amount of shipping. This downward trend ended after the Second World War as British exports were replaced by American coal. Since the latter could not offer return cargoes for tramps bringing bulk goods to Europe, the traditional joint-production model broke down. This not only resulted in higher freight rates but also in an increasing separation between the major bulk trades.[23]

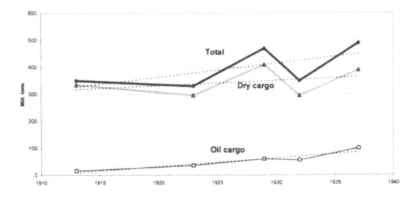

Figure 4: World Maritime Transport, 1913-1937

Sources: See figure 2.

Another well-established market – Atlantic passenger liners – fared slightly better. While emigration to the US diminished after the passage of restrictive legislation in the early 1920s, the number of other travellers increased on these routes, and liner companies made good profits before the Great Depression. Prospects seem to have been promising even in the 1930s, as the building of ships like *Normandie*, *Queen Mary* and *Queen Elisabeth* demonstrate (although they did receive state subventions). A number of other passenger trades also prospered, and the importance of the this sector was

[22]Sarah Palmer, "The British Coal Export Trade," in David Alexander and Rosemary Ommer (eds.), *Volumes Not Values: Canadian Sailing Ships and World Trades* (St. John's, 1979), 333; Isserlis, "Tramp Shipping," 85; and Woytinsky and Woytinsky, *World Commerce*, 457.

[23]Kaukiainen, "Ocean Tramp Freights," 27.

demonstrated by the fact that in 1939 passenger-cargo ships still comprised at least one-fifth of global merchant tonnage, exceeding tanker tonnage by almost fifty percent. Indeed, it was only in the late 1950s that the development of air travel threatened the big Atlantic passenger ships.[24] In any case, a plausible hypothesis – albeit one that requires further testing – seems to be that many sectors of liner shipping grew, or at least did not contract, while the traditional ocean tramp trades, in particular those connected with British coal exports, experienced a downward trend in the 1920s and 1930s.

The Second World War resulted in remarkable structural changes in the global merchant fleets. Because of vigorous shipbuilding in North America, overall tonnage grew by a quarter despite substantial war losses. The growth, however, took place almost exclusively in the tanker and dry-bulk fleets; at the same time, the tonnage of passenger ships, many of which served as troop carriers or floating hospitals, declined by about a third.[25] In addition, wartime demand for liquid fuels accelerated the long-term growth of oil transport.

Figures 5, 6 and 7 depict the most essential changes in the structures of global tonnage and maritime transport. In both cases, the data for the 1950s and 1960s are still quite rough and lack detail. Moreover, the production estimates ignore the passenger trades, although passenger tonnage decreased substantially during the war, a trend that continued until the early 1970s (see table 1). Thereafter, a noticeable recovery began, boosted by the breakthrough of modern car-passenger ferries, so that by 2000 passenger tonnage exceeded the levels of the 1930s by at least fifty percent. Keeping this in mind, from the late 1930s to the early 1970s overall maritime transport grew somewhat more slowly than is suggested by the estimates of goods transport, while the opposite holds true for the last quarter of the twentieth century.[26]

---

[24]Scholl, "German Merchant Marine," 206-207; Woytinsky and Woytinsky, *World Commerce*, 451; and Hope, *New History of British Shipping*, 402-404.

[25]Woytinsky and Woytinsky, *World Commerce*, 451; and Gustav Adolf Theel, *Weltschiffahrts-archiv* (Bremen, 1959), 192.

[26]This was also suggested by the first estimates of world maritime transport. The 1950 series based on tonnages entered and cleared (which implicitly included passenger traffic) showed a decline of eleven percent from 1937 to 1949, while figures for freight loaded/unloaded, measured in tons (which only included the commodity trades), showed a growth of two percent over the same period. Of course, the former was not a true measure of transport because it lacked a reduction for unused cargo or passenger space.

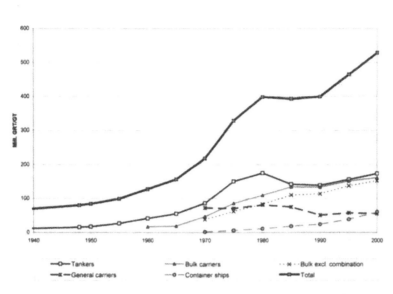

Figure 5: World Merchant Tonnage (grt), 1939-2000: Distribution by Ship Type

Sources: See figure 1.

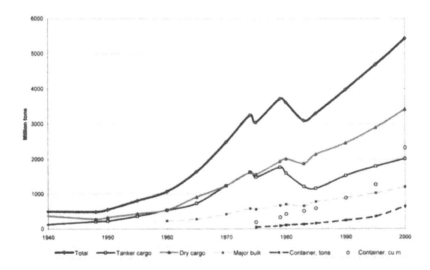

Figure 6: Structure of Maritime Transport, 1940-2000

Note: "Major bulk" refers to ore, coal and grain.

Sources: See figure 2; and Martin Stopford, *Maritime Economics* (London, 1988; 2nd ed., London, 1997), 362 (with extrapolations backward and forward).

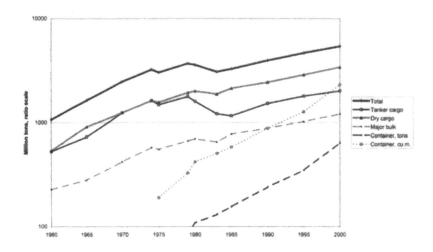

Figure 7:   Maritime Transport, 1960-2000: Overall and Sectoral Trends

Sources: See figure 6.

Table 1
World Passenger Tonnage, 1939–2000

Year	1000 GRT/GT
1939	12,560
1952	8210
1965	4370
1972	3050
1986	9100
2000	21,430

Note: According to W.S. Woytinsky and E.S. Woytinsky, *World Commerce and Government: Trends and Outlooks* (Baltimore, 1955), 451, world merchant tonnage in 1939 and 1952 amounted to about 14.6 and 10.6 million grt, respectively.

Sources: 1939 and 1952: Gustav Adolf Theel, *Weltschiffahrts-archiv* (Bremen, 1959), 192; 1965 and 1972: ISL, *Shipping Statistics* (Bremen, 1966 and 1973); and 1986 and 2000: ISL, *Shipping Statistics Yearbook* (Bremen, 1987 and 2001).

Nonetheless, it is clear that the growth of maritime transport was unusually rapid in the 1960s and early 1970s. There was a distinct turning point in the late 1970s – indeed, this becomes even more conspicuous if we look at structural trends. The dominant feature in the period 1950-1980 was the rapid growth of oil tanker tonnage. Whether measured in grt or dwt, overall loading capacity grew about ten-fold, which implies an average growth rate of no less than eight percent per year. Other shipping sectors also grew, albeit at much slower rates. Excluding tankers, the annual growth rate of world tonnage dropped to 4.5 percent, only marginally better than the long-term average for the entire 1850-2000 period. In this light, the spectacular boom seems to have been produced almost exclusively by a single sector.

The demand for oil transports, on the other hand, grew even faster than tanker tonnage, rising by almost ten percent a year in the 1960s and early 1970s, although it slowed after the initial oil shock. As a result, the overall rate for the period 1950-1980 was about 7.3 percent a year. Since the absolute volume of tonnage continued to grow well into the 1970s, a substantial surplus developed in the tanker sector, making it abundantly obvious that the preceding era of strong growth had led shipowners to become over-optimistic. Moreover, in the late 1960s demand for tanker tonnage increased more than demand for crude oil because of the closure of the Suez Canal in the summer of 1966, forcing oil shipments to Europe and the east coast of North America to be rerouted around the Cape. This "surplus" demand vanished after the reopening of the Canal in 1975, which strengthened the effect of the oil shocks.

About 1960 the volume of oil transport approached that of all dry cargo (or even exceeded it by some estimates).[27] The role of coal had declined steadily since the 1930s, and from the late 1950s to the late 1970s most that was transported overseas was for metallurgical purposes.[28] Until 1960 iron ore was by far the most important bulk cargo, accounting for more than twice the volume of coal and growing about three-fold until 1973. Although this also increased demand for coking coal, overall consumption grew more slowly.

Table 2
Average Growth Rates of Different Cargoes, 1960-2000,
(percent per annum)

	1960-1973	1973-1979	1979-2000
Tanker Cargo	9.1	1.3	0.6
Iron Ore	8.7	1.5	1.6
Coal	6.5	7.3	5.8
Three Major Bulk Cargoes*	6.9	3.6	2.9
Other Cargo**	8.9	5.1	2.7
Total Maritime Transport	8.7	2.1	1.8

Note: *Iron ore, coal and grain; **Total dry cargo minus three major bulk cargoes.

Sources: OECD, *Maritime Transport*, various years; and ISL, *Shipping Statistics Yearbook* (based upon Fearnleys *Review*), various years.

---

[27]For the differences between various estimates, see note 7 above.

[28]Stopford, *Maritime Economics*, 320-321.

Still, the demand for different dry cargoes, even including major bulk commodities (see table 2), grew more than the respective tonnages (between 1960 and 1973, tanker tonnage grew on average by 8.2 percent per annum and the remainder of the merchant fleet by five percent). This is even more remarkable because the average haul of iron ore and coal also increased at the same time.[29] It is reasonable to conclude that the technical efficiency of bulk-cargo ships improved, and this was actually the period when the modern bulk carrier was developed. The transition can be followed in tonnage statistics, which began to specify a new category of "ore and dry-bulk carriers." As can be seen in figure 5, this class increased rapidly – between 1963 and 1973 by more than four-fold – eventually surpassing the "general cargo" ships (which obviously not only referred to liners but also to bulk-cargo tramps of more traditional design). Accordingly, the bulk sector grew almost as fast as the tanker market, and in terms of technical development it probably surpassed it.[30] The first phase of the "container revolution" even improved the efficiency of liner shipping, but the total tonnage was still so small that its overall effect was not great.

When comparing the tanker and dry-bulk sectors, one important factor must be considered. Since the 1950s a linkage has gradually developed between these two markets. Combination carriers – first ore/oil and since the 1960s ore/bulk/oil (OBO) carriers – were developed to enable ships again to be deployed in some kind of joint production. In practice, however, the geography of maritime transport – the most important destinations not only for oil, ore and coal but also for grain were in Europe and Japan[31]– effectively limited the scope of joint production after the demise of British coal exports, and it became more typical for combination carriers periodically to alternate between oil and bulk transports according to the respective freight levels. From the late 1960s until the first oil shock, the overwhelming majority of this tonnage was used in the "tanker mode," but it shifted to the bulk sector in the

---

[29]*Ibid.*, 125.

[30]See, for example, Watson, "Bulk Cargo Carriers," 77-78; and D.K. Fleming, "Modern Trampships, Bulk Carriers and Combination Carriers," in Robert Gardiner (ed.), *The Shipping Revolution* (London, 1992), 22-24. New bulk carriers were much bigger than traditional tramps and enjoyed improved economies of scale, but their most important feature was the provision for more efficient cargo handling. Instead of small hatches (often battened down with heavy timber sleepers or layers of tarpaulin), they had wide hydraulic openings; indeed, their decks became a series of hatches which allowed efficient unloading by large grabs. On the other hand, oil had been pumped in and out ever since the first tankers.

[31] See, for example, the maps of major sea routes in Harlaftis, *History of Greek-Owned Shipping*, 248-255.

late 1970s.[32] At the peak of the oil boom the actual tanker tonnage accordingly was even larger than the statistics indicate. The obverse was that the active bulk tonnage was smaller, which confirms the productivity growth in that sector.[33]

The late 1970s and the first half of the 1980s have generally been dubbed "the great shipping crisis." This was also seen in the development of world tonnage, which grew slowly through the initial phase of the crisis, peaking in 1982 but then sinking by some five percent. It regained the earlier levels by 1990 and then grew by a fifth through 2000 (see figure 5 above). As might be expected, tanker tonnage decreased most, falling by about a quarter during the 1980s; in the following decade, it grew by a third and exceeded the 1980 leve by about four percent. These fluctuations roughly followed the pattern of demand. Bulk carriers increased steadily throughout and enjoyed an overall tonnage growth of some forty percent during these two decades. This brought them almost to the same level as tanker tonnage, and not surprisingly the overall volume of dry cargo surpassed that of oil by the latter half of the 1970s.

The growth of dry-bulk cargo depended mainly on the growing demand for coal. From the end of the 1970s to 2000, coal shipments increased more than three-fold, or on average by six percent a year. The term "coal boom" indicates that coal was increasingly substituted for oil to produce energy in new heating plants. Indeed, even the trade in iron ore slowed in the late 1970s, and the volume of coal cargoes exceeded that of ore in the 1990s. The net result was that, with the exception of 1973-1985, the total transport of major bulk commodities increased slightly slower than all dry cargoes or total maritime transport. Although the growth of demand in this sector exceeded the increase in tonnage, this was easily compensated for by the large fleet of combination carriers which shifted to dry bulk – in fact, this spread both the tonnage surplus and the crisis from the tanker market to bulk shipping. These experiences began (or at least coincided with) the decline in combination tonnage, which gradually fell from about twenty-six million grt in 1980 to 9.3 million by the end of the millennium. It is obvious that the returns earned by such ships did not match the higher building and maintenance costs, and the multi-purpose concept has thus far lost out compared with increased specialization.[34]

---

[32]Tenold, "Shipping Crisis," 121-122.

[33]In tonnage statistics combination carriers were classified as dry-bulk ships. By the end of the 1970s, combination-carrier tonnage had grown to over twenty-six million gross tons, or almost a third of actual bulk tonnage.

[34]Construction prices, of course, were increased by dual cargo-handling systems. In the late 1960s the price difference was just a couple of percent per

The dominant trend during the shipping boom of the 1960s and 1970s was the rapid increase of tankers and bulk carriers. Accordingly, their rise – as well as the sub-average growth of general cargo – suggests a proportional decline of liner tonnage. This was confirmed by investigations carried out by the ISL in the 1960s. According to its estimates, total world liner tonnage in 1965 amounted to some thirty-two million grt, or about sixty percent of contemporary tanker tonnage. But this did not account for passenger ships; if they are included, the total would rise to slightly above thirty-six million tons. This tonnage represented only about twenty-three percent of the world merchant fleet or thirty-five percent of dry-cargo tonnage. Indeed, the ratios depict a massive relative decline since the 1930s and suggest that the global liner fleet had experienced no real growth in more than three decades.[35] The investigation also revealed fairly large variations between different national fleets. In many Western industrial countries, such as Britain, the US, the Netherlands, Belgium, Portugal and Denmark, the proportion of liner tonnage amounted to forty percent or more, but surprisingly this list was topped by two socialist countries, Poland and East Germany. On the other hand, Norway and Greece represented an opposite situation with ratios below ten and five percent, respectively.

The entire 1960s was marked by a declining trend. The proportion of liners in the British merchant marine fell from about half in 1960 to forty percent in 1965, and the ISL statistics for 1967 recorded an aggregate liner tonnage that was about one million tons smaller than it had been two years earlier.[36] This negative trend resulted from two parallel developments: the

---

deadweight ton (dwt), but this increased with growing demand to about twenty percent in the 1970s, according to "Newbuilding Prices," *Fearnleys Review* (Oslo, various years). Moreover, since all the pipelines of an ore/bulk/oil (OBO) carrier had to be placed on deck so as not to interfere with the unloading of dry cargoes, they were subjected to corrosion and mechanical damage. As well, both the piping and the requirement for longitudinal stiffness resulted in relatively narrow hatches which made the unloading of dry cargoes less efficient. In tanker mode, OBOs also experienced problems with the tightness of hatch covers and – because they could not have a central longitudinal bulkhead – the sloshing of oil cargoes sometimes caused stability problems.

[35]ISL, *Shipping Statistics 1966* (Bremen, 1966), 31-34. The ISL statistics for the passenger fleet (ships with at least 100 passenger berths) were for 1 March 1966. Surprisingly, ISL reckoned the liner share (excluding passenger ships) of total tonnage at 23.5 percent, which implies a total tonnage of only 136 million (while the actual mid-year figure for 1965 was about 157 million). The estimates presented above suggest that in 1933 the world liner fleet amounted to some thirty-eight million gross tons.

[36]In 1960, the total tonnage of British liners was estimated at almost three times the volume of tramps; at that date, thirty-one percent of the country's tonnage consisted of tankers, which means that the overall share of liners was almost exactly

growth of air travel, which thinned the ranks of luxury ocean liners,[37] and the undermining of the profitability of liners by rapidly rising stevedoring costs. At the same time, revenues did not increase significantly even during the Korea and Suez booms. Moreover, the development of modern, efficient bulk carriers made typical cargo liners obsolete in the carriage of bulk commodities and deprived them of substantial marginal income. This trend was amplified by certain developments in the freight markets and by the strategies adopted by shipowners. As early as the 1920s and 1930s time-charters, often covering periods of several years, were becoming increasingly popular, in particular among independent tanker owners. This trend continued after the Second World War, and in addition to regular time-charters (which gives the charterer fairly wide powers in operating the ship), other types of long-term contracts, involving either the transport of specified large volumes of goods or a number of consecutive voyages, became common. For example, about half of all Norwegian tankers and bulk-carriers sailed on various long-term charters by 1977, and these ratios seem to have been below the average in international shipping.[38] Being a kind of compromise between liner and tramp strategies, it is quite possible that long-term chartering attracted many owners who in the 1930s would have hoped for more stable and predictable incomes by entering the liner business.

The trend seems to have been reversed, however, during the 1970s. A Dutch estimate for 1973 and a Japanese one for 1980 set global liner tonnage at about fifty-one to fifty-three and seventy or seventy-one million grt, respectively.[39] These figures suggest a substantial tonnage increase after 1965,

---

one-half; Davies, "Liner Trades," 194; and ISL, *Shipping Statistics 1968* (Bremen, 1968), 18-19.

[37]For example, *Queen Mary* was withdrawn from regular service in 1967, *Queen Elisabeth* in 1968 and *United States* in 1969.

[38]Tenold, "Shipping Crisis," 170-175.

[39]H.J. Molenaar, "The World's Liner Tonnage," in *The Future of Liner Shipping* (Bremen, 1976), 43-48; and Y. Koike, "Market Situation and Future Development in Liner Shipping," in *Conference Report: International Symposium on Liner Shipping III* (Bremen, 1984), 26-34. The first measured tonnage in dwt; the figure was about fifty-six million, which in a "typical" contemporary liner fleet with a high proportion of 'tweendeckers suggests a gross tonnage of only five percent smaller. The second estimate was produced by the Japanese liner firm Nippon Yusen Kaisha (NYK); it did not present any explicit estimate of total liner tonnage, but the author indicated that the proportion of full-container ships was sixteen percent of total gross liner tonnage. Since the gross tonnage of such container vessels, according to Lloyd's, was around 11.3 million grt, total liner tonnage in this estimate must have been around 70.6 million grt.

but since both indicate that the world liner fleet amounted to eighteen or nineteen percent of all merchant tonnage (or thirty-three or thirty-two percent of dry-cargo tonnage, respectively), this growth was still slower than average. Nonetheless, liner shipping seems to have increased even during the shipping crisis when overall tonnages stagnated. The detailed tonnage statistics available after 1985 enable fairly realistic identification of potential liner tonnage.[40] As table 3 demonstrates, the figure for 1985 was clearly higher than the one estimated by the Japanese and thereafter practically all categories of liners – except traditional two-deck, general-cargo carriers – grew at a good pace. By 2000, their share of world merchant tonnage was approaching one-quarter.

Table 3
Potential Liner Tonnage, 1986 and 2000
('000 grt)

	1986	2000
General-Cargo Ships, Multi-Deck	42,064	25,630
Container Ships	17,916	55,101
Reefers	5688	6960
Ro-ro Ships, Cargo/Passenger Ferries	11,275	22,586
Passenger and Passenger/Cargo Ships	4076	8794
Total	81,019	119,071
Percent of Total Merchant Fleet	20.6	22.5
Percent of Dry-Cargo Fleet	33.6	35.4

Sources: ISL *Shipping Statistics Yearbook* (Bremen, 1986 and 2000); and the sources for total tonnage cited in figure 1.

It is possible that the growth in the 1990s was exaggerated slightly by the transition to the new measurement system which increased substantially the tonnages of certain types of passenger and cargo ferries. Yet there were real elements of growth based upon the firm foundation of the so-called "container revolution" which had been brewing for more than three decades. The concept had been developed in the North American coastal trades, as well as those between the US west coast and Hawaii, in the late 1950s, and container ships

---

[40]Of course, there is a substantial "grey area" between liner and non-liner tonnage. Above all, this concerns single-deck, "general cargo" ships. Before the era of bulk carriers they were typical tramps carrying all kinds of bulk goods. But today they can also include fairly modern ships designed to carry certain types of "break bulk" cargoes, such as timber, pulp, paper and steel rolls. Interestingly, their tonnage doubled during the 1990s, from about fifteen million to twenty-eight million tons gross, which indicates that the share of old-fashioned tramps was declining rapidly. Therefore, some fraction of these ships should be regarded "potential liners," and the tonnage estimate in table 3 can be regarded as a minimum rather than a maximum, in particular for the 1990s.

began to cross the North Atlantic and the Pacific around 1966-1967. Traffic between Europe and East Asia began in 1972, and during the same decade containerization became established as a global system.[41] In terms of tonnage, however, its impact remained modest for a long time. About 1980 container ships only comprised about three percent of world grt, and even ten years later the percentage had only doubled. At the same time, the fleet of "general-cargo ships" (as the tonnage statistics call them), although steadily declining, still exceeded container tonnage by seven times in 1980 and two times in 1990 (see figure 5).

It is no surprise that container tonnage did not grow more rapidly. The demand for capital was high during the technical transition; in the late 1960s a new container ship, including the necessary three sets of containers, may have cost about three times as much per grt as a conventional two-deck liner, and in many cases shipping companies had to invest in cargo-handling equipment in their terminal ports.[42] The obverse was that such new ships – because of much faster turnaround times in port – were able to replace a number of traditional liners.[43] Since many of the latter still had years of useful service left, they were either redeployed on secondary routes or sold in the second-hand market – but in both cases they remained at sea. In the North Atlantic, and in particular in short-sea traffic, the container system also had – and still has – a serious competitor, the roll-on, roll-off concept (unitized cargo moved on wheeled trailers through ramps and stern or bow doors) which required less fixed equipment in ports. Finally, it must be remembered that the diffusion of containerization cannot be fully appreciated by looking only at the growth of dedicated ("cellular") container tonnage, since vast numbers of containers were also carried on other types of ships. On many liners, for example, some of the existing holds were converted to container cells, and containers were also carried as deck cargo on ro-ro vessels and even on the

---

[41]Frank Broeze, The *Globalisation of the Oceans: Containerisation from the 1950s to the Present* (St. John's, 2002), 32-37 and 51-60; and Sidney Gillman, "Container Shipping," in Gardiner (ed.), *Shipping Revolution*, 43-44.

[42]Broeze, *Globalisation*, 29. The example presented by Broeze compares ship prices per dwt, which is not very meaningful because a container ship required maximum cargo space, plus space for deck-cargoes, rather than a large dwt. Accordingly, the price ratio per gross ton was 1:1.6 rather than 1:2.3.

[43]*Ibid.*, 45. The passage cited by Broeze claims that one container ship was able to replace five or six traditional vessels, but it also reminds us that modern vessels were "several times larger." Thus, it remains unclear how large the improvement in transport efficiency actually was. According to Koike, "Market Situation," 26, the NYK believed that the transport efficiency of container ships was six times that of conventional vessels. It therefore seems possible that productivity improvements exceeded those experienced when steam replaced sail.

hatch covers of bulk carriers. As late as 1986, almost half of total world TEU capacity was found on vessels other than "full" container ships, and in 2000 their share still amounted to twenty-eight percent.[44]

Even compared with total maritime transport, the proportion of container cargo remained surprisingly low for a long time. In 1980 it was estimated at almost three percent and at six percent in 1990; in both cases the percentages were almost identical with the shares of container tonnage. It must be remembered, however, that the percentages refer to volumes measured in tons and that the ton – as was noted earlier – is a poor yardstick for volume cargo. If instead we estimate the volume of container cargo in cubic metres (as is also done in figures 6 and 7), the scale becomes totally different. By 1990, the volume of container cargo was almost the same as that of the three major bulk cargoes, and in 2000 it was roughly comparable with all tanker cargo.[45]

After the first oil crisis, containerization was the most dynamic and rapidly-growing sector of world shipping. The great shipping crisis did not hamper it; in the 1980s, the tonnage of container ships grew on average by 7.4 percent per year, and this increased to over nine percent in the next decade. The growth of container cargo fluctuated around ten percent throughout the period 1975-2000. The last five years of the twentieth century were marked by a real spurt in the container "revolution," as the average growth of cargo rose to almost thirteen percent and the overall tonnage of cellular container ships exceeded that of conventional "general-cargo" vessels.

A complimentary development to the trends in container and liner traffic has been the growth of ro-ro and ferry traffic.[46] Because such shipping often provides feeder services to worldwide container lines, there is a direct connection between these sectors. On the other hand, since the 1960s ro-ro ferries have been carrying passengers and cars across narrow seas, so a substantial part of their market is detached from international commodity

---

[44]*Containerisation International Yearbook* (1987), 14; and (2001), 6.

[45]Since grain and crude oil have specific gravities of less than sea water, their metric cubic volumes are slightly larger than their weights in metric tons. But measuring heavy cargoes, like iron or copper ore, by volume is as meaningless as measuring light cargoes by weight. Thus, their real "freight ton" is the ton(ne), while for light cargo it is really the cubic metre. In the tariffs published by liner conferences, light cargo was also charged according to its cubic volume.

[46]The roots of roll-on roll-off (ro-ro) shipping go back to rail ferries across the Channel and between Danish islands. By the 1930s two car-ferry lines were in operation from Denmark to Norway and Sweden. On the North Atlantic, the pioneer of the concept was the Swedish Broström Company, which built specialized vehicle carriers to serve Swedish car exports. See Bruce E. Marti, "Passenger Ships," in Gardiner (ed.), *Shipping Revolution*, 84; and Pekka Sörensen, *Siljarederiet och de samseglande* (Åbo, 1979), 20-23.

trades. During the last two decades of the twentieth century, such traffic has grown vigorously, particularly on the Baltic, North and Mediterranean seas and between Western Europe and West Africa (including the Canary Islands). In addition, passenger ships which carry no cargo, above all cruise ships, have recently increased rapidly.[47] Overall, the tonnage of passenger vessels grew three-fold between 1980 and 2000. Accordingly, the earlier decline of passenger shipping has turned into a new rising trend.

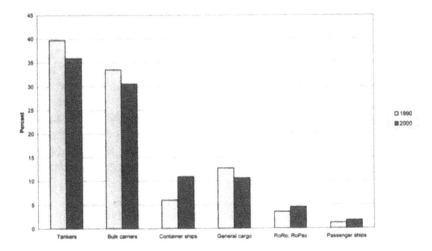

Figure 8:   World Merchant Tonnage (grt), 1990 and 2000: Distribution by Ship Type

Source: ISL, *Shipping Statistics Yearbook*, various years.

The latter half of the twentieth century thus may be described as a period of successive shipping revolutions. The first consisted of the rapid growth in tanker size; the second was connected with the development of the modern bulk carrier; and containerization was the last. The first two depended upon rising demand for energy and raw materials in the industrial world and therefore resulted in the spectacular growth of bulk shipping. It was only after the oil shocks and the great shipping crisis that growth shifted from bulk to general cargo and liner shipping. So far, liner shipping has not regained the dominant position it had before the Second World War. On the other hand, containerization has increased the distinction between liner and tramp (bulk) trades; while small amounts of bulk goods are sometimes sent in containers, cellular container ships cannot alternate between liner and tramp trades. Still, it is useful to remember that today the amount of so-called "break-bulk"

---

[47]Today's biggest cruisers are also the biggest passenger ships ever built, and it has been claimed that the cruising business is the fastest-growing sector of shipping.

goods, such as timber products, paper and steel, is almost as large as container cargo and that such commodities are typically carried by multi-purpose "general-cargo" ships which may also load containers.[48]

Economies of Scale and Specialization

The modern freight market is not only segmented into a number of fairly autonomous sub-markets, but these markets can be divided into a number of "layers" according to ship size.[49] This, of course, has always been the case, and the optimal size has been a function of both the routes plied and the ports frequented, as well as the size of the local or regional markets which the ships serve. Actual sizes, however, have grown significantly during the last half century. In the early 1950s the typical workhorses in all bulk trades were ships of about 10,000 dwt, like the so-called "Liberty" ships, and practically all merchant vessels, aside from the biggest Atlantic liners, were able to transit both the Suez and Panama canals. Today, a ship of 6000 dwt is regarded as small, while the biggest container ships are approaching 200,000 dwt, bulk carriers are nearing 400,000 dwt, and tankers had already exceeded 500,000 dwt in the 1970s (although few of this size are still in service today.) In terms of economies of scale, the overall range has widened a good deal.

Economies of scale, of course, favour big ships, but since the biggest ones only can visit a fraction of world ports, the greatest scale effects are limited to the principal intercontinental sea routes with high and steady demand for transport. Economies of scale also favour specialized vessels with optimal layout of holds and cargo-handling systems with regard to the commodities to be carried. This last feature is also connected with the development of ports and their equipment, which has been particularly rapid since the 1960s. World-class ports today have such sophisticated cargo-handling systems that ships no longer need any shipboard gear to load or discharge their cargo.[50] This has led to a new division of labour between port and ship, with the most substantial savings both in capital and labour costs accruing to the latter, which no longer requires either expensive equipment or skilled labour. While ports understandably charge ships more for the use of their equipment than in the past, the overall result has been improved economies of scale. With present turnaround times, cargo-handling gear on an ocean-going ship would lie idle for sixty to seventy percent of the time, while in busy ports quayside gear will

---

[48]See, Stopford, *Maritime Economics*, 328-329, 343, 362 and 398-400.

[49]See Tenold, "Shipping Crisis," 32.

[50]The only major exceptions are tankers which use shipboard pumps (and in cold weather, cargo-heating systems) when unloading. On the other hand, tanker systems were the most advanced for a considerable period of time.

be in use daily. The results of this new type of diversification are clearly seen in the structure of tonnage: among container ships, practically all those over 2000 TEU (about 30,000 dwt) were gearless by the mid-1990s, while for bulk carriers the corresponding dividing line is around 50,000 dwt.[51]

Smaller vessels serving minor markets are necessarily less cost efficient. If they call at ports that lack cargo-handling equipment they need their own gear to load and discharge, which adds to overhead costs. This is the case especially for shipping serving developing countries; indeed, the resulting diseconomies of scale (often also connected with poor port and governance infrastructures) are the main reason that the foreign trade of these countries is burdened by higher than average freight costs.[52]

Even in the industrialized world, specialization is limited by certain constraints on more peripheral routes. If commodity flows are only moderate, but frequent regular services are still required, shipping companies tend to opt for multi-purpose tonnage which can handle both containerized and break-bulk goods rather than highly specialized, single-mode ships. The price of flexibility will, of course, be paid in the form of somewhat higher capital costs.[53]

Bigger ships and increasing specialization are therefore prominent features of the busy ocean highways, and such forms of transport enjoy massive economies of scale. Calculations made in the early 1970s indicated that a 120,000-dwt bulk carrier could carry freight over moderately long distances at about a third of the cost per ton-mile of a 15,000-dwt ship. On the other hand, similar-sized vessels incur lower costs when steaming on long routes instead of short.[54] This reminds us that scale effects depend not only on size and other features of a ship but also on terminal (port) costs. Since the latter are basically a flat-rate overhead which remains the same irrespective of voyage length, they add a proportionally smaller amount to the costs of long-distance than to short-sea voyages. It seems that the old "tyranny of distance" has been replaced by a "tyranny of scale," as Keith Trace has noted.[55]

---

[51]Stopford, *Maritime Economics*, 390-407.

[52]Kaukiainen, "Ocean Tramp Freights," 33-36.

[53]Stopford, *Maritime Economics*, 392 and 397-400. Ro-ro ships are a good example of modern vessels with some built-in flexibility. Since they carry a loading/unloading system onboard (stern/side/bow doors and ramps), they can be compared to conventional geared ships.

[54]Stopford, *Maritime Economics*, 404.

[55]Keith Trace, "For 'Tyranny of Distance' Read 'Tyranny of Scale:' Australia and the Global Container Market," *The Great Circle*, XXIII, No. 1 (2001), 21-46.

The new tyranny of scale, the cheapening of long-distance transport between major world "hubs," has led to a substantial restructuring of a number of commodity trades. Traditionally, most ships carried their cargoes from exporting ports directly to their final destinations. But today a "hub-and-spoke" pattern has evolved, with massive cargoes transported to regional hubs from which they are re-distributed by smaller vessels, or "feeders." An absolute condition for the viability of such a system has been a substantial decline in transhipment costs. In the case of certain valuable goods, like coffee, this had already occurred by the end of the nineteenth century, when coffee exported from Brazil was sent to Hamburg and then distributed throughout Scandinavia and the Baltic. Still, the system only became common in the wake of the "port revolution" which began in Western Europe in the 1960s. But many dry-bulk trades remain an exception because the low value of these commodities renders transhipment less economical.

Globalization and the Demise of National Fleets

In the nineteenth century, large and efficient merchant navies were the pride of Western nations. Even in a legal sense, they were regarded as extensions of the territory of their domestic states, as manifested by the ensigns they flew. Most maritime nations were prepared to make financial sacrifices to promote their fleets; direct subsidies were paid, for example, by Austria, France, Italy and Japan; indirect support was given in the form of mail subsidies by many more; and even after the repeal of earlier navigation acts foreign competition could be restricted in various ways, such as by reserving coastal traffic (cabotage) for domestic vessels.[56]

In spite of strong currents of nationalism, the nucleus of a global maritime economy also existed in the late nineteenth century. This globalism, however, was the result of the European colonial system, and its most important agent was the British Empire. Between 1850 and 1914, about eighty percent of world tonnage was owned in Europe and North America, and about half of that was British.[57] This North Atlantic supremacy was born in the seventeenth and eighteenth centuries, and the industrial development of the nineteenth century further strengthened the position of the most advanced economies. When iron replaced wood as the primary shipbuilding material, the most important comparative advantages were transferred to countries with well-developed iron industries which also possessed the new engineering skills;

---

[56]See, for example, Hope, *New History of British Shipping*, 302 and 335.

[57]Lewis R. Fischer and Helge W. Nordvik, "Maritime Transport and the Integration of the North Atlantic Economy, 1850-1914," in Fischer, McInnis and Schneider (eds.), *Emergence of a World Economy*, II, 526.

Britain became the "shipbuilder for the world," a position it retained for the next half a century or so.

The latter half of the nineteenth century was also marked by the development of an international maritime labour market. High-wage countries, above all the US but also the UK, attracted thousands of sailors from Scandinavia and other low-wage areas.[58] Obviously, this supply of foreign labour – in particular after the traditional restrictions on foreign labour were repealed in Britain in 1853 – helped to keep maritime wages lower than they otherwise would have been and alleviated one inherent competitive disadvantage of a developed economy.[59]

This movement towards global markets for shipping capital and labour was reversed with the growth of protectionist policies, especially after the First World War. Subsidies to shipping and shipbuilding industries were granted in most maritime countries, and direct discrimination against foreign flags also was common.[60] Direct and indirect restrictions on foreign labour also reappeared. This was exacerbated by the growth of seamen's unions in Britain and America: as might be expected, the unions considered inexpensive foreign labour to be a substantial challenge and tried to secure priority for their own people. To some degree they were supported in this endeavour by governments. In Britain, for example, the old profession of crimping was eradicated during the war, and a National Maritime Board, controlled by the union and the shipowners' federation, was founded to manage the hiring of seamen. Not surprisingly, the share of foreign sailors began to decrease. In 1912 the British merchant marine employed more than 30,000 foreign seamen, excluding lascars, or about fifteen percent of its workforce, but by 1938 this figure had fallen to 7000.[61] Since the British merchant navy still was by far the largest in the world, its experience tells us a lot about general trends.

Practically everywhere in the Western world seamen's unions gradually managed to improve the lot of sailors, both in terms of wages and

---

[58]For respective wage differentials, see Lewis R. Fischer, "Around the Rim: Seamen's Wages in the North Sea Ports, 1863-1900," in Fischer, *et al.* (eds.), *The North Sea: Twelve Essays on the Social History of Maritime Labour* (Stavanger, 1992), 59-73. An international maritime market that attracted labour from Germany and southern Scandinavia existed in the Dutch Republic in the seventeenth century.

[59]Hope, *New History of British Shipping*, 288 and 342.

[60]*Ibid.*, 360-362 and 366-367; Thorsten Rinman and Rigmor Brodefors, *Sjöfartens historia och utveckling under de senaste 200 åren* (Kungsbacka, 1982), 107 and 123-126; and Atle Thowsen and Stig Tenold, *Odfjell: The History of a Shipping Company* (Bergen, 2006), 256-257.

[61]Hope, *New History of British Shipping*, 344, 355 and 383.

working conditions. An important stage on this road was the general
movement from the traditional two-watch to a three-watch system, which in
many countries took place in the late 1940s and early 1950s. This reform gave
seamen an eight-hour work day, at least in principle, albeit decades after this
had been achieved by landward labour. Actual weekly working time was
gradually shortened, and longer annual paid vacations were introduced. Since
in practice this meant that ships needed more men than there were jobs, a
system of rotation gave sailors increasingly longer time off after each voyage,
and in many cases seamen spent as much time on vacation as at sea. Such
working conditions became common in Europe in the 1970s, just before the
great shipping crisis.[62]

The corollary of all this of course was that maritime labour costs
increased rapidly in most Western nations. In the early 1980s, total wages in
the leading group of high-cost countries typically amounted to four times those
in flag-of-convenience nations.[63] It thus was not surprising that shipowners
were tempted to move their vessels to these "convenience" registers to tap
sources of much cheaper labour or to avoid heavy taxes in their home country.
Trade unions opposed such schemes, and in 1958 the International Transport
Workers Federation – with the support of European shipowners' unions –
actually managed to slow down "flagging out" by declaring a boycott against
ships sailing on open registers.[64] At that time, the developed industrial
countries of Europe and North America – including Japan but excluding the
socialist countries – still owned about four-fifths of world merchant shipping,
while the Liberian and Panamian registers comprised no more than about ten
percent. But in the long run the flight of shipping from high-cost countries was
difficult to staunch. By 1970 the share of tonnage on open registers was
already a fifth, and ten years later it was a third. In particular, the British
merchant navy suffered from this flight (see figures 9 and 10).

---

[62]See, for example, Kaukiainen, "Ocean Tramp Freights," 45.

[63]ISL, *Shipping Statistics Yearbook 1984* (Bremen, 1984), 89-90. According
to these data, crew costs in a typical, handy-size, bulk-carrier of 25,000 dwt amounted
to about US $2.7 million per year in the US and Japan, US $1.5 million in West
Germany, around US $1 million in the UK and Greece and US $.55 million for a flag-
of-convenience vessel. Similar relative variations were also observed in other types of
ships. See also ISL *Shipping Statistics Yearbook 1977* (Bremen, 1977), 203.

[64]Gelina Harlaftis, *Greek Shipowners and Greece 1945-1975: From Separate
Development to Mutual Interdependence* (London, 1993), 55-56.

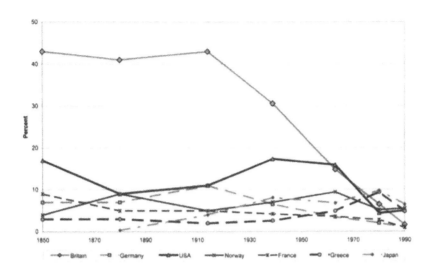

Figure 9: Large National Fleets, 1850–1990: Percentages of Total World Tonnage

Sources: 1850 and 1880: Fischer and Nordvik, "Maritime Transport," 526; 1914: Ronald Hope, *A New History of British Shipping* (London, 1990), 362; subsequent years: Lloyd's Register of Shipping, *Statistical Yearbooks*.

At the same time, many less-developed countries began to challenge the shipping hegemony of the Western world. An example of this was the adoption in the early 1970s of UNCTAD's "Code of Conduct for Liner Conferences" which reserved for all countries an automatic participation in liner shipping serving their ports. This agreement only became effective in 1983; although it was never ratified by either the US or Japan, and while it was hardly more than a declaration of fair principles, it may have helped a number of developing countries to establish their own liner services.[65] In any case, the role of developing economies was growing, albeit quite slowly: in 1970, they owned about six percent of world tonnage, and ten years later their share was ten percent.

---

[65]Stopford, *Maritime Economics*, 350 and 451.

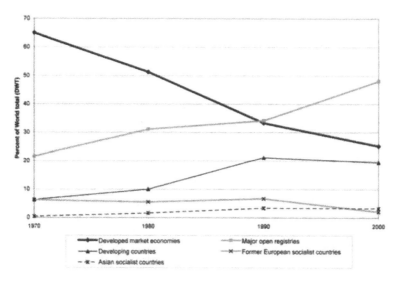

Figure 10: World Merchant Fleet by Country (Register) Group, 1970–2000

Source: UNCTAD, *Review of Maritime Trade* (2001), table 13.

    The major transformation began in the wake of the shipping crisis. By coincidence, this also was the time when many industrial countries started to liberate capital transfers to foreign countries. When oil and dry-bulk freights plummeted, Western shipowners found new opportunities to transfer their fleets to countries where crew cost only a fraction of their national levels. In the course of just a few years, many European countries lost the best part of their tanker and bulk tonnage to various open registers, and this trend has continued. The merchant shipping tonnage registered in developed economies only accounted for a third of the world total in 1990 and for a quarter in 2000. The majority of transfers benefited the major open registries (Panama, Liberia, Cyprus, the Bahamas, Malta and Bermuda), but ships were also transferred to a number of smaller registries in developing countries. In January 2000, about 14,000 ships representing over sixty percent of world dwt were flying flags which had nothing to do with the nationality of their beneficial owners.[66]
    A number of countries tried to prevent the exodus of merchant tonnage by allowing domestic shipowners some of the benefits enjoyed under flags of convenience, such as tax relief and the option to hire low-wage foreign labour. In most cases this was done by establishing a second, "international" register which ships engaged in foreign trade were allowed to enter. The prototype of such registers is the Norwegian International Shipping Registry

---

[66]UNCTAD, *Review of Maritime Transport 2001* (Geneva, 2001), table 16.

(NIS), started in 1987, which was followed by similar Danish (DIS), German (GIS) and French (FIS) systems. Even the UK and the US have their own "offshore" registers (Isle of Man, Bermuda, Gibraltar and the Marshall Islands).[67] The Norwegian and Danish systems have been particularly successful, since about half of the tonnage owned by the citizens of these two countries still flies the national flag.

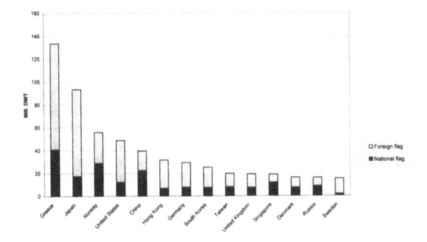

Figure 11: Major Shipowning Countries and Territories, 1 January 2000

Source: UNCTAD, *Review of Maritime Trade* (2001), table 16.

Dramatic as the results seem, flagging out was not a true revolution in ship ownership. As figure 11 demonstrates, most important maritime countries and territories in 2000 were still the same as in the early 1970s, and about sixty-three percent of world tonnage was owned in the developed market economies. This proportion was slightly smaller than in 1970, when sixty-five percent of global tonnage was flying the flags of developed countries (and to which should be added some twenty percent of shipping which already had been flagged to convenience registers). The two fleets which have regressed the most are those of Britain and the US, which in the 1960s were still the two

---

[67]The International Transport Workers' Federation (ITF) includes the French International Shipping Registry (FIS) and the German International Shipping Registry (GIS) in its list of flags of convenience; see www.iftglobal.org/flags-convenience/flags-convenien-183.cfm, accessed December 2007. In addition, a few countries like Finland have created special registers for ships in international trade. These vessels enjoy tax relief and certain exemptions from national manning regulations, but these registers are not open to foreigners in the same sense as the Norwegian International Shipping Register (NIS) or the Danish International Shipping Registry (DIS).

biggest in the world. They have now been replaced by Greece, Japan and Norway, which together around 2000 commanded almost forty percent of world tonnage. Another group which has increased its tonnage are the East Asian "tigers" (China, Hong Kong, South Korea, Singapore and Malaysia), which in 2000 owned about twenty percent of world tonnage, a figure which corresponds closely to the relative decline of shipping in the West. Thus, a modest global levelling took place during the last two decades of the twentieth century, although the developed and industrialized countries have remained the major powers in shipping. In particular, they have retained their position in the quality end of shipping: in 2005, for example, seventy-four percent of container tonnage was owned in countries which were members of the OECD.[68]

Much more important than the moderate changes in national ownership shares, at least in terms of globalization, has been the removal of huge amounts of tonnage beyond the reach of the legal authorities of the countries in which the actual shipowners reside. While the ships have nominally become subjects of their new flag countries, the latter have fairly limited power – even if they had the necessary determination – to exercise effective control over them. This means that the powers of the owners are extraordinarily broad. Such circumstances have created an odd non-national economic environment – a kind of no man's land – which resembles certain nineteenth-century colonial enclaves.[69]

Technology, Markets and the Cost of Ocean Transport

The commonly repeated axiom that the cost of maritime transport has declined substantially since the mid-nineteenth century is logical, plausible and supported by a good deal of empirical evidence. Yet we are still far from being able to present a precise and systematic description of the development of freight rates from 1850 to 2000. As I pointed out before, this is because there are no reliable quantitative data that cover the entire period. Nor are there data for all the various sectors of shipping, in particular for liners.

Thanks to the data collected from 1869 onwards by the London shipbrokers, Angier Bros., published by the shipping journal *Fairplay*, and its continuation until 1951, we have a fairly representative series of tramp (or spot) freights for a period of 118 years. These data were first used by the British statistician Dr. L. Isserlis in 1938, and quite recently it has again been exploited in two articles on the development of freight rates, one by Saif I.

---

[68]ISL, *Shipping Statistics Yearbook 2005* (Bremen, 2005), table 1.1.10.

[69]See Heide Gerstenberger and Ulrich Welke, *Arbeit auf See: Zur Ökonomie und Ethnologie der Globalisierung* (Münster, 2004), 28-69.

Shah Mohammed and Jeffrey G. Williamson and another by myself.[70] As far as the time before the First World War is concerned, these studies demonstrate that there indeed was a remarkable decline in the freight rates for important bulk commodities between the early 1870s and 1910s (see figure 12). The linear trend computed from the Isserlis index (expressed in fixed prices) implies an overall decrease of almost one-third, or one percent per year on average, while the other two unanimously suggest an even larger decline of about forty-five percent, or 1.5 percent a year.

Figure 12: Freight Rate Indices, 1870-1914 (fixed prices, 1884 = 100)

Note: 1: Isserlis index; 2: "Global index" calculated by Mohammed and Williamson; 3: Average freights of grain and coal carried for 5000 nautical miles calculated by Kaukiainen. Linear trends have been inserted.

Sources: Isserlis, "Tramp Shipping;" Saif I. Shah Mohammed and Jeffrey G. Williamson, "Freight Rates and Productivity Gains in British Tramp Shipping, 1869-1950," *Explorations in Economic History*, XLI, No. 2 (2004), 172-203; and Yrjö Kaukiainen, "Journey Costs, Terminal Costs and Ocean Tramp Freights: How the Price of Distance Declined from the 1870s to 2000," *International Journal of Maritime History*, XVIII, No. 2 (2006), 17-64.

Unfortunately, no dedicated liner freight indices exist for this period, although Angier's data does include rates for goods normally carried by liners, such as "sugar, etc.," "coffee, etc.," "light freight" or "general." But the data

---

[70]See notes 1 and 2 above; and Kaukiainen, "Ocean Tramp Freights," 23-24. From the 1950s my research is mainly based upon samples of detailed published chartering data.

are neither systematic nor continuous, which is likely why no one has tried to squeeze them into a special index, but the general impression is that in most cases the freights are more or less on the same scale as, for example, those of grain.[71] The Angier data have no quotations for manufactured goods, however.

On the other hand, a few contemporary freight indices did include liners. In 1904 the British Board of Trade published freight data covering the twenty years between 1884 and 1903. The material was a combination of tramp and liner freights to and from the UK, and there seems to be a slight liner bias in the routes chosen.[72] Figure 13, which compares the overall freight index (undeflated) with Isserlis' tramp index, shows that both fluctuated quite similarly. But somewhat surprisingly, the Board of Trade index had a stronger downward trend than the Isserlis figures; indeed, it correlates quite well with the global index constructed by Mohammed and Williamson.

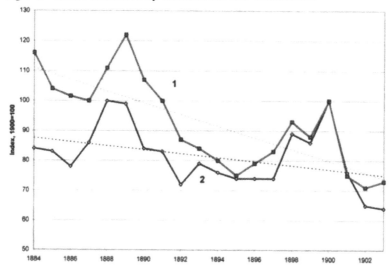

Figure 13: Comparison of Freight Indices by the British Board of Trade and Isserlis, 1884-1903 (Current Prices; 1900 = 100)

Notes: 1: Board of Trade index; 2: Isserlis index. Linear trends have been inserted.

Source: Isserlis, "Tramp Shipping," 57 and 122.

---

[71]A typical feature in such quotations is that instead of tons or other common measurements they refer to different freight scales (Bombay Scale, Colombo New Scale, Cochin Scale, etc.). Such scales allowed the actual measures of different goods to be adjusted according to their stowage factors, weights or cubic volumes.

[72]Isserlis, "Tramp Shipping," 55-57.

The comparison suggests that liner freights may have fallen as fast as tramp freights. Because liners carried many inexpensive bulk goods, these two markets were not effectively separated, so this is not totally unexpected. It also suggests that at least for a number of "colonial products" the actual freight levels did not differ much from those of better-paying bulk cargoes like grain. On the other hand, it is clear that the freight rates for such "liner goods," which were shipped in fairly small consignments and for which tramps did not compete, must necessarily have paid much more per ton than grain. It is also possible that their freights did not fall as much as those for bulk goods. Unfortunately, such "special" freights did not affect the freight indices because it would have been too difficult to record the entire range of "general goods" in the statistics.

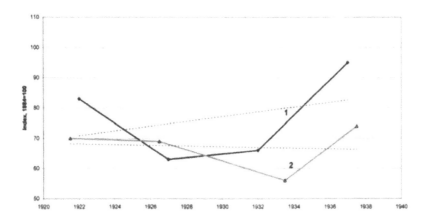

Figure 14: Freight Rates, 1920-1939 (Fixed Prices; 1884 = 100)

Notes: 1: Mohammed and Williamson's "global index;" 2: Average freight, grain and coal carried for 5000 nautical miles calculated by Kaukiainen. Linear trends have been inserted.

Sources: Mohammed and Williamson; "Freight Rates; and Kaukiainen, "Journey Costs."

During the First World War, freight levels rose rapidly, but in real terms they regained the prewar levels by the beginning of the 1920s. During the Great Depression of the 1930s nominal freights fell considerably, but because prices also declined their real value (compared to producers' prices) did not sink as much. On the other hand, it seems that the earlier trend of falling transport costs did not continue. Figure 14 presents two estimates in constant currency, Mohammed and Williamson's "global index" and the average freights of grain and coal which I have constructed. The former

suggests that there in fact was a slightly rising trend while the latter does not
show any clear trend at all. As the corresponding index values for the early
1910s were around eighty, and the projected trend values around seventy (see
figure 12), it seems clear that there was a turning point somewhere between
1910 and 1920.

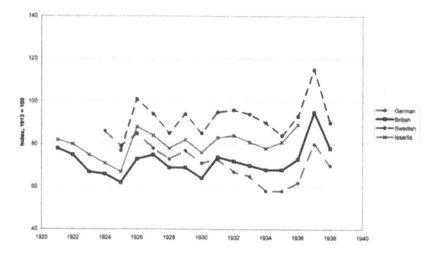

Figure 15: Comparison of German, British and Swedish Freight Indices, 1921-1938
(Fixed Prices; 1913 = 100)

Note: Original current value indices deflated by the respective national
               wholesale or producer-price indices.

Source: *Statistical Year-Book of the League of Nations* (Geneva, various years),
               tables of "index numbers of ocean freight rates."

It also appears that trends in freight rates were not uniform in the
1920s and 1930s. Figure 15, which presents contemporary British, German
and Swedish national indices, shows that they differed in both levels and
trends. The British index calculated by *The Economist* agrees quite well with
Isserlis, as does the Swedish (calculated by Handelsbanken), while the German
(by Statistisches Reichsamt) depicts an exceptionally steep decline from the end
of the 1920s. The differences likely reflect the foreign trade, particularly
exports, of the respective countries. During this period Sweden experienced
brisk industrial growth, and its exports grew steadily, while Germany's
economy fared far worse in the 1930s.[73] While differences in freight rates

---

[73]See, for example, *Statistical Year-Book of the League of Nations* (Geneva,
various years), tables of imports and exports; and Angus Maddison, *Phases of*

obviously reflected variations in demand, they may also have been affected by discontinuities in certain freight markets. In a period of increasing protectionism, states tried to promote liners, while subsidies for tramps were rare.

All three indices seem to have comprised both liner and tramp freights. Since they correlate well with the Isserlis index for tramps, there is nothing to indicate that liner tariffs increased substantially in either real terms or compared with tramp freights. But the indices obviously did not include tankers. Since this was a growing sector, it would be reasonable to assume that freight rates held up better than in other sectors.

The Second World War again triggered a steep rise in ocean freight rates; according to Mohammed and Williamson, they increased in real terms by 160 percent over the levels of the late 1930s. But after the peace the return to prewar levels was fairly gradual: during the latter half of the 1940s, Mohammed and Williamson's index shows that the general level of tramp freights in real terms (compared with producer prices) was almost one-quarter higher than in 1910-1914, or was at roughly the same level as in the 1890s. Nor was there any distinct decline in the following decade. Indeed, there were two strong booms: in 1951-1952, coinciding with the Korean War, and 1955-1957 during the first Suez crisis when freight rates exceeded the levels of 1945-1949 by some forty percent.[74]

According to the index compiled by the *Norwegian Shipping News* (see figure 16), it was only after 1958 that trip freights permanently sunk below the levels of the late 1940s. About 1965 a new decline set in, interrupted only by peaks in 1970 and 1973-1974. When the shipping crisis spread to the dry-bulk sector, trip freights plummeted between 1980 and 1982 by no less than a third, which brought them in real terms to about one-half of the freight levels of the early 1960s. Thereafter, rates stabilized at a new plateau, and the fluctuations since then have been fairly modest. The net result was that dry-bulk freight rates fell in real terms to less than a third between the late 1940s and 2000. Most of the decline took place before 1985 at an average rate of about three percent a year. My own estimates of grain and coal freights agree fairly well with the Norwegian index.[75] For the dry-bulk market, the

---

Capitalist Development (Oxford, 1982), appendices. Sweden and Finland first benefited from the fact that Russia's exports of sawn wood practically stopped after the Revolution. Subsequently, Swedish exports of pulp and paper increased rapidly.

[74]Mohammed and Williamson, "Freight Rates," table 3. Their data for the late 1940s, however, were very thin (on average only two quotations a year). Kaukiainen, "Ocean Tramp Freights," 51 and 53-54, suggests a smaller difference between the late 1940s and early 1910s (but it only included 1948 and 1949).

[75]*Norwegian Shipping News* Index (NSN), as printed in Statistics Norway, *Historisk statistikk 1978* (Oslo, 1978), table 201; and Kaukiainen, "Ocean Tramp

period since the end of the 1950s has been characterized by a decline in freight rates comparable to what occurred in the late nineteenth century.

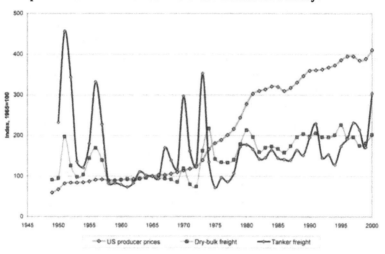

Figure 16: Development of Dry Bulk (Trip) and Tanker (Spot Market) Freights, 1949-2000 (Current Prices; 1965 = 100)

Sources: Dry bulk: *Norwegian Shipping News*, trip freight index, as printed in *Historisk statistikk 1978* (Oslo, 1978), table 201. Tankers: until 1973, *Norwegian Shipping News* index, according to Intascale and Worldscale points; from 1973 according to spot-market quotations, "dirty fixtures" from Arabian Gulf to North Europe, expressed in US $ per cargo ton, published in ISL, *Shipping Statistics Yearbook*, various years. Prices: until 1966, British wholesale price index; thereafter, US producer price index.

Freights," 53-54. Nominal indices were deflated by the British wholesale price index until 1966, and later by the US producer price index (during the 1960s, the US dollar replaced sterling as the primary currency in which ocean freights were quoted). Mohammed and Williamson also continued their global index by linking it with a new index devised by Hummels, "Have International Transportation Costs Declined?" But it is not clear how the linking was done because their data ended in 1950 and Hummels' started in 1952, with the Korean boom separating these two dates (indeed, it still affected freights in 1952), Mohammed and Williamson, "Freight Rates," table 3, claim a much steeper real-value decline than the NSN index, no less than ninety-six to ninety-seven percent between 1945-1949 and 1995-1997. This may partly result from the linking problems mentioned above, but it may also reflect the fact that Mohammed and Williamson used the British producer price index as the deflator for the entire period from 1950 to 1997. As British prices rose much more than in the US (if both prices in 1970 equalled 100, the British index in 1997 was 750 while the US index was 349), this makes a substantial difference. If we apply the NSN index, a realistic value for 1995-1997 would have been around thirty-six (1884 = 100) instead of seven, as in Mohammed and Williamson's table.

After the Second World War there is no need to use the data for dry bulk freights as a surrogate for other ocean transport costs, since series for tankers exist from the late 1940s onwards and for liners from the mid-1950s. Nonetheless, there are certain problems with the data. First, tanker freight rates have not usually been fixed in shillings or dollars per ton but in relation to standard freight scales (today called Worldscale), which were revised regularly according to changes in fuel prices and other costs. Yet a Worldscale index should not be regarded as a real fixed-price freight index, and trends computed from it cannot safely be compared with those of other indices, whether nominal or real.[76] Therefore, the index for tanker freights in figure 16 was based on actual dollar-per-ton quotations as far as possible.

Figure 16 clearly indicates that tanker freights were even more volatile than those in other sectors: the two booms of the 1950s, while corresponding perfectly with what was happening in the dry-bulk sector, were much more precipitous and were followed by two more in the early 1970s. On the other hand, the steep decline in 1974 and 1975 also was extremely sharp, although it was followed by a partial recovery. A new decline in the early 1980s took tanker rates in real terms to about half of their 1965 level, and they continued to decline moderately thereafter until the brief boom at the turn of the millennium.

Although the trends in freight rates in figure 16 have only been compared with the buying power of the dollar, it should be understood that this is not a perfect universal deflator. As long as the Bretton Woods system managed to maintain fixed exchange rates, there was no real problem, but after the system collapsed the dollar (which became the principal universal currency for ocean freights after the British pound was devalued in 1967) experienced a faster inflation than certain other currencies, such as the German *mark* or the Japanese *yen*. This means, of course, that dollar-based rates became cheaper in terms of such stronger currencies. Thus, from the early 1970s there was not just one real value for freights but several. For German shippers, for example, the average dry-bulk freights fell from 1965 to the late 1990s by about fifteen

---

[76]These scales were developed from the system by which the US and British governments compensated the owners of requisitioned tankers during the Second World War. In order to guarantee a "fair" return, a standard freight was computed by estimating voyage costs of "nominal" or benchmark ships. The present Worldscale is in principle based upon similar semi-annual estimates for different tanker routes, and on spot markets the actual freights are quoted as a percentage of the respective standard freight. This means that the freights are, in a way, related to a basket of costs, a built-in (albeit very narrow) deflator. The great weight given to fuel prices during the 1970s often caused the Worldscale rates to fluctuate quite differently than ordinary producer price indices (see, for example, ISL, *Shipping Statistics Yearbook 1990* [Bremen, 1990], 180). Moreover, since the standard freights are not published, the system is far from transparent.

percent more than the corresponding real value in dollars.[77] Still, the latter may be tolerably close to an international average.

The available data on liner freights for most of the period is limited only to the German liner trade index, which is based on data collected for liner cargo entering and clearing major German and Dutch ports (see figure 17).[78] While it probably covers quite well the Atlantic and Europe-East Asia trades, it cannot reflect trends on Pacific lines. This risk, however, has diminished in recent years due to the emergence of large-scale alliances of container lines and the beginning of around-the-world services which have made liner markets much more uniform than in the days of the traditional conferences. Moreover, the ease of container transhipment prevents the existence of exceedingly high rates on any of the major routes.[79] In any case, alternative freight series only became available in the late 1980s when container freights began to be published. In the beginning, however, the data mainly concern conference tariffs, which could differ substantially from the rates actually negotiated.[80] For this reason, the German index remains the only real choice.

The German index, being a part of national price statistics, was naturally computed in *marks*. But this does not seriously impair its validity as an international yardstick because liner companies (or rather, conferences) tried to compensate for the effects of dollar devaluation by levying a special surcharge known as the "Currency Adjustment Factor" (CAF). In Germany, at least, this seems to have been updated regularly, and we may therefore expect that most of the effects of exchange rate fluctuations were eliminated. The only exception were the years 1981-1985 when the exchange rate of the *mark* to the dollar experienced a substantial decline, and this fluctuation obviously was not compensated by CAF surcharges.[81] Of course, some proportion of freights

---

[77]In 1965 1 US dollar was worth about four *Deutschmarks* (DM), but in the late 1990s it was only worth DM 1.75 (www.measuringworth.com/datasets/exchangeglobal/, accessed December 2007). During the same period, German wholesale prices doubled while US prices quadrupled.

[78]Concerning the data and methods, see "Neuberechnung des Indizes der Seefrachten auf Basis 1991," *Wirtschaft und Statistik*, No. 3 (1996), 193-194.

[79]See, in particular, Trace, "For 'Tyranny of Distance,'" 23-27.

[80]*Ibid.*, 24-25. Beginning in 1988, a selection of conference rates was published annually in OECD, *Maritime Transport*, and from 1994 onwards on a quarterly basis in *Containerisation International*.

[81]H.L. Beth, "Fluctuations of Exchange Rates – Their Impact on Liner Shipping," *Report on the International Symposium held at Bremen, October 24th-26th, 1979* (Bremen, 1980), 39-60. Exchange rates between the US $ and DM were calculated according to www.measuringworth.com/datasets/exchangeglobal, accessed

were also negotiated in *marks* and other currencies, and since these normally were not added by currency surcharges they may have increased more slowly.[82] It is thus probable that the German liner index – with the exception of the mid-1980s – slightly underestimates the average growth of liner freights.

Figure 17: German Liner Freight Index, 1954–2000 (Fixed Prices; 1965 = 100)

Notes: 1: German liner index; 2: *Norwegian Shipping News* dry-bulk trip-freight index. The German liner index has been deflated by the German wholesale price index. The Norwegian index, as in figure 16, has been deflated by the UK/US producer price indices, chained at 1966.

Sources: ISL, *Shipping Statistics* and *Shipping Statistics Yearbook*, various years.

Figure 17 presents the real-value trend of the German liner index. It tells a rather interesting story which differs dramatically from other freight developments. Until the end of the 1960s, liner freights were remarkably

---

December 2007. In 1980 one US $ was worth DM 1.82, but in 1985 the rate was DM 2.94; the earlier rate was again restored in 1987.

[82]"Neuberechnung des Indizes," 194, informs us that in 1995 half of basic freights (*Grundraten*) were paid in US dollars, forty-six percent in DM and four percent in other currencies (but it does not specify in which currencies the surcharges – which of course were included in the data – were paid). On the other hand Beth, "Fluctuations of Exchange Rates," 39, estimates that some eighty percent of German shipowners' income was earned in US dollars. While these two rates are not mutually exclusive – German shipowners carried freight to all parts of the world, and ships from many countries carried German imports and exports – it is possible that the proportion of freight payable in DM increased. That would further emphasize the possibility that the German index slightly underrates the average international trend.

stable: there were hardly any fluctuations and only a slowly rising real-value trend. The 1970s were characterized by rapid growth which clearly exceeded the general rate of inflation; compared with German producer prices there was a seventy percent increase. This was followed by a modest decline, which covered the worst years of the shipping crisis, and a brief peak in 1984-1985. As the latter was connected with the temporary decline of the German *mark*, however, it obviously had no similar counterpart in dollar rates.[83] After that a distinct and fairly continuous decline ensued, bringing the rates down approximately to the levels of the late 1970s. At the turn of the millennium there was a short boom, but the rates sunk to their earlier levels after 11 September 2001.

The amazing rise of liner freights obviously resulted from the inherent stability of conference tariffs and the strong positions of the respective cartels.[84] Surcharges were an efficient tool to compensate for increases in different costs; in addition to the CAF, a parallel "Bunker Adjustment Factor" (BAF) was particularly important in a period when fuel costs grew five-fold – indeed, the BAF seems to have been the main reason why liner freights in the 1970s rose much faster than prices in general. On the other hand, it also contributed to the decrease after oil prices began to fall in the 1980s. Moreover, the non-transparency of liner freights helped to maintain the stability of cartel prices. Still, in the 1970s most conferences charged even containerized cargo according to traditional tariffs which contained several hundred individually priced items. It was only in the late 1980s that simple "box" or "FAK" (freight of all kind) rates became common, thus making it much easier for shippers to compare actual transport costs.[85]

---

[83]While it is obvious that the index expressed in DM in 1981-1986 exceeded the current freights in dollars by some margin, the difference cannot be estimated reliably since there are no systematic data on the ratio of the US dollar and the DM in actual freight transactions, nor do we know for sure whether any Currency Adjustment Factors (CAF) were added in these years to freights denominated in DM.

[84]Even the US exempted liner conferences from its antitrust legislation, mainly to prevent Soviet penetration into the international liner business; see "Solving the Intermodal Puzzle," *Containerisation International Yearbook* (1978), 12.

[85]*Ibid.*, 15; "Shippers Seize Power," *Containerisation International* (April 1996), 31-32; and W.B. Jackson, "Shipper's Point of View on Re-designing of Liner Tariffs," in *Future of Liner Shipping*, 196. The first line to offer "Freight of All Kind" (FAK) rates was the Taiwanese "outsider" Evergreen in 1975.

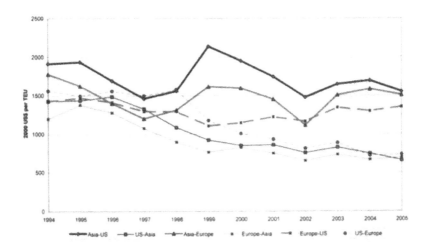

Figure 18: Negotiated Container Freights on Major Routes, 1994-2005 (Fixed Prices in 2000 US $)

Note: Rates refer to the second quarter of each year and include all typical surcharges (CAF, BAF and the Terminal Handling Charge [THC], which has been collected since 1991); actual rates deflated by the US producer price index.

Source: *Containerisation International*, "Freight Rates Indicators," second quarter (usually published in September), various years.

The downward trend which began in the late 1980s seems to have been connected with a change in liner markets. It has been claimed by some that the power of the traditional conference system to regulate the market and control prices started to decline in the 1980s and that during the next decade the conferences lost almost half of liner markets to independent carriers. Accordingly, intensifying competition and slowly accumulating "surplus" tonnage started to affect freight levels. Figure 18 confirms the message of the German liner index: container shipping freight rates have declined in real terms by some twenty percent between 1994 and 2005. On the other hand, a bifurcation of freight rates was imminent: the most massive decline, about fifty percent, was accounted for on low-demand legs of global routes, while on high-demand sides the decline was only slightly more than ten percent.[86] This indicates that demand was influencing liner freights more powerfully than before, although so far the sinking trend has been quite moderate. According to the German liner index, freight rates declined by only fifteen percent

---

[86]For the imbalance of the main container trades, see Stopford, *Maritime Economics*, 366-370.

between 1989 and 1999, and in the latter year the index was still in real terms about fifty percent higher than in the mid-1960s.

Table 4
Estimates of the Real-Value Trends in Tramp (Dry-Bulk) Freights, c. 1870-2000
(Index, 1870-1980 = 100)

Period	Grain/Coal (5000 nm)	M&W/NSN index
1870-1880	100	100
1905-1914	54	57
1925-1934	47	51
1950	62	62
1953-1956	75/82	64
1998-2001	15/19	20

Notes: Grain/coal per 5000 nm refer to my estimates, representing the average freights of grain and coal projected to a distance of 5000 nautical miles. Before the Second World War, freight rates included all stevedoring costs (i.e., the ship had to pay for them; this was called "gross rate" terms), but by the 1950s it had became common in the bulk trades for ships not to pay for discharge ("free discharge" [FD] terms), and in the 1970s they no longer paid for loading ("free in and out" [FIO]). For comparability, such changes have been compensated for by adding estimated loading or loading and discharge costs (plus associated port charges) to respective nominal freights. For 1953-1956 and 1998-2001, the lower figures refer to nominal, FD or FIO freights, while the higher includes corrections. M&W/NSN refer to the Mohammed and Williamson global index continued from 1950 by the trip freight index in the *Norwegian Shipping News*. Its level in 1950 has been set to equal the grain and coal average.

Sources: Kaukiainen, "Journey Costs," table 1; Mohammed and Williamson; "Freight Rates;" and *Norwegian Shipping News* index, as printed in *Historisk statistikk 1978*, table 201.

The overall development between about 1870 and 2000 can only be sketched for that part of the freight market which has been called tramp or the dry-bulk trades (table 4). But even this picture is based upon limited data; while there are a number of freight indices for both 1920-1939 and from the late 1940s onward, they lack continuity during the Second World War. This gap has only been bridged by real freight series of grain and coal plus the fairly scanty data on which the index by Mohammed and Williamson was based. Nonetheless, it seems quite clear that the decline of freights was a two-stage process. The first phase, marked by a fall in rates by about half, was terminated by the First World War and reversed by the Second: freights stayed above the level of the late 1930s until the last years of the 1950s. The second phase culminated in the 1980s, but a slow decline continued until the end of the twentieth century. About 2000, average real dry-bulk freights only amounted to about a fifth of what they were a century and a half earlier. While it is possible that the trends in liner freights were roughly similar before the Second World War and even for a couple of decades thereafter, it is clear that since 1970 their development has differed fundamentally from what happened in the bulk sectors.

Main Cost Elements: The Role of Ports

When trying to explain the decline in ocean transport costs, it is important to bear in mind that such costs contain two different, at least partly separate elements: voyage (journey) costs and terminal (port) costs. Since port costs accumulate regardless of the length of transport, the relative weight of these elements varies greatly on short and long routes. In a recent article, I tried to estimate the role of terminal costs in the long-term development of grain and coal freight rates. This was done by comparing the nominal rates to the respective lengths of hauls; in the resulting regression equation the intercept, or residual, included those elements which did not depend upon distance and which mainly represented terminal costs (as well, of course, as statistical errors). The development of this "terminal component" is presented in table 5.

Table 5
Terminal Component as a Proportion of Average Freights
of Grain and Coal, Selected Distances, 1872-2001 (percent)

	Freight at 2000 nm	Freight at 5000 nm	Freight at 10,000 nm
1872-1880	63	41	27
1907-1913	54	34	21
1953-1956	61	41	29
1998-2001	81	61	44

Note: All percentages computed according to the so-called "gross terms" (see table 4, note).

Source: Kaukiainen, "Journey Costs," 29, table 1.

It must be pointed out that the estimates may involve significant errors. Nonetheless, it is obvious that terminal components have always represented a major share of overall transport costs and that over shorter distances they regularly exceeded journey costs. The data suggest that there was a universal declining trend during the late nineteenth century, which implies that the decline of voyage costs was a little slower than freight rates. On the other hand, the high level of freights after the Second World War seems to have depended more on port than journey costs. This has persisted ever since: while terminal components have declined in real terms, they have fallen at a slower rate than overall freights. By 2000 terminal costs exceeded journey costs on average voyages of 5000-6000 nautical miles. This means that during the latter half of the twentieth century long-distance transports have, relatively speaking, declined faster than short ones. Such a difference may have given an additional boost to the process of globalization.

The decline of terminal components in the late nineteenth century suggests that port efficiency had improved; since stevedoring costs, at least in London, grew quite modestly in real terms between 1870 and 1910, it seems reasonable to suppose that there may have been some improvement in labour productivity. A contributing factor may also have been intensifying competition between major ports. Later, however, stevedores' wages increased faster than production: from 1910 to 1940, loading costs in London doubled again, and between 1950 and 1975 they grew four-fold.[87] Thus, it is not surprising that terminal components rose during and after the Second World War.

Until the 1950s stevedoring was overwhelmingly manual labour: indeed, it has been claimed that while power cranes were common, they improved "working conditions [more] than cargo handling speed."[88] Thus, there was a real demand for the so-called "port efficiency revolution" which began in Western European ports in the late 1950s. Mechanization and increasing proportions of skilled labour improved productivity; for example, in Antwerp the tons handled by a waterside worker grew four-fold between 1950 and 1970, and the revolution spread in the following decades.[89] It therefore seems surprising that the proportion of terminal costs continued to increase. The actual value of the terminal component, however, declined by more than one-half between the late 1970s and 2000. That the decrease was less than that of voyage costs can at least in part be explained by the new division of labour between ship and port; as I have already mentioned, big ships today have no cargo-handling gear but rely exclusively on port equipment. European and

---

[87]Research by P.M. Alderton, quoted in Gillman, "Container Shipping," 42. The data concern the London-Sydney liner trade and suggest that loading costs for liners were somewhat higher than for bulk-carriers: in London about 1960, these amounted to 0.73 pounds per dwt (8.9 in 2000 US dollars), while the discharge of one ton of heavy grain in the late 1950s usually was about 1.5 dollars (about $7 in 2000 US dollars); see Kaukiainen, "Ocean Tramp Freights," 63. Unloading costs for grain, however, usually included a port charge based upon the volume of cargo, while the liner example obviously only concerned stevedoring costs.

[88]Gillman, "Container Shipping," 42.

[89]See Kaukiainen, "Ocean Tramp Freights," 48-49, and the literature cited in table 7.

American ports also had the comparative disadvantage of being unable to hire cheap labour from the less-developed world. Moreover, terminal components are interesting because they tend to increase during shipping booms. This is, of course, caused by port congestion which leads to slower turnaround times and, not infrequently, to additional charges for overtime.

One more landward factor is also worth noting. Huge improvements in ship-to-shore and shore-to-ship communications have produced savings by allowing ship movements to be rationalized. In the late nineteenth century long-distance vessels often left a loading port without knowing their final destination; thus, they had first to enter a "port for orders" to pick up a letter or telegram telling them where to unload. Ships today can receive orders without losing time entering a port for orders, and they can even be directed to a berth just in time to start loading or unloading without any lay-days. Since the operating costs of large ships may exceed US $10,000 per day, a lot of money can be saved by modern communications.

Shipping Technology and Markets

The decline of ocean transport costs has traditionally been explained in terms of technological development, or "revolutions," which produced more efficient and economical vessels.[90] Broadly speaking, this can be taken as an axiom, since it is difficult to perceive how modern commodity flows could be handled by relying on nineteenth-century shipping technology. It would have been almost impossible to build and maintain sufficient wooden tonnage, and manning such vessels would require some ten million seamen. On the other hand, for at least two reasons the "mechanical invention" argument by itself is not sufficient to explain the amount or timing of decreases in freight rates. First, it does not take into account the role of ports (or rather the synergy between shipping and ports); and second, it seems to imply a belief that more efficient technology would automatically lead to lower prices. But a top modern ship is seldom cheaper than a second-best vessel, and those who have

---

[90]Douglass C. North opposed this view by claiming that organizational improvements were the dominant factor in the developments of the early nineteenth century, but some of his conclusions were effectively challenged twenty-five years ago by C. Knick Harley who, using new empirical data, came to the conclusion that a general decline of freights only started after 1850 and that it was caused by "metal ships and steam propulsion" (Harley, "Ocean Freight Rates and Productivity," 851-876). This line of thought has quite recently been further developed by Mohammed and Williamson, "Freight Rates." As far as more recent times are concerned, a good example of the "mechanical invention" paradigm is Martin Stopford´s emphasis on "two technical revolutions" – the containerization of liner shipping and the development of the modern bulk carrier – which have been central to the rapid development of shipping after 1960 (Stopford, *Maritime Economics*, 4).

invested in the former expect that it will produce returns as high as possible. Therefore, lower prices normally presuppose some kind of intervention by a competitive market.

In principle, technological development can improve ships' cost-efficiency in two ways: by increasing the actual transport performance and freight income or by decreasing capital and operating costs. These two do not necessarily go hand in hand; for example, the transition from sail to steam increased operating costs by adding a new element, fuel expenses, and steamers also were more expensive to build. Such additional costs were balanced by greater efficiency because steamers were able to carry three or four times more cargo in a given time than sailing vessels. The actual superiority, as well as cost differences, varied according to economic cycles and actual trades; as is generally known, sail remained competitive in long-distance trade decades after being displaced on shorter routes.[91]

It has already been mentioned that the overall volume of maritime transport has grown faster than world merchant tonnage. The difference between the respective growth rates suggests that the actual transport performance of ships has grown on average by more than one-half of one percent per year. This very crude measurement suggests that modern ships in any given time might carry about three times as much cargo per gross ton (or five times as much per net ton) as their predecessors 150 years ago. But it is quite another thing to assume that they can do this as cost-effectively as the old sailing vessels with low-wage crews and no fuel costs.[92]

The most important indicator of improving cost-efficiency – and one which can be followed from the 1860s or 1870s to 2000 – is the growth of average ship size (see table 6). It is generally understood that for each ton of cargo capacity large ships not only are cheaper to build but also less expensive to operate. In this respect, two periods of rapid change stand out: the four decades before the First World War and the 1950s, 1960s and 1970s, in particular the two latter decades. The only, and quite modest, backlash was recorded in the 1980s, mainly because a number of super-tankers were permanently laid-up or sent to breakers' yards.

---

[91]The comparative advantages of steamers depended not only on their ability to sail regardless of the wind but also on their shorter port turnarounds because of two novel features: water ballast in double-bottom tanks and steam-powered cargo-handling gear. Moreover, steam power could also be used in other heavy work, like mooring or weighing anchor.

[92]As an example, around 1875 an able-bodied seaman (AB) hired in Britain was paid about £3 per month. In the 1990s, a Filipino AB received on average about US $1300 dollars a month, including overtime and social security; see Stopford, *Maritime Economics*, 163. The real value of £3 in 1875 was about $200-220 in 1995.

Table 6
Growth of Average Ship Sizes, 1870-2000

Year	GRT/GT	Year	GRT/GT
1880	500	1948	3000
1900	1100	1970	5600
1913	1600	1980	9800
1921	2200	1990	9700
1939	2500	2000	11,400

Note: Excludes fishing and other non-trading vessels; numbers of ships before 1921 according to *Veritas* statistics.

Source: See figure 1.

The important question, of course, is how strong a correlation existed between the growth of ship sizes and the decrease in freight rates. At first glance, the trends seem parallel, at least before the First World War: between 1880 and 1913, average vessel size trebled and tramp freights decreased by about forty percent. Yet later data suggest a contrary conclusion. While average size jumped between 1910 and 1921, this was not followed by a real decline in tramp freights. Even more perplexing was that after the World War II ship sizes grew rapidly until 1980 but were accompanied by only a modest sinking trend in freights, although masked by strong cyclical fluctuations. Moreover, the lowest real levels in dry-bulk and tanker freights in the 1980s coincided with a moderate decrease in average ship size. Neither was there a good correlation between the growth of ship sizes and the decline of capital costs. Between the mid-1950s and 1980, the average size of grain carriers grew three-fold and coal carriers more than five-fold, yet the price per ton of both fell only modestly. Between 1980 and 2000, on the other hand, while the relative growth of both types of bulk carriers was slower (a fifty percent increase for grain and 100 percent for coal carriers), respective ton-prices fell by sixty or seventy percent.[93] Thus, it can be concluded that technological development alone affected the level of capital costs less than did the balance between supply and demand. This agrees well with the fact that ship prices, both new and second-hand, correlate strongly with freight-rate cycles.[94]

Liner shipping, and the container sector in particular, also experienced a fairly rapid growth in ship sizes, which were estimated to have halved operating costs per TEU-mile until 1985.[95] Yet there was no real-term

[93]Kaukiainen, "Ocean Tramp Freights," 43-46.

[94]Stopford, *Maritime Economics*, 101-110.

[95]Trace, "For 'Tyranny of Distance,'" 28; and Broeze, *Globalisation*, 94.

decline during the 1970s – in fact, the contrary occurred – and not even the massive new building of "fourth-generation" Panamax ships caused any sudden decline of freights, although they seem to have saturated the market and caused a moderate tonnage surplus. As was mentioned earlier, liner cartels (conferences) still controlled a good share of the market during the 1980s.

Declining freights are exactly what can be expected when supply exceeds demand, provided of course that there is a competitive market. A tonnage surplus seems to have been connected with earlier phases of freight decline or depressed rates. In the 1930s the situation was considered so severe that after a recommendation by an international shipping conference, several maritime nations introduced systematic ship-scrapping programs. It also seems that in the late nineteenth century the increase of global merchant tonnage in terms of actual transport capacity exceeded the growth of international trade.[96]

The development of tonnage surpluses is not infrequently associated with shipping "revolutions." When leading shipowners modernize their fleets, new buildings are regularly financed in part by selling older ships in the second-hand market. Thus, these vessels will still stay at sea and, since they are relatively cheap, remain competitive despite being less modern and efficient. Bursts of modernization thus produce a growth of low-cost shipping. Even if that does not result in surplus at the quality end of the shipping market, the additional tonnage will affect other segments of the freight market, usually tramp or dry-bulk trades or more peripheral liner shipping.

The bursts of modernization, or investment booms in shipping, tend to begin when freights are at good, or at least firm, levels. This was true after 1945; according to the profit-and-loss statements of British cargo companies collected by *Fairplay*, 1949-1953 and 1954-1958 were the two best peacetime quinquennia on record.[97] According to a director of P&O, shipowning then was "a delightful profession," so it is no wonder that it attracted invest-ment. It also seems that the new growth of liner tonnage in the 1970s was connected to the fact that income in this sector did not fall as in the bulk trades.

In all developed countries an additional motive for modernization was increasing labour costs, both in ports and aboard ships. Many states also paid direct or indirect subsidies to shipping and shipbuilding, which seem to have

---

[96]According to current estimates (Maddison, *Phases of Capitalist Development*, 254), the volume of international trade quadrupled between 1870 and 1913. If sail tonnage is added to steam tonnage multiplied by three – as was done by Fischer and Nordvik, "Maritime Transport," 532 – the theoretical transport capacity of world tonnage grew six-fold during the same period.

[97]*Fairplay*, annual reports of liner and cargo companies (based upon large samples). Profits compared to the book-value of respective fleets amounted in 1949-1953 to 39.5 percent and in 1954-1958 to twenty-six percent; comparable profits were only realized in 1914-1918 (28.5 percent).

sustained high levels of investment.[98] Similar factors can also be found behind the earlier phases of modernization; national subsidies were common at least from the 1850s, and British investment in steam shipping grew rapidly in the 1860s and 1870s when net returns from shipping were still at a respectable level.[99] The obverse was that after 1870s, as well as after the 1960s, declining freight rates also correlated with declining returns on capital.

To sum up, it seems that the long-term decline in freight rates has been discontinuous. While technological development was a permanent underlying factor, its economic effect on transport costs has been modified by the long-term rhythm of investment and market cycles in shipping. Ports have also contributed to this development, although it seems that terminal costs have not declined as fast as journey costs in the twentieth century. Therefore, ocean transport costs have sunken faster over long than over short distances.

Conclusion

Over the past 150 years ocean shipping has changed dramatically. The scenes in ports and at sea are totally different than in the 1850s: forests of masts have been replaced by the outlines of gantry cranes, and the scale and tempo of activities have increased significantly. Brunel's huge "leviathan," the 15,000-dwt steamer *Great Eastern* (launched in 1858 and until 1899 the biggest ship ever built), would today hardly rank as a "handy size" bulk carrier, and the present annual throughput in the port of Rotterdam exceeds the entire world's estimated maritime transport in 1913.[100] Another significant visual change is the sample of national flags flown by ships: the Red Ensign and other Western European and North American flags, flown by three-quarters of merchantmen about 1913, have become quite rare.

The huge overall growth of maritime transport has, of course, been closely connected with modern economic growth and especially with international trade (so far, the growth of air transport has remained a marginal element). Yet for shipping, derived demand does not seem a satisfactory expression of this co-variation. If average ocean freights were halved during the late nineteenth century and – at least for bulk shipping – more than halved again in the late twentieth, the old axiom of declining transport costs as a catalyst for trade growth merits serious consideration.

If ocean transport costs were five times higher in the mid-nineteenth century than today, it is not difficult to imagine that the "tyranny of distance"

---

[98]See note 51 above.

[99]Palmer, "British Shipping Industry," 92, table 2.

[100]Ewan Corlett, *The Iron Ship* (Frome, 1990), 197; and www.portofrotterdam.com/mmfiles, accessed December 2007.

in the earlier period substantially affected the interaction of supply and demand. Across fairly moderate distances, the exchange of goods was limited to those for which the producer enjoyed a comparative or absolute advantage. When these costs were lowered – as in the late nineteenth century – a new equilibrium was created. Depending on the actual terms of a transaction, this led to in improvement in producers' prices, a lowering of importers' prices or both. In all cases, though, the most likely outcome was an increase in the volume of goods traded. Less expensive transport also meant that products from distant areas were able to enter the "world" market, boosting the international division of labour and further increasing the volume of trade.[101]

Yet if we want to view the development of shipping in a wider context, another variable must also be considered. Customs duties and similar surcharges could add substantially to the prices of imports and often were used to protect domestic industries or to prohibit undesirable imports; typically, finished products were taxed more heavily than raw or semi-finished goods. It seems probable that before the mid-nineteenth century, transport costs still counted heavily, in particular for bulky products, but that the general lowering of duties from the 1840s to the 1870s changed matters considerably. The decline of transport costs during the latter half of the century probably triggered the new rise of protectionism during the 1920s and 1930s; in any case, it tipped the scales and made customs dues and tariffs often a more important barrier than distance. Since customs dues for oil, coal and raw materials in general were relatively low, the first phase of the postwar "shipping revolution" was connected with the growth of bulk shipping. The inexpensive long-distance transport of crude oil satisfied the growing demand for energy in the developed world, and by the 1970s even dry-bulk freights fell enough to make the shipping of iron ore from Australia to Western Europe an economic option. At the same time, a new wave of free trade, manifested in both the regional and multilateral reductions of duties (under the auspices of GATT and, more recently, the WTO) lowered customs barriers, especially for non-agricultural goods. This removed a major barrier from the trade in high-value manufactured goods, but another obstruction – the relatively high level of liner freights – remained. Therefore, the beginning of the decline of liner freights in the late 1980s was a more important catalyst for globalization than it would have been otherwise.[102]

---

[101]See, in particular, Harley, "Late Nineteenth Century Transportation," 595.

[102]O'Rourke and Williamson, *Globalization and History,* 30-41; and Estevadeordal, Frantz and Taylor, "Rise and Fall of World Trade." I presented a rough sketch of the role of customs relative to transport costs – which conforms quite well with the conclusion reched by Estevadeordal, *et al.* – in "Foreign Trade and Transport," in Jari Ojala, Jari Eloranta and Jukka Jalava (eds.), *The Road to Prosperity: An Economic History of Finland* (Jyväskylä, 2006), 162-163.

Norwegian Shipping in the Twentieth Century

Stig Tenold[1]

Norway is the greatest ship-owning country, relative to size, in the world. The explanation is not far to seek. The meagre resources of the land are insufficient to support the population. The natives are compelled to turn to the sea for their livelihood...In spite of the fact that shipping is one of the poorest paying businesses of the world, Norwegian capital and labor perforce must go to sea...By reason of its surplus of cheap, efficient labor and its serviceable fleet, Norway is prepared to do the cheap freighting of the world better and cheaper than any rival.[2]

From ancient times the Scandinavian peoples have been, in a prominent degree, engaged in shipping. In that way they introduced themselves for the first time in the history of Western Europe, in a rather violent manner by the Viking expeditions; while the Norwegians, or Norwegian colonists, discovered Iceland, Greenland, and even the North American continent nearly five centuries before the discoveries of Columbus. And in our day the Scandinavian flags, covering a seafaring trade far beyond what might be expected from the small population of these countries, wave in every part of the world.[3]

More than 100 years after the renowned shipping statistician A.N. Kiær wrote the above paragraph in the *Journal of Political Economy*, Scandinavian – and, in particular, Norwegian – shipping continues to play an important role inter-

[1]The author would like to thank Jan Tore Klovland, Lars Fredrik Øksendal and participants at the seminar in Oslo in October 2006 for comments.

[2]H.C. Calvin and E.G. Stuart, *The Merchant Shipping Industry* (New York, 1925), 221 and 266.

[3]A.N. Kiær, "Historical Sketch of the Development of Scandinavian Shipping," *Journal of Political Economy*, I, No. 3 (1893), 329.

nationally. Is the substantial Norwegian involvement in shipping an indication of the Norwegians' ability to stand their ground in one of the most competitive sectors in the world, or is it – as H.C. Calvin and E.G. Stuart argued – a result of limited shore-based alternatives? While the latter element has limited explanatory power in today's liberalized global economy, except through tradition and path-dependence, it was undoubtedly important for pre-petroleum Norway when domestic markets were more detached. Nonetheless, shipping still plays a significant role in Norway's economic fabric.

Table 1
Tonnage per 1000 inhabitants, Eleven Largest Maritime Nations,
1890 and 2000

Effective Tonnage per 1000 Inhabitants, 1890		Deadweight Tonnage per 1000 Inhabitants, 2000	
Norway	1100	Norway	12454
United Kingdom	547	Greece	12217
Denmark	252	Hong Kong	4732
British North America	200	Singapore	4669
Sweden	158	Denmark	3016
Australia	160	Taiwan	887
Greece	138	Japan	737
United States	64	South Korea	537
Germany	60	Germany	357
France	59	United Kingdom	318
Spain	59	United States	173
Western Average	146	World Average	121

Note: Kiær's data refer to "effective tonnage," where steam tonnage has been assigned a value three times higher than sail tonnage. The 2000 figures refer to "country of domicile" rather than country of registry. British North America includes Canada and Newfoundland.

Sources: 1890: A.N. Kiær, "Historical Sketch of the Development of Scandinavian Shipping," *Journal of Political Economy*, I, No. 3 (1893), 360-361; 2000: United Nations Conference on Trade and Development (UNCTAD), *Review of Maritime Transport 2000* (Geneva, 2000), 28, divided by population data from World Bank, *World Development Indicators* (Washington, DC, 2000); and, for Taiwan, United States, Central Intelligence Agency, *World Factbook 2000* (Washington, DC, 2000).

The aim of this article is to sketch some of the main trends in Norwegian shipping in order to illuminate the industry's contribution to the economy and to evaluate the country's position in international shipping. The focus is on long-term development. Accordingly, periods that are historically important, such as the two world wars, are not discussed in detail – these should be considered anomalies in the longer perspective. The aim is to highlight some of the factors that have enabled Norway to sustain its significant role in international shipping, a position that had already been established at the start of the twentieth century. In this essay I will present a broad overview of five different aspects of Norwegian shipping: networks and economic integration; fleet development, technological transitions and major trades; business organization and ownership; centres of activity; and shipping policy.

But first we need to establish Norway's position. Kiær used fleet size, divided by population, to illustrate the disproportionate Scandinavian participation in shipping. Norway's leading position by this measure was maintained more than a century later. Table 1, which cites and updates Kiær's data on "carrying power per inhabitant," shows that shipping continues to be much more important in Norway than in other countries.

Networks and Economic Integration

The shipping sector's position in the economy has been substantially more significant in Norway than in practically any other developed nation, perhaps with the exception of Greece. The maritime industries played a crucial role in the modernization of the Norwegian economy in the nineteenth century, and shipping was the country's leading export sector until it was eclipsed by oil revenues in the late 1970s. Figure 1 illustrates the crucial role of shipping in Norwegian exports. In addition to earning export revenues, the shipping sector has had important economic roles in other respects: as a basis for employment, as a buyer of Norwegian-built vessels and as hub in a network of auxiliary service providers – often referred to as "the maritime cluster."

In the nineteenth century, Norway's three leading exports were timber, fish and shipping services, together comprising more than three-quarters of all exports in the final quarter of the century. There was initially a close interrelationship between the three. At the beginning of the century the modest fleet primarily transported Norwegian exports and imports in northern and Baltic waters.[4] In 1860, the revenues from the transport of goods between other countries (third-country shipping) for the first time exceeded those related to the country's own trade.[5] By 1880 the Norwegian merchant marine

---

[4] A good introduction to Norwegian shipping in the late nineteenth and early twentieth century is Helge W. Nordvik, "The Shipping Industries of the Scandinavian Countries, 1850-1914," in Lewis R. Fischer and Gerald E. Panting (eds.), *Change and Adaptation in Maritime History: The North Atlantic Fleets in the Nineteenth Century* (St. John's, 1985), 117-148.

[5] For an analysis of this development, see Camilla Brautaset, "Norsk Eksport 1830-1865" (Unpublished PhD thesis, Norwegian School of Economics and Business Administration, 2002), 129-167.

had become the world's third largest, and Norwegian vessels served ports all over the world. This position was more or less maintained over the next century.

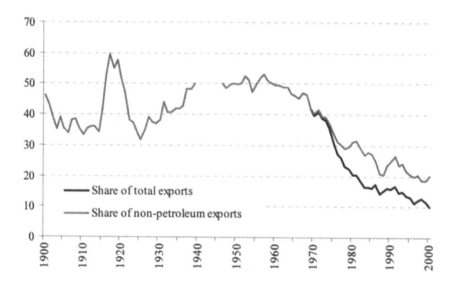

Figure 1:   Gross Freight Earnings from Shipping, 1900-2000 (Percent of Exports)

Sources: For the period before 1970: Statistics Norway, *Historisk Statistikk 1994* (Oslo, 1994); for subsequent years, Statistics Norway, *National Accounts* (Oslo, 2007), table 09.01.29 (web file at http://www.ssb.no/emner/09/01/nr/tab-29.html).

International demand developments, which will be dealt with later, are of course important to explain this transformation from home-based to world-wide shipping. But there was also a strong domestic supply stimulus. Norwegian merchants, subsequently evolving into specialized shipowners, learned the trade when transporting goods to and from Norway. As demand for shipping increased at the international level, cities and towns along the coast could use their advantages to supply transport capacity. Maritime experience, coupled with a low domestic wage level due to limited employment opportunities ashore, secured efficient and relatively inexpensive labour. Vessels were usually built at local shipyards with local inputs, and the vast forests provided ideal raw materials for the building of wooden sailing ships.

Although demand for Norwegian seamen continued to increase for more than century after 1850, the link between domestic shipbuilding and the shipping industry gradually diminished. Norwegian shipyards were tied to a dying technology. They had no comparative advantage in the construction of the new iron and steel steam vessels, and the abundance of second-hand sailing tonnage in the international market meant that used wooden tonnage could be bought cheaply. After 1861 ships bought from foreign shipowners for the first time outweighed the domestic supply of new tonnage. In the early 1880s ships built abroad became much more important than locally-built vessels, and from 1898 onwards imported steam tonnage exceeded the imports of sailing vessels.[6] In the years 1910-1913 the amount of imported tonnage was five times as high as that delivered from Norwegian yards.[7]

The position of the domestic shipyards as the main providers of tonnage to Norwegian owners waned, but some domestic shipbuilding and ship repair activities were maintained. During the 1930s Norwegian owners turned their backs on the traditionally important British shipbuilders, forging strong links with Swedish and Danish yards.[8] Norwegian yards struggled in this period, but new opportunities appeared after the Second World War. Substantial demand for new tonnage and limited foreign currency reserves led to a partial revitalization of the domestic shipbuilding industry. Partly as a result of direct and indirect public support policies, the shipbuilding industry was able to expand rapidly in the 1950s and 1960s.[9] Between the second half of the 1940s and the first half of the 1970s, tonnage delivered from Norwegian yards to domestic owners grew by a factor of more than ten, but the number of ships was halved due to the massive increase in average size. Nevertheless, the strong appetite of Norwegian shipowners for modern tonnage meant that the majority of their acquisitions were still built abroad. In the years 1963-1970, domestic yards accounted for less than twenty percent of new tonnage delivered to Norwegian owners. Over the same period, though, these same owners purchased more than seventy-five percent of the tonnage built at Norwegian

---

[6]Statistics Norway, *Tabeller vedkommende Norges skibsfart i aaret 1898* (Kristiania, 1900).

[7]Statistics Norway, *Historisk Statistikk 1948* (Oslo, 1949), 244.

[8]The British failure to maintain their most valuable foreign customers was partly related to a reluctance to build tankers; see Lewis Johnman and Hugh Murphy, *British Shipbuilding and the State since 1918* (Exeter, 2002); and Edward H. Lorenz, "An Evolutionary Explanation for Competitive Decline: The British Shipbuilding Industry, 1890-1970," *Journal of Economic History*, LI, No. 4 (1991), 915-916. After World War II, the reduction in Norwegian orders continued with even more force; see Johnman and Murphy, "The Norwegian Market for British Shipbuilding, 1945-1967," *Scandinavian Economic History Review*, XLVI, No. 2 (1998), 55-78.

[9]The scale and effects of the authorities' support have been analyzed in detail in Hans K. Mjelva, "Tre storverft i norsk industris finaste stund" (Unpublished PhD thesis, University of Bergen, 2005).

yards. It is evident that while Norwegian shipowners were extremely important to the country's shipbuilding industry, the significance of domestic yards for Norwegian shipping was much more limited.[10]

Just as the Norwegian shipbuilding industry thrived on orders from domestic owners, a number of other businesses evolved in the slipstream of Norwegian shipowners. Domestically-based companies have gained substantial market shares in a number of auxiliary services. The classification society Det Norske Veritas – with around sixteen percent of the international ship classification market – may be the best example of this linkage between the Norwegian fleet and shipping-related business activities.[11] Norwegian enterprises also play important roles within other support functions. Two of the world's three leading ship finance institutions have their shipping headquarters in Oslo, and two Norwegian insurance companies have an aggregate market share of fifteen percent. Norway is also home to the world's second largest shipbroker, as well as a plethora of smaller brokers. Moreover, despite the reduced importance of domestic yards, Norwegian companies control shipbuilding facilities both at home and abroad. Several leading international ship equipment producers are Norwegian-based, and their products have succeeded in following Norwegian (and international) ship orders, for example, to yards in East Asia.

Norway's economic history is thus intrinsically linked to the sea. While today's high GDP *per capita* hinges largely upon offshore oil production, the exports of fish and, in particular, shipping services played equally important roles in earlier periods. In an international setting Norway has been a peculiar case; for more than a century at least one-third of foreign revenues came as a result of the export of services. This accomplishment reflects the ability of the Norwegian maritime community to adapt to shifting circumstances in the international market.

Fleet Development, Technological Transitions and the Major Trades

Norway's share of the world fleet has been substantial since the mid-1850s. The country's share of world population reached a peak of approximately 0.15 percent around 1900, but the Norwegian-owned share of the world fleet has never dipped below 4.5 percent and at times has been more than ten percent. In the year 2000, the Norwegian-flagged and Norwegian-owned shares of the world fleet were 3.9 and 7.6 percent, respectively, while the country had only

---

[10]Data on Norwegian acquisitions come from Statistics Norway, *Historisk Statistikk 1978* (Oslo, 1978), 377-378.

[11]The history of Det Norske Veritas has been published by Håkon With Andersen and John Peter Collett, *Anchor and Balance: Det Norske Veritas 1864-1989* (Oslo, 1989).

0.07 percent of the global population.[12] Despite the relative consistency of the Norwegian share of the world fleet, the strategies and skills that lie behind this have shifted along the way. In a broad perspective, it is possible to identify three major transformations, with the two world wars as convenient breaking points. These shifts, illustrated in table 2, characterize both fleet development and market focus.[13]

Table 2
Three Transformations in Norwegian Shipping

Period	Technological transition	Market development
Pre-WWI	Expansion, then sail to steam	Domestic basis to third-country shipping
Interwar	Steam to motorships and tankers	Classic tramp to tank and liner services
Post-WWII	Larger ships, then specialization	Liquid and dry bulk to special segments

Source: Courtesy of the author.

The technological transitions and changes in the main markets are closely related processes. The following presentation looks first at fleet development, then at changes in employment. Norwegian owners have been characterized as "laggards" during the first major technological transition from sail to steam.[14] The reluctance to embrace new technology was partly a result of conservatism. A more important explanation, however, is that Norwegian owners, given the domestic cost structure and the properties of their major trades, could use the old technology efficiently and profitably longer than owners in many other countries.[15]

---

[12]Population data are from Angus Maddison, *The World Economy – Historical Statistics* (Paris, 2003); fleet data are from UNCTAD, *Review of Maritime Transport, 2000*.

[13]This schematic presentation of course involves a substantial degree of generalization and does not take into account the gradual and overlapping nature of the transformations.

[14]Håkon With Andersen, "Laggards as Leaders: Some Reflections on Technological Diffusion in Norwegian Shipping, 1870-1940," in Kristine Bruland (ed.), *Technology Transfer and Scandinavian Industrialisation* (Oxford, 1992), 307-331.

[15]Ole Gjølberg, "Økonomi, Teknologi og historie: Analyser av skipsfart og økonomi 1866-1913" (Unpublished PhD thesis, Norwegian School of Economics and Business Administration, 1979). For an alternative to Gjølberg's macro-perspective, see

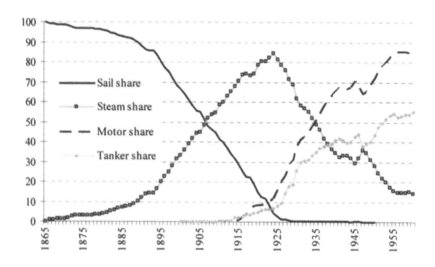

Figure 2:   Structural Transformations, 1865-1960: Shares of Sail, Steam, Motor
                 and Tankers in the Norwegian Fleet (percent of tonnage)

Sources: Statistics Norway, *Historisk Statistikk 1948* (Oslo, 1949); Statistics
                 Norway, *Statistisk Årbok for Norge 1963* (Oslo, 1963); and *Historisk
                 Statistikk 1994*.

Figure 2 illustrates the transition from sail to steam and the rapid
spread of motorships and tankers after World War I. In the early twentieth
century the laggards became leaders; Norwegian shipowners were pioneers in
a number of fields. The shift from steam to motorships occurred earlier in
Norway than in other major shipping nations. By 1939, motorships comprised
more than sixty-two percent of the Norwegian fleet but less than one-quarter of
the world total.[16] Parallel and subsequent transformations to more specialized
tonnage – oil, gas and chemical tankers, cruise shipping, dry bulk and combination carriers and roll on-roll off (Ro-Ro) and heavy lift vessels – also were
areas in which Norwegians were pioneers. These innovative strategies are
partly explicable by the relatively small, non-bureaucratic and entrepreneurial-
minded companies that dominated Norwegian shipping. Another explanation is
that Norway in the postwar period developed into a country with high labour

Berit Eide Johnsen, *Rederistrategi i endringstid: Sørlandsk skipsfart fra seil til damp og
motor, fra tre til jern og stål, 1875-1925* (Kristiansand, 2001).

[16]Data from the *Lloyd's* register, reprinted in S.G. Sturmey, *British Shipping
and World Competition* (London, 1962), 84. Due to definitional differences, the share
of motorships deviates from that shown in figure 2.

costs. The combination of increasing wages and strict manning requirements obliterated the image of the inexpensive Norwegian seaman of the late nineteenth century. Consequently, productivity improvements from economies of scale related to vessel size or from technological superiority were necessary to compensate for higher wage bills.

The shifts in Norway's major trades have of course been heavily influenced by the developments sketched above. There have been at least three significant transformations in the employment pattern. The first transition occurred during the nineteenth century, when the main activity shifted from servicing the country's foreign trade to shipping goods between foreign ports, the so-called "cross-trades." The second transition took place in the interwar period, when Norwegian shipowners took advantage of opportunities in the rapidly increasing market for oil transport and also made temporary inroads into the liner business. The final shift has been the gradual focus on increasingly specialized niches, a transformation that began in the postwar period but escalated during and after the shipping crises of the 1970s and 1980s. To some extent the specialization was helped by Norway's position as an offshore oil producer, thus – at least initially – reflecting a return to home waters.

Explanations of the three transformations must rely on a combination of external and internal factors, with particular emphasis on global demand development and Norwegian cost structures. The repeal of the British Navigation Acts in 1849 enabled the strong growth in third-country shipping in the second half of the nineteenth century. From 1850 to 1860 the volume of Norwegian tonnage clearing British ports increased by 191 percent; only the United States had a larger absolute increase in the British market.[17] Norwegian shipowners were able to take advantage of this opportunity as a result of their rich maritime traditions and comparative advantages in the provision of efficient and inexpensive transport services.

The strong growth of Norwegian tanker shipping was premised upon oil companies outsourcing their transport requirements. Yet to explain why Norwegian shipowners, rather than those in other countries, engrossed much of this trade it is necessary to look closer at the characteristics of tanker investors. First, it is evident that tanker owners comprised primarily new or relatively small companies rather than the established shipping aristocracy. Second, while second-hand purchases have been important in some cases, a more general explanation of the tanker expansion can be found in the relationship between the new tanker owners, with limited financial resources, and shipyards abroad willing to offer generous credits for tanker orders. Non-bureaucratic companies, with little to lose and a willingness to take risks, were

---

[17]John Glover, "On the Statistics of Tonnage during the First Decade under the Navigation Law of 1849," *Journal of the Royal Statistical Society of London*, XXVI, No. 1 (1863), 14.

well-suited for new and unknown ventures in the tanker sector.[18] Some established operators, on the other hand, moved out of the tramp segment and into the liner business. This partly reflected encroachment by liners on tramp transport in a depressed market, but there appears to have been a tendency to overestimate the importance of the Norwegian owners' foray into liner shipping.

Liner shipping did become more important in the interwar period, and some companies – such as Wilh. Wilhelmsen – managed to attain a position among the world's leading liner companies. Nevertheless, Norway was underrepresented in the liner trade. The liner share reached a peak around 1930. According to international sources, approximately a third of the Norwegian fleet was involved in liner services at the time compared with more than fifty percent for the world fleet.[19] But many of the Norwegian ships in this trade did not conform to our common understanding of a liner. Some of the Norwegian "lines" had a distinctly tramp-like flavour. This applied both to the manner in which the services were organized and the characteristics of the vessels used in these services. Some ships operated in the tramp market on parts of the journey, some were time-chartered to foreign liner interests, and some "lines" were based on long-term contracts with shippers rather than on fixed sailing schedules.[20] As such, the term "quasi-liner services" is perhaps a more appropriate description. Regardless of the actual extent of Norwegian liner involvement, one thing is clear; the downward liner trend that started in the early 1930s increased in the postwar period. By 1975 only four percent of Norwegian tonnage was engaged in liner shipping.[21]

The final transformation, towards increased specialization, in fact involved two partly overlapping processes. Until the early 1970s mammoth tankers and bulk carriers dominated the Norwegian fleet. While the strong growth of the international trade in raw materials provided the demand for this development, the domestic cost structure gave a supply-side impetus for capital-intensive tonnage that utilized economies of scale to neutralize labour-cost dis-

---

[18]See Stig Tenold, "The Norwegian Interwar Tanker Expansion – A Reappraisal," *Scandinavian Economic History Review*, LV, No. 3 (2007), 244-261.

[19]Christopher von Schirach-Szmigiel, *Liner Shipping and General Cargo Transport* (Stockholm, 1979), 32. According to data quoted in Osborne Mance, *International Sea Transport* (Oxford, 1945), 68, the share of the Norwegian fleet accounted for by tramp tonnage declined from eighty-four percent in 1914 to forty percent by 1933. The data indicate a massive increase in the share of the fleet contributed by liners but do not take into account Norwegian involvement in the tanker sector.

[20]See, for instance, the discussion of the County Line or the Fern Line in John. O. Egeland, *Kongeveien – Volume II* (Oslo, 1973), 81-84.

[21]Norway, Parliament, Stortingsmelding No. 23 (1975-1976), "Om sjøfolkenes forhold og skipsfartens plass i samfunnet," 89.

advantages. Yet even during this transformation, some shipowners chose technologically advanced niche tonnage, rather than sheer size, to compensate for uncompetitive wage bills and to take advantage of the relative abundance of equity capital within Norway. Norwegians were among the first movers in a number of new segments, investing, for instance, in gas and chemical tankers, cruise vessels and car carriers. When the shipping crises violently hit the "staple" liquid and dry-bulk markets in the second half of the 1970s and first half of the 1980s, the mammoth vessels lost their dominant position in the Norwegian fleet.[22] At the same time, niche operators, some of whom had managed to gain substantial market shares in their chosen segments, became much more important. Another rapidly growing segment was the offshore oil sector. Norwegian shipowners invested heavily in offshore rigs and service vessels – supply ships, diving support craft and tugs. By the year 2000 offshore service vessels comprised approximately twelve percent of the value of the Norwegian fleet – thirty-five years earlier, such vessels had been practically non-existent. Though originally based upon Norwegian oil exploration, by 2000 the majority of Norwegian mobile offshore units operated outside the domestic sector.[23]

As previously shown, the income from shipping has traditionally comprised a substantial part of Norwegian export revenues. Figure 3 illustrates the importance of the various types of ships and charters in a long-term perspective. Unfortunately, the available data are differentiated by propulsion before World War II and by cargo thereafter. For the period until 1939, the left-hand side of the figure shows the relative shares of gross freight earnings from sailing vessels, steamships and motor vessels. The earnings for the latter two groups have been divided into voyage and time freights. It is likely that a substantial part of motorship earnings came from tankers. After World War II the manner of reporting changed, and the right-hand side of figure 3 shows the relative shares of liners, dry cargo vessels and tankers. Again, earnings for the latter two groups have been divided into voyage (trip) and time freights.

Figure 3 illustrates the shifts in the various types of shipping revenues, but there are reasons for caution in interpreting the data as the types' and segments' relative contributions to the Norwegian economy. First, the proportion of "imports" needed to produce revenues varied. For instance, sailing vessels had relatively small expenses abroad compared with steam and motorships. Second, even among steam and motorships, costs accrued abroad differed. In particular, liners tended to have substantially larger costs abroad than liquid and dry-bulk vessels. During the 1970s liners comprised around five percent of the fleet but accounted for almost a third of gross freight earnings.

---

[22]See Stig Tenold, *Tankers in Trouble: Norwegian Shipping and the Crisis of the 1970s and 1980s* (St. John's, 2006).

[23]Norges Rederiforbund, *Kvartalsinformasjon om skipsfart og offshorevirksomhet* (Oslo, 2000), 6 and 8.

This is not an indication of particularly high profitability but rather reflected the fact that the liner trade is a high-cost shipping segment. Finally, the shipping market is characterized by sharp fluctuations in freight rates but more stable operating costs. This implies that during booms incomes increase faster than costs. This becomes evident if we look at costs abroad relative to gross freight earnings. During the World War I boom, disbursements abroad made up approximately thirty percent of gross freight earnings. This was fifteen to twenty percentage points lower than levels either before or after the war.

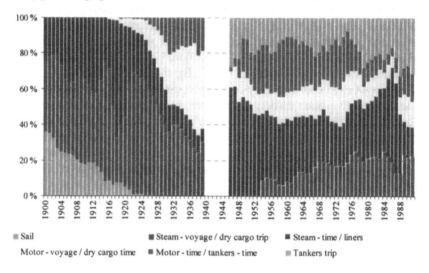

Figure 3: Relative Gross Freight Earnings by Ship Type/Employment, 1900-1991

Note: Dry-cargo trip freights are included in the category "liners" for the period 1946-1953.

Sources: *Historisk Statistikk 1948*; and *Historisk Statistikk 1994*.

Geographically, shifts in the employment of the Norwegian fleet mimic developments in international trade. In the last part of the nineteenth century European ports were particularly important, accounting for more than two-thirds of the Norwegian ship arrivals. Subsequently, more services arrived at Asian and American ports; by 1960 the US alone accounted for almost seventeen percent of Norwegian ship arrivals, an increase from 7.6 percent in 1895. The British share (including Ireland) fell from almost twenty-eight percent in 1895 to slightly more than seven percent by 1970. In the latter part of the period the increasing importance of oil exports from the Gulf was evident – their share of Norwegian tonnage arrivals grew from less than eight percent in 1960 to more than fourteen percent a decade later.

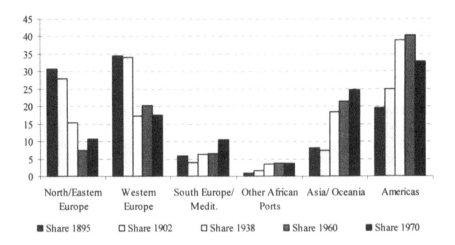

Figure 4: Employment of the Norwegian fleet (Percent, Net Tonnage)

Note: Shares are based on arrivals and tonnage. Arrivals in Norway included.

Sources: Statistics Norway, *Tabeller vedkommende Norges skibsfart i aaret 1895* (Kristiania, 1897); Statistics Norway, *Tabeller vedkommende Norges skibsfart i aaret 1902* (Kristiania, 1904); *Historisk Statistikk 1948*; *Statistisk Årbok for Norge 1963*; and Statistics Norway, *Statistisk Årbok for Norge 1973* (Oslo, 1973).

Figure 4 shows the spatial shifts in the trading pattern from the early twentieth century to 1970. While the data are not wholly consistent across time and regions, the figure can be seen as a crude approximation of shifts in the employment of the Norwegian fleet. But it is important to note the limits of these data. First, the manner in which "arrivals" were registered and defined varied, both with regard to ships in ballast and the treatment of multiple "arrivals" in a single country. Second, the data can only give an indication of the importance of the various geographic segments. There is no differentiation between short and long voyages, and this has to be taken into account if we want to compare the relative importance of ports in different regions.

Business Organization and Ownership

The organization and structure of shipping companies has differed from other enterprises. Although the main unit of analysis has been – and should be – the *rederi* (management company), the vessels have in the twentieth century usually been legally owned by holding companies, which may or may not have been controlled by the same person or people as the *rederi*. The incorporation of the holding companies has varied, but most grew out of the traditional nine-teenth-century form of ownership – the *partsrederi* (usually translated as part-nership, part-ownership or joint-ownership).

In the early expansionary phase of Norwegian shipping, the *partsre-deri* was the dominant form of ownership. Individuals bought one or more parts in a vessel, a method of raising capital and distributing risk that mirrored early maritime organization in many countries.[24] The investments were usually confined to a specific ship, and the partnership was dissolved when the ship was sold, broken up or lost. The partnerships were a convenient means of rais-ing funds. Parts were sometimes paid for in kind, and while loan capital was hard to come by for the *rederi*, part owners were able to raise individual loans using their shares or other assets as collateral.

Due to the limited possibilities of obtaining mortgages on ships in the nineteenth century, the *partsrederi* was relatively long-lived in Norway com-pared with other countries. Only in the first part of the twentieth century were partnerships, with prorated liability, replaced by limited-liability, joint-stock companies (*aksjeselskap* or *skipsaksjeselskap*). Behind this development were legal changes, including improved acceptance of ships as collateral, as well as the growing demand for funds as ships became more expensive.

Before World War I the old partnerships co-existed with single-ship, limited-liability companies, some of which had been transformed from partner-ships. There was also an increased tendency to "consolidate" interests in multi-ship, limited-liability companies. But the degree to which the various organiza-tional forms were used differed among geographic regions and trades.[25] The transformation to single-ship, limited-liability companies in Norway gathered momentum after the turn of the century, at least thirty years after similar de-velopments in British shipping. Yet the consolidation into "proper enter-prises," built for longevity rather than tied to individual vessels, appears to have been primarily an interwar phenomenon.

---

[24]Similar types of ownership, for instance, were the British "sixty-fourthers" or the Spanish *porciones*; see Gordon Boyce, "64thers, Syndicates, and Stock Promo-tions: Information Flows and Fund-Raising Techniques of British Shipowners before 1914," *Journal of Economic History*, LII, No. 1 (1992), 181-205; Jesús M. Valdaliso, "Spanish Shipowners in the British Mirror: Patterns of Investment, Ownership and Finance in the Bilbao Shipping Industry, 1879-1913," *International Journal of Mari-time History*, V, No. 2 (1993), 1-30; and Gelina Harlaftis and John Theotokas, "Euro-pean Family Firms in International Business: British and Greek Tramp-Shipping Firms," *Business History*, XLVI, No. 2 (2004), 219-255.

[25]See Atle Thowsen, "Vekst og strukturendringer i krisetider 1914-1939," *Bergen og sjøfarten IV* (Bergen, 1983), 29-44, for a more detailed discussion of the various forms of ownership.

In the postwar period there were two important changes in the manner in which shipping was organized. The first was the growing use of *kommandittselskap* (limited partnerships) as holding companies. *Kommandittselskap* became attractive primarily for tax reasons, and the proportion of the Norwegian fleet owned by such companies increased from 2.5 percent in 1970 to about twenty percent by 1985.[26] The second important change was the introduction of "managerial capitalism" approximately a century after this had caught on internationally. The separation of ownership and management became relatively common in Norwegian shipping companies from the 1970s onwards.[27] While many companies fell victim to the shipping crisis before the owners vacated the helm to outsiders, several companies that managed this transition subsequently increased the spread of ownership through such devices as stock exchange listings.

A relatively recent phenomenon is the disentanglement of Norwegian shipping companies from domestic equity capital. Some Norwegian shipping companies with long histories, such as Bergesen, have been acquired by foreign owners but continue to operate out of Norway and are still listed on the Oslo *Børs* (stock exchange). In several Norwegian shipping companies, the proportion of foreign shareholders is relatively high. This reflects both "real" foreign capital and investor vehicles registered abroad for tax or other reasons, but with ultimate ownership by Norwegian entities.

The issue of ownership raises a number of interesting questions. First, how does the turnover (birth and death rates) of shipping companies compare with other Norwegian sectors – and the shipping sector in other countries? Second, what were the initial advantages of the number of new successful shipping companies established during the twentieth century? Preliminary research indicates that both "reverse mergers" following inheritance or other family settlements and new companies established by personnel from existing companies have been important. Third, the manner in which the business was organized – with the separation of the *rederi* from the holding companies – raises a number of interesting "corporate governance" issues. Did managers – who could live comfortably on their annual commissions – "starve" shareholders by keeping dividends unduly low? What determined the distribution of ships among holding companies related to the same *rederi* but with different shareholders?

---

[26]See Stig Tenold, "The Shipping Crisis of the 1970s: Causes, Effects and Implications for Norwegian Shipping" (Unpublished PhD thesis, Norwegian School of Economics and Business Administration, 2002), 298-306, for an introduction to changes in the incorporation of shipping companies in the period 1970-1985.

[27]The separation of ownership and management refers to the hierarchy within shipping companies and not to the use of external management companies to operate fleets.

To answer these questions, a combination of macro and micro studies will be necessary. The macro studies will enable us to analyze differences in ownership across time and geographic regions and to gain knowledge about the changes in the population of shipping companies. The micro studies will give complementary insights, for instance with regard to differences among market segments, and will also make it possible to address questions regarding ownership, strategy and "corporate governance" in more detail.

Centres of Activity

The dispersion of ownership among a large number of companies was also reflected in a broad spatial distribution of shipowners. All along the coast, shipping was an important business in cities, towns and villages. But the main centres of activity varied over time. Until the last decades of the nineteenth century ports on the south coast were particularly important; in the late 1870s the county of Agder, with approximately 150,000 inhabitants, controlled two percent of world shipping tonnage.[28] Bergen, on the west coast, was a leader in the transition from sail to steam, mainly because of its prominent position in the fish and fruit trades where speed was more essential than in other markets.

Figure 5 shows that in the early twentieth century there were substantial regional differences – and also major differences among ports in the same region – with regard to the proportion of "modern" tonnage. The figure below the geographic category indicates the amount of steam and motor tonnage in gross tons. The black squares show the average share of steam and motor tonnage in various regions (as percentages of the total fleet), while the lines reveal the "span" in this proportion between the various ports in a region.

In the interwar period shipowners based in Oslo assumed a much more important role, in part due to their massive investments in tankers. Nevertheless, the role of the capital city was relatively limited compared with the concentration in many other maritime nations, at least until the shipping crisis of the 1970s and 1980s. Until the early 1970s, thirty ports along the coast, some of which were relatively small places, owned ships engaged in international shipping. Today, the two leading cities account for almost three-quarters of all Norwegian tonnage; Oslo is a leading international maritime centre, and Bergen hosts major participants in a number of shipping niches. The activity in other places with long maritime traditions is either non-existent or confined to a handful of companies. Figure 6 illustrates the changes in the registration of the Norwegian fleet across time based upon public statistics.

---

[28]The subsequent decline of this region is discussed in Johnsen, *Rederistrategi i endringstid.*

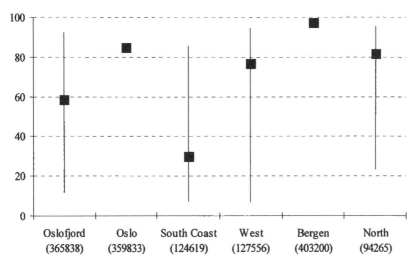

Figure 5: Shares of Steam and Motor Tonnage, 1910 (Percent, Gross Tonnage)

Note: Oslofjord: Halden, Sarpsborg, Fredrikstad, Moss, Drøbak, Hamar, Dram-
men, Holmestrand, Horten, Tønsberg, Sandefjord, Larvik, Brevik, Pors-
grunn, Skien and Langesund; South Coast: Kragerø, Risør med Lyngør,
Tvedestrand, Arendal, Grimstad, Lillesand, Kristiansand S., Mandal, Far-
sund and Flekkefjord; West: Sogndal, Egersund, Stavanger, Sandnes,
Skudeneshavn, Kopervik, Haugesund, Odda; North: all ports north of Bergen. Ports with an aggregate tonnage lower than 1000 gross registered tons
have been excluded.

Source: *Historisk Statistikk 1948*, 254.

Unfortunately, the Norwegian statistics do not accurately reflect the
changes in the importance of the various regions. There are three main reasons
for this. First, some shipping companies conducted their business from one
region but registered their ships in other ports. This typically leads to an un-
derestimation of Oslo's share, as several large companies were based there but
registered their vessels elsewhere. This problem affects the data throughout the
period. Second, in the early part of the period, the disproportionate shares of
steam and sail tonnage implies that the regions' share of "effective tonnage"
deviated from their share of net tonnage. Finally, in the latter part of the period two problems occur. A substantial number of ships have not been assigned
to a specific region, reflected in the less than 100 percent aggregate in 1987.
Second, the propensity to register ships abroad varied between regions. Consequently, there were regional differences between the share of the Norwegian-
registered fleet and the Norwegian-controlled fleet. Table 3 illustrates how
different definitions of the fleet affected the importance of various regions.

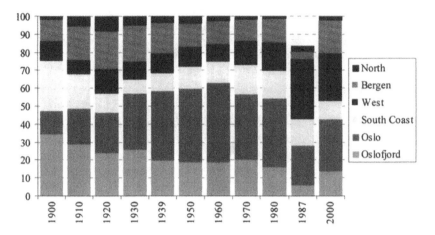

Figure 6:   Regional Distribution of the Fleet (Percent, Gross Tonnage)

Note: Data for 1900 refer only to vessels in foreign trade. Geographic categories
         are the same as in figure 5.

Sources: 1900: Statistics Norway, *Tabeller vedkommende Norges skibsfart i aaret
            1900* (Kristiania, 1902), *Historisk Statistikk 1948*, 253-260; and Statistics
            Norway, *Historisk Statistikk 1978* (Oslo, 1978), 387. 1910-1970: Statistics
            Norway, *Statistisk Årbok 1981* (Oslo, 1981), 198. 1980; Statistics Norway,
            Statistisk Årbok 1988 (Oslo, 1988), 304. 1987: Statistics Norway,
            Sjøtransport (Oslo, 2007), table 06.17.09. 2000: web file at http://www.
            ssb.no/handelsfl/arkiv/tab-2002-06-17-09.html.

Table 3
Regional Distribution of the Fleet (Percent, Gross Tonnage)

	1900 I	1900 II	1987 I	1987 II	1987 III	1987 IV	1987 V
Oslofjord	31.9	34.6	5.9	7.1	12.0	4.5	4.3
Oslo	14.2	12.6	22.2	26.7	34.0	69.8	59.7
South Coast	19.3	28.2	14.6	17.6	14.8	14.8	18.9
West	11.1	10.7	33.2	39.9	30.6	2.4	3.0
Bergen	21.2	12.2	4.1	4.9	7.6	7.5	13.9
North	2.3	1.7	3.2	3.9	1.1	1.07	0.1

Note: See the text for a discussion of the various categories.

Sources: 1900: *Tabeller vedkommende Norges skibsfart i aaret 1900*, 3-10. 1987 I and
            II: *Statistisk Årbok 1988*, 304. 1987 III, IV and V: Stig Tenold, "The Ship-
            ping Crisis of the 1970s: Causes, Effects and Implications for Norwegian
            Shipping" (Unpublished PhD thesis, Norwegian School of Economics and
            Business Administration, 2002), 258-283.

Columns 2 and 3 in table 3 illustrate how the regional shares of the fleet changed if we look at "common" tons (1900 II) or adjust for the fact that steam and motor are more efficient than sail (1900 I). The differences between the two columns reflect, for example, the relatively high proportion of modern tonnage in Bergen and the limited share of steam and motor tonnage on the South Coast.

The five columns depicting the status in 1987 are based on the following definitions of the Norwegian fleet. 1987 I shows the proportions of gross tonnage as they appear in the public statistics. Approximately seventeen percent of the fleet have not been assigned to a specific port. 1987 II, like 1987 I, is based on gross tonnage data in the public statistics, but the unspecified tonnage has been assigned to the various ports based upon their shares of the recorded tonnage. 1987 III shows the proportions from a purpose-built database compiled from the Veritas register. Only foreign-going tonnage, defined as ships above 5000 gross registered tons (grt), has been included. These vessels have been assigned according to their ports of registry. The basis for 1987 IV is the same as for 1987 III, but the tonnage of two large shipping companies, Sig. Bergesen d.y. and Wilh. Wilhelmsen, has been assigned to Oslo, where the companies had their headquarters, rather than to the ports in which their ships were registered.[29] Accordingly, the category "The West," which includes Stavanger, the port of registry for the Bergesen ships, lost approximately ninety percent of its fleet. Finally, 1987 V is drawn from the same database as 1987 III and IV. Here, however, ships registered abroad but managed by Norwegian companies have been included and assigned to the regions in which they had their headquarters. The differences between this column and 1987 IV reflect the fact that there was a relatively high propensity to register vessels abroad among companies in Bergen and on the South Coast.

This exercise illustrates that even for a relatively simple question, such as how to measure and present the spatial distribution of the Norwegian fleet, it is important to understand what the public statistics actually show. Moreover, it is important to evaluate whether the statistics in fact provide a suitable basis for answering our questions.

Shipping Policy

It may seem strange that shipping's important economic role has been only tangentially related to policies designed specifically to promote the industry.

---

[29]The changes following from this adjustment – including a more than doubling of Oslo's share – are massive. This reflects the fact that the two companies in question were relatively successful during the shipping crisis of the 1970s and 1980s and kept their tonnage on the Norwegian register. If the same adjustment were performed, for instance, in 1970, Oslo's share of the Norwegian fleet would only have increased by 10.8 rather than by 35.8 percentage points.

Until the middle of the 1970s few, if any, policies were targeted directly at subsidizing or helping Norwegian shipowners.[30] Yet this does not at all imply that policies have been unimportant in securing Norway's position in international shipping. First, policies in other countries – the repeal of the Navigation Acts, which benefited Norwegian shipping, or the introduction of flag preference and cargo reservation, which held it back – have been extremely important. Second, owners were banned from registering ships abroad – Norwegian ships had to fly Norwegian flags. This delayed the flight to flags of convenience and was undoubtedly crucial for the size of the Norwegian-flagged fleet until the liberalization of this regime in the early 1980s. Third, Norwegian policies *per se*, though not directly intended as aids to shipping, have had substantial effects. In particular, the tax regime, with generous depreciation allowances, made shipping investments attractive. Furthermore, regulation of manning and seamen's wages, as well as restrictions on the transfer of capital abroad, have shaped the investment pattern – and thus the business strategies – of Norwegian shipowners.[31]

After the mid-1970s the authorities introduced a number of policy measures specifically targeted at the shipping sector.[32] We can thus see the familiar pattern of expansion without public support in good times and accommodating support policies for sunset industries in times of crisis. The 1975 establishment of the Norwegian Guarantee Institute for Ships and Drilling Vessels Ltd., the first "direct" transfer of public funds to the shipping sector, eased the financial pressure on a number of Norwegian shipping companies. This was motivated, however, by a desire to avoid potential problems for shipyards and financial institutions as well as a concern for shipowners. A more important policy measure was the gradual liberalization of the access to register ships abroad, which finally paved the way for the establishment of the

---

[30]One exception was a brief period of preferential access to foreign exchange during the reconstruction of the early postwar years (1945-1947). This was followed, however, by a period of strict licensing (1947-1948) and eventually a virtually total ban on new contracts abroad (1948-1950); see Atle Thowsen, "Skipsfart og planøkonomi. Kontraherings- og lisensieringspolitikken overfor norsk skipsfart i den første etterkrigstiden (1945-53)," *Sjøfartshistorisk Årbok 1985* (Bergen, 1986).

[31]See Camilla Brautaset and Stig Tenold, "Waiving the Rules to Rule the Waves: Globalisation and Norwegian Shipping Policy, 1850-2000," *Business History*, C, No. 3 (2008), 565-582, for a more thorough discussion of this element.

[32]It could be argued that even before the 1970s, subsidies to Norwegian shipbuilders represented an indirect financial support to their most important customers, the Norwegian shipowners. But given the international character of the market for ships, this argument is not entirely convincing. In the absence of subsidies to the Norwegian shipbuilding industry, Norwegian owners would have been able to acquire identical ships in the world market at practically the same price.

Norwegian International Ship Register (NIS) in 1987. The NIS made it possible to combine Norwegian capital and competence with low-cost foreign labour and brought a much needed revitalization of the Norwegian flag after a period of severe hardship. Fortuitously, a concurrent improvement in freight rates led to a massive reinvestment in shipping, more or less neutralizing the decline during the shipping crises.

Concluding Remarks

Ever since the middle of the nineteenth century, Norway has been an atypical country in international shipping. Its share of the international shipping market has been substantially higher than its shares of world population or international trade would suggest. There are three main reasons for the sustained role of Norwegian shipowners in the international market. The first is "path dependence" – the role of maritime traditions and experience acquired in an era when the alternatives to shipping for Norwegians were limited. Until the 1970s this was strengthened by a regulatory regime that restricted the ability of Norwegian shipowners to invest in shipping companies abroad and in ships flying foreign flags. The second reason is skilful adaptation to the shipping market, in particular a willingness to innovate and enter new market segments. It is likely that the relatively small and non-bureaucratic organizations can explain why Norwegian shipowners were at the forefront in grasping – and even creating – new investment opportunities. Finally, policy changes played an increasingly important role in the final part of the twentieth century. The introduction of the NIS gave Norwegian shipping a new life, enabling the combination of low-cost foreign labour and Norwegian maritime expertise.

The Greek Shipping Sector, c. 1850-2000

Gelina Harlaftis

With more than 3000 ships over 1000 gross registered tons (grt), and eighty-five million grt in total, Greek-owned shipping entered the twenty-first century as the world's largest maritime power, followed by Japan, Norway and the US (see table 1). It is remarkable that two of the smallest countries in Europe, lying at the northeast and southeast tips of the continent, owned fleets larger than those possessed by the world's economic leaders.

Table 1
Ten Largest Maritime Powers in Terms of Actual Ship Ownership, 2000

Country	Number of Ships	Thousand Grt
Greece	3251	84,910
Japan	2922	69,222
Norway	1688	39,670
US	1440	31,882
Germany	2103	15,087
China	2214	26,494
Hong Kong	548	20,104
South Korea	903	17,368
Great Britain	819	14,622
Taiwan	519	13,021
Total of Top Ten	16,407	342,380
Fleet Total	35,157	540,675
Percentage of Top Ten	47%	64%

Note: Includes only vessels larger than 1000 grt.

Source: Lloyd's Register of Shipping, *World Fleet Statistics 2001* (London, 2001).

Greeks, who became the main eastern Mediterranean grain carriers by the late eighteenth century, maintained this position after the formation of the Greek state in the 1830s and consolidated their place as the most important owners of bulk cargo tonnage in the Mediterranean during the era of the *Pax*

Britannica.[1] Greek-owned shipping, which developed almost exclusively as international cross-traders, evolved into a global tramp shipping fleet in the twentieth century. Its main strength was a tight maritime business network in Europe in the nineteenth century and globally in the twentieth.

For the Greek economy, shipping was a major source of capital accumulation and was second only to agriculture as a contributor to Gross Domestic Product (GDP) until the First World War. During the twentieth century shipping income covered a large part of the country's balance-of-payments deficit, while shipowning capital, considered officially as "foreign," was invested in industry, transport, tourism and banking. The international business networks of Greek shipowners meant that shipping income earned abroad influenced national economic development. This essay will follow the path of Greek shipping over the past 150 years in the international economy and will analyze its impact on the national economy.

Greek Fleet in World Shipping

In 1850, just twenty years after the formation of the Greek state, the underdeveloped nation owned a fleet almost equivalent to those of Holland and Norway. Table 2 depicts the relative importance of Greek shipping in a European context. Although by 1880 the Greek fleet could not compare to those of Britain, Norway, Italy, France or Germany, it was in the same league as Russia, Sweden and Spain and was larger than those of Denmark, the Netherlands, Austria-Hungary or Portugal. In 1910 Greece had the ninth largest fleet in Europe. It consisted almost exclusively of ocean-going tramp vessels for the transport of bulk cargoes in the international cross-trades. By comparison, the fleets of Russia, Austria-Hungary, Italy, France and Spain consisted mostly of liners sailing on regular routes and owned by large, often subsidized companies which essentially carried passengers and industrial or package products.

It is not surprising that European countries owned the largest share of world tonnage. Due to technological innovations, their international merchant fleets were able to carry an increasing volume of cargoes between continents with greater speed and lower cost than their competitors. By 1900 Britain was still the undisputed world maritime power, owning forty-five percent of world carrying capacity, followed by the US, Germany, Norway, France and Japan (see table 2). Over ninety-five percent of the world fleet belonged to only fifteen countries that formed the so-called "Atlantic economy" (or what today comprise the "developed" nations of the Organisation of Economic Cooperation and Development). Meanwhile, in the Pacific Japan was preparing to become the rising star of world shipping in the twentieth century.

---

[1]Gelina Harlaftis, *A History of Greek-Owned Shipping: The Making of an International Tramp Fleet, 1830 to the Present Day* (London, 1996).

Table 2

Largest Commercial Fleets of Europe, 1850-1910

Country	1850	1860	1870	1880	1890	1900	1910
Britain	3,565,133	4,658,687	5,690,789	6,574,453	7,978,538	9,304,108	11,556,663
Germany			982,355	1,181,525	1,433,413	1,941,645	2,903,570
Norway	298,315	558,927	1,022,915	1,518,658	1,705,699	1,508,118	1,525,727
France	688,153	996,124	1,072,048	919,298	944,013	1,028,726	1,451,648
Russia				666,192	794,685	974,536	1,116,356
Italy			1,012,164	999,176	740,716	948,008	1,107,192
Spain				560,133	618,182	774,579	789,457
Sweden	214,248	175,675	361,806	502,742	510,947	613,792	772,679
Greece				389,351	331,194	332,471	619,256
Denmark			179,366	249,466	302,194	408,440	546,838
Holland	292,576	433,922	389,614	328,281	255,711	346,923	534,275
Austria-Hungary					236,648	299,725	509,851
Portugal			329,377	322,612		116,002	114,037

Note: Includes sail and steam in net registered tons (nrt).

Sources: For Greece: Gelina Harlaftis and George Kostelenos, "Tertiary Sector and Economic Development: The Shipping Income, 1835-1914," in Th. Kalafatis and E. Prontzas (eds.), *Elliniki Oikonomiki Istoria, 19th-20th Centuries* (Athens, forthcoming), appendix 1. For other countries: Adam W. Kirkaldy, *British Shipping: Its History, Organisation and Importance* (London, 1914), appendix XVII. The data are based on "Progress of Merchant Shipping in the United Kingdom and Principal Maritime Countries," Cd. 6180, 1912, appendix 1.

Table 3
Largest Fleets of the Twentieth Century (million grt)

Country	1914		1937		1963		1992 "Real" Ownership (including all flags)	
	Grt	%	Grt	%	Grt	%	dwt	%
Britain	21.0	43%	20.6	31%	21.6	15%	23.6	3.4
Germany	5.5	11%	3.9	6%	5.0		16.9	2.4
US	5.4	11%	12.4	18%	23.1	16%	59.1	8.5
Norway	2.5	5%	4.3	6%	13.7	9%	54.1	7.8
France	2.3	5%	2.8	4%		4%	7.0	1
Japan	1.7	4%	4.5	7%		7%	90.2	12.3
Italy	1.7	3%	3.2	5%	5.6	4%	11.7	1.7
Holland	1.5	3%	2.6	4%	5.2	4%		
Sweden	1.1	2%	1.5	2%	4.2		12.2	0.3
Austria/ Hungary	1.0	2%	-	-	-	-	-	-
Russia/ USSR	1.0	2%	1.3	2%	5.4	4%	19.2	2.8
Spain	0.9	2%	1.0	1%	2.0		5.1	0.7
Greece	0.8	2%	1.9	3%	15.0	10%	100.6	14.5
Hong Kong			0.3		0.8		31.6	4.5
China			0.6		0.5		27.5	3.9
South Korea					0.1		18.2	2.6
Total of 10 Largest Fleets					108.3	74%	441	63%
World Total	49.1	100%	66.7	100%	145.9	100%	694.6 (444.3)	

Sources: Lloyd's Register of Shipping, 1914; Lloyd's Statistical Tables, 1990 and 1992; and Gelina Harlaftis, *A History of Greek-owned Shipping: The Making of an International Tramp Fleet, 1830 to the Present Day* (London, 1993), table 6.3.

The international economy never recovered in the two decades after World War I, a dislocation which altered its entire structure and led in 1929 to the worst economic crisis in the history of the industrial world. During the interwar period world shipping faced severe problems stemming from a contraction of seaborne trade, decreased migration and increasing protectionism. World War I weakened Britain and allowed competitors to challenge its maritime hegemony. The withdrawal of British ships from trades not directly related to the Allied cause opened the Pacific to the Japanese. Moreover, both Norway and Greece were neutrals (although Greece did enter the war in 1917), which meant that their fleets profited from high wartime freight rates. Norwegian and Greek vessels traded at market rates for three years while most of the British fleet was requisitioned and worked for low, fixed remuneration. Freight rates in the free market remained high until 1920, after which they plummeted; while there was a brief recovery in the mid-1920s, the nadir was reached in the early 1930s.

Table 3 records the development of the fleets of the main maritime nations from 1914 to 1937 and beyond. Between 1914 and 1937 the world fleet grew at only about one-third of its prewar rate. While the British fleet was virtually the same size it had been almost a quarter century earlier, its share of global tonnage fell from forty-three to thirty-one percent due to more rapid increases elsewhere. The interwar period was characterized by the unsuccessful attempt of the US to maintain a large national fleet through costly subsidies to shipowners. Most of the increase of the world fleet in the interwar period outside the US was due to the Japanese, Norwegians and Greeks; their fleets proved to be the most dynamic merchant marines of the century. Their growth was connected largely with the carriage of energy. Indeed, the most important change in world trade during the interwar period was the gradual decrease of the coal trade and the growing importance of oil.

The second half of the twentieth century was marked by a sharp increase in world trade that towards the end of the century was increasingly described as the "globalization" of the world economy. Growth was especially rapid until the 1970s, as world trade rose from about 500 million metric tons in the 1940s to more than three billion metric tons in the mid-1970s. If the history of world maritime transport in the first half of the twentieth century was largely a story of coal and tramp ships, in the second half the main features were oil and tankers.[2] During this period, bulk seaborne trade was divided into liquid and dry cargo. Almost sixty percent of the growth was due to the unprecedented increase in the carriage of liquid cargo at sea, especially petroleum and its derivatives. The growth of the next five main bulk cargoes – ore, bauxite, coal, phosphates and grain – was almost as impressive. To carry the enormous volumes required by the industries of the West and East Asia, the size of ships carrying liquid and dry cargoes increased. The second half of the century was characterized by the gigantic sizes of ships and specialization according to cargo. The last third of the century was also marked by the introduction of container ships. These "ugly" vessels revolutionized the carriage of industrial goods and world transport while straining existing port systems almost to the point of collapse.[3]

---

[2]Gelina Harlaftis and John Theotokas, "Maritime Business during the Twentieth Century: Continuity and Change," in Costas Th. Grammenos (ed.), *Handbook of Maritime Economics and Business* (London, 2002); and Harlaftis, *History of Greek-Owned Shipping*, chapter 9.

[3]Frank Broeze, "At Sea and Ashore: A Critical Review of the Historiography of Modern Shipping since the 1970s," *NEHA Bulletin,* XIII, No. 1 (1998), 3-37; and

Until the 1960s the main maritime nations remained the same, with Britain and the US clinging to their decreasing shares of world shipping, followed by Greece, Japan and Norway. Although flags of convenience were widely used, in the immediate postwar years they were resorted to more extensively by Greek and American owners. Flags of convenience, which were later called "open registries," became a key component of US maritime policy and a determining factor in guaranteeing low-cost bulk shipping.[4] After the freight-rate crises of the 1980s they were used extensively by all maritime nations.

The 1970s marked the start of a new era characterized by the final loss of the predominance of European maritime nations with the exception of the Greeks, who maintained their leadership (as they have to the present day) and Norwegians (who despite the great slump of the 1980s retained their market share in the 1990s). During the last third of the twentieth century the growth of the world fleet continued, albeit at a slower rate. The United States has resorted even more than in the past to flags of convenience, yet its share of world tonnage has declined, while Japan has remained steadily in second place. The rise of new maritime nations in Asia has been striking: by 1992 China owned more tonnage than Britain, and South Korea was close behind. The division of labour in world shipping had shifted dramatically.[5]

Development of Trades and Technological Transitions

Timely adjustments to changes in world trade and to technological shifts kept Greek shipowners in the forefront of world shipping. As the Black Sea region became Europe's granary in the nineteenth century, grain exports from the eastern Mediterranean competed with those from North America, while at the same time the transition from sail to steam and the opening of the Suez Canal

---

Broeze, *The Globalisation of the Oceans: Containerisation from the 1950s to the Present* (St. John's, 2002).

[4]For an insightful analysis, see Alan W. Cafruny, *Ruling the Waves: The Political Economy of International Shipping* (Berkeley, 1987). For a classic study of flags of convenience, see Basil N. Metaxas, *Flags of Convenience: A Study of Internationalisation* (Aldershot, 1985). For the resort of Greeks to flags of convenience, see Gelina Harlaftis, "Greek Shipowners and State Intervention in the 1940s: A Formal Justification for the Resort to Flags-of-Convenience?" *International Journal of Maritime History*, I, No. 2 (1989), 37-63.

[5]See Helen A. Thanopoulou, "The Growth of Fleets Registered in the Newly-emerging Maritime Countries and Maritime Crises," *Maritime Policy and Management*, XXII, No. 1 (1995), 51-62. See also Thanopoulou, "A Fleet for the 21st Century: Modern Greek Shipping," in Athanasios A. Pallis (ed.), *Maritime Transport: The Greek Paradigm* (Amsterdam, 2007), 23-61.

brought the Mediterranean back to equal importance with the larger oceans.[6] This was also the period of major transformations in the eastern Mediterranean, where in 1800 the Ottomans still reigned. In the 1830s the first nation to gain its independence from the disintegrating Ottoman Empire was Greece, which was followed by the rest of the Balkan states in the 1870s.

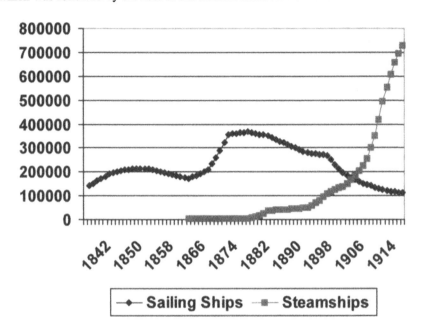

Figure 1: Greek-owned Fleet, 1841-1911

Note: Includes both sail and steam tonnage.

Source: See table 2.

The Greek sailing ship fleet, which was really an international carrier between third countries (a "cross-trader" in maritime terms), flourished on forty or so islands in the Aegean and Ionian seas, and its growth was directly related to the grain trade, which was handled largely by the diaspora merchants in the various Greek commercial communities that spread from the

---

[6]Gelina Harlaftis and Vassilis Kardasis, "International Bulk Trade and Shipping in the Eastern Mediterranean and the Black Sea," in Şevket Pamuk and Jeffrey G. Williamson (eds.), *The Mediterranean Response to Globalization before 1850* (London, 2000), 233-265.

Black Sea to the North and Baltic seas.[7] These vessels transported grain from the ports of the Black Sea to the Western Mediterranean and Northern Europe, and on the return route carried coal to the Mediterranean. The spectacular growth of Black Sea grain exports compensated for the decline of freight rates, which had been maintained at a reasonably high level during the dominance of sail up to the 1870s and provided the capital for the subsequent transition from sail to steam by Greek shipowners that was completed at the turn of the twentieth century (see figure 1).

Technological innovations continued in the twentieth century, and the choice by entrepreneurs whether to adopt them determined the path of world shipping. The first half of the century was marked on the one hand by the replacement of steam propulsion by diesel and on the other by the massive standard shipbuilding projects during the two world wars. Diesel engines, which first appeared in 1890, were only used on a massive scale by motorships during the interwar period, particularly in Germany and Scandinavia, because the cost of oil was thirty to fifty percent lower than for coal. Standardization was introduced into shipbuilding during World War I after the Germans sunk a high proportion of the Allied fleets in an unprecedented submarine war. The world had not yet realized what industrialization and massive weapons production could do. The convoy system had been abandoned, and battleships armed with complex weapon systems were ready to confront the enemy. But it was the Allied merchant steamers that were the arteries of the war supply chain, and these unarmed ships were easy targets for German submarines. From 1914 to 1918, 5861 ships, representing half of the combined Allied fleet, were sunk.

The replacement of the vessels that were lost took place between 1918 and 1921 in American and British shipyards. For the first time standard types of cargo ships were built on a large scale. These "standards" became the main type of cargo ship during the interwar period; they were steamships of 5500 grt. It was these vessels that Greeks, Japanese and Norwegian tramp operators purchased *en masse* on the British second-hand market to expand their fleets between the world economic crises. For similar reasons, during World War II the US and Canada launched the most massive shipbuilding programmes the world had ever known, using welding to speed the process. As a result, within four years they managed to build 3000 so-called "Liberty ships" which became the standard dry-bulk cargo vessels for the next twenty-five years.[8] Greek, Norwe-

---

    [7]Gelina Harlaftis, "Mapping the Greek Maritime Diaspora from the Early 18th to the Late 20th Centuries," in Ina Baghdiantz McCabe, Gelina Harlaftis and Ioanna Pepelasis Minoglou (eds.), *Diaspora Entrepreneurial Networks: Four Centuries of History* (Oxford, 2004), 147-171.

    [8]For more on this subject and further bibliographic suggestions, see Harlaftis, *History of Greek-owned Shipping,* chapters 6 and 8.

gian, British and Japanese tramp operators all came to own Liberty ships in one way or another and operated them up to the late 1960s.

Part of the Greeks' success during the postwar period was due to their entry into the tanker market in the late 1940s and the 1950s. The first ship-owners to do so were Aristotle Onassis and Stavros Niarchos, both of whom benefited from the Norwegian experience in tankers at this propitious international conjuncture. The most important independent tanker owners internationally during the interwar years were the Norwegians. As Stanley Sturmey noted, it was the Norwegians who, after buying a few dozen tankers from Anglo-Saxon Oil complete with time charters in the late 1920s, created by 1939 the world's largest independent tanker fleet.[9] Their entry into the tanker market was an example of businessmen willing to take a risk to enter what for them was a new market. They saw the gap in the market and exploited it successfully. Twenty years later, Greek shipowners made the same move successfully, exploiting the inability of the hitherto dominant Norwegians to respond to rapidly increasing demand. The Greeks invested in tankers and in the end conquered the market. The inability of the Norwegians to respond was linked to a postwar foreign exchange crisis in Norway; due to the lack of reserves, the Norwegian government prohibited the purchase of ships abroad between 1948 and 1951.[10] Thus, Norwegian shipowners were unable to exploit the "golden age" of the freight market which was created by the Korean War.

The gap was filled immediately, not only by Stavros Niarchos and Aristotle Onassis but also by several other Greek shipowners who rushed to copy them.[11] In the early postwar years, Onassis and Niarchos were able to finance their expansion from their own capital. Following the same tactic as the Norwegians, they bought tankers with time charters from American oil companies in the 1940s and 1950s. Through the competition between them, these two pioneering shipowners further developed the methods of financing ships. Instead of ordering one tanker at a time, they began placing orders for a series of such ships, with only one charter contract as a guarantee. Moreover, ordering a series of ships in a single shipyard reduced costs and ensured long-term employment for the yards. Shipyards in Germany and Great Britain accepted mass orders for ships in the early postwar years. A little later, less expensive Japanese yards took their place, and in the 1960s and 1970s Greeks became their best customers.

Niarchos' and Onassis' expansion strategy was quickly followed by many of the successful "traditional" shipowners, primarily those who had set-

[9]S.G. Sturmey, *British Shipping and World Competition* (London, 1962), 61-97.

[10]Atle Thowsen, *Shipping and a Planned Economy* (Bergen, 1986), 35.

[11]Harlaftis, *History of Greek-owned Shipping*, chapter 9.

tled in New York during the Second World War. The trailblazers' success also created access to the American financial market for other Greek shipowners. By 1974 the Greek-owned tanker fleet had become the largest in the world, comprising seventeen percent of the global total. Starting from scratch in 1945, this fleet reached 8,200,000 grt in 1965, 14,700,000 grt in 1970 and 21,800,000 grt in 1974. Tankers represented between forty and forty-eight percent of the overall capacity of the Greek-owned fleet in the years 1958-1975.

After the first oil crisis (1973-1974), the situation in the freight markets for liquid cargoes changed dramatically. The decline in demand, in conjunction with surplus capacity, created crisis conditions, which lasted – with only short respites – until the end of the 1980s. During this period, the oil companies undertook strategic restructuring, which led to a decrease in the number of self-owned tankers. This strategy provided an opportunity for the independent tanker owners, but in the charter sector it favoured the creation of a free market to the detriment of time charters. Whereas in the early 1970s about a fifth of the tanker fleet was chartered in the open market, by the early 1990s this share had risen to over seventy percent.[12]

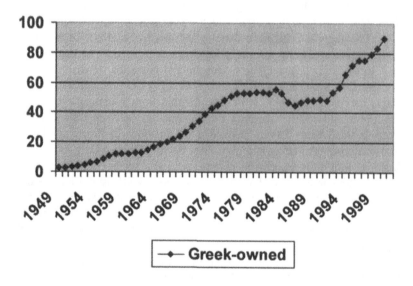

Figure 2:   Greek-owned Shipping, 1949-1997 (million grt)

Source: Harlaftis, *History of Greek-owned Shipping*, chapter 10.

---

[12]Martin Stopford, *Maritime Economics* (London, 1988; 2nd rev. ed., London, 1997), 29.

As a result, new Greek shipowners began to enter the liquid-cargo freight markets at an increasing rate using Piraeus as their base. The crises in 1973-1974, 1978 and 1981-1986, led – in many cases forced – Greek shipowners to reduce their participation in the liquid-cargo sector. The Greek-owned fleet began to contract in 1983 and reached its nadir in 1986. By 1985 the percentage of tankers in the Greek-owned fleet had dropped to thirty-eight percent, the lowest level since the early 1960s. Thereafter, however, the percentage began to rise again, and throughout the 1990s tankers accounted for over forty percent of the fleet. The year 1991 was the critical point of the recovery, and by the end of the century the Greek-owned fleet had surpassed 100 million grt (see figure 2).[13]

The critical innovation in postwar dry-bulk shipping was the introduction of bulk carriers, which began to transport a large share of the cargoes traditionally carried by "classic" cargo tramps. Factors that favoured this move were increases in demand and the distances to be covered, the need to exploit economies of scale and a desire to reduce the average cost of transport. The growing needs of the industrial nations, especially Japan and in Europe, for large quantities of the five staple bulk cargoes (iron ore, coal, grain, bauxite and phosphates) also favoured the bulk carrier. The economies of scale achieved by tankers applied also to bulk carriers, although the latter were limited to much smaller sizes by the harbours where they could dock as well as to the fact that iron ore and coal were the only cargoes transported in quantities in excess of 100,000 dwt. Only a small percentage of the bulk carrier fleet today is of the "Capesize" category (those with capacities greater than 100,000 dwt). These ships are used mainly to carry iron ore and coal on specific routes, and they dock in specially-equipped harbours. A large number of bulk carriers were on the order of 75,000 dwt (known as "Panamax" ships because this was the maximum size that could navigate the Panama Canal). The increase in the participation of bulk carriers in the world fleet was spectacular, reaching twenty percent in the 1970s and over thirty percent in the 1980s. Indeed, in the 1980s the capacity of bulk carriers surpassed that of tankers. In the Greek-owned fleet the percentage of the bulk carriers in 1980 was thirty-six percent compared to forty percent for tankers; by 1990 the percentage of bulk carriers equalled that of tankers at forty-six percent.[14]

---

[13]Ioannis Theotokas and Gelina Harlaftis, *Leadership in World Shipping: Greek Family Firms in International Business* (London, forthcoming), chapter 1.

[14]Harlaftis, *History of Greek-owned Shipping*, table 9.5.

"Flagging-out"

"Flagging out," or transferring ships from traditional registers to flags of convenience, has been a major feature of post-World War II international shipping. Flags of convenience are registers which levy low taxes and allow lax conditions of employment and operation. Basil Metaxas has defined "flags of convenience" as the national flags of states under which shipowners registered their vessels in order to avoid tax obligations and the terms and conditions of employment and production to which they would be subject if their ships were registered under the flag of their own states.[15] The establishment of "cheap flags" by various small, developing countries directly dependent upon either American or European interests became a characteristic feature of the second half of the twentieth century. There has been an ever-increasing number of countries that have "opened" their registries; in addition to Panama, Liberia and Honduras (the infamous "PanHoLib" flags), Costa Rica, Bermuda, the Isle of Man, Cyprus, Vanuatu, Lebanon, Malta, Bangladesh, the Marshall Islands, Saint Vincent, the Cayman Islands, the Bahamas and Hong Kong, among others, have created such registries.

Although Greek shipowners generally attribute their use of non-Greek flags after 1945 to hostile domestic maritime policy, political instability and the power of Greek unions, the main reasons for their behaviour in fact appear to be exogenous. The US government explicitly supported the growing use of such registries in the immediate postwar period through its financial institutions; most Greek shipowners who bought ships on credit from American banks were "urged" to sail under flags of convenience. High domestic labour costs, which kept American ships from being competitive, and the need to retain control over a large part of the world's merchant fleet for strategic and political reasons, led US maritime policymakers to support flags of convenience. The adoption of such flags by US-controlled oil companies and independent owners meant that powerful lobbies were established to ensure their continued existence.[16] During the second half of the 1940s and the 1950s, eighty to ninety percent of the Liberian fleet and forty-five percent of the Panamanian were operated by Greeks.[17] The demise of the domestic Greek register throughout the 1950s is evident in figure 3. The boycott against flags

---

[15]Basil N. Metaxas, *The Economics of Tramp Shipping* (London, 1971; 2nd ed., London, 1981), 197. For a detailed discussion of flags of convenience, see Metaxas, *Flags of Convenience*.

[16]Mike Ratcliffe, *Liquid Gold Ships: A History of the Tanker, 1859-1984* (London, 1985), 314.

[17]Gelina Harlaftis, *Greek Shipowners and Greece, 1945-1975: From Separate Development to Mutual Interdependence* (London, 1993), table 8.4.

of convenience in 1959 led to a brief revival of the Greek flag, but the decline of freight rates in the mid-1960s reversed this. Rising rates after 1967 and the establishment of a Greek dictatorship that granted concessions and provided a taxless regime, policies that were continued after the return of democracy in 1974, again led to an increase in the domestic flag, and by 1980 almost four-fifths of Greek-owned tonnage was registered domestically. The crisis of the 1980s brought an end to this trend, something which continued in the 1990s.

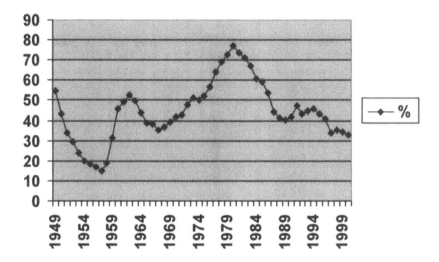

Figure 3: Percentage of Greek Flag in Greek-owned Shipping. 1949-1999

Source: *Naftika Chronika* (various issues); and Ioannis Theotokas and Gelina Harlaftis, *Leadership in World Shipping: Greek Family Firms in International Business* (London, forthcoming).

The effects of the shipping crises on the various national fleets were important in two main ways. First, the slumps led traditional fleets to restructure their capacity by upgrading their ships technologically. Second, it led to a reversion to flags of convenience. The share of world tonnage accounted for by flags of convenience rose from 31.1 percent in 1980 to 48.1 percent in 2000. But these moves simply delayed the effects of growing competition. At the same time, the developing countries, and especially those characterized as the "New Maritime Countries," increased their share of the world fleet.[18] So extensive was the reduction of the national fleets of many traditional countries that from the mid-1980s some of them attempted to reconstitute their national

---

[18]Thanopoulou, "Growth of Fleets," 60.

fleets by creating international shipping registers that allowed shipowners to keep their ships under a national flag while enjoying the benefits of an internationalized market for factors of production, especially labour. The effectiveness of this move is debateable, however, since for shipping to survive requires a range of interconnected activities that constitute a nexus, and the international shipping registers could not by themselves construct this.[19]

Table 4
Ten Largest Fleets, 1970-2000 (million grt)

Country	1970		1980		1990		2000	
Liberia	1	33.3	1	80.3	1	54.7	2	51.5
Japan	2	27	2	41	3	27.1	10	15.3
Britain	3	25.8	4	27.1				
Norway	4	19.3	7	22	5	23.4	7	22.6
US	5	18.5	8	18.5	7	21.3		
USSR	6	14.8	6	23.4	4	26.7		
Greece	7	11	3	39.5	6	20.5	5	26.4
Germany	8	7.9						
Italy	9	7.4	9	11.1				
France	10	6.5						
Panama			5	24.2	2	39.3	1	114.3
China			10	6.9	9	13.9	9	16.5
Cyprus					8	18.3	6	23.2
Bahamas					10	13.6	3	31.4
Malta							4	28.2
Singapore							8	23.5
Total 10	171.5		294.1		258.8		350.9	
FOC		33.3		104.5		125.9		270.1
10/FOC		19.4		35.5		48.6		77%
Total		227.5		419.9		423.6		558.1

Source: Lloyd's Register, *Statistical Tables*, 1990.

The data in table 4 are indicative of the realignments of the national fleets during the postwar period, as well as the increase in the percentage of tonnage on flags of convenience in the world fleet. In 1970, the ten biggest maritime powers – except for the then-Soviet Union and Liberia, a flag-of-convenience country – were all members of the OECD. In 2000, the list of the largest biggest flags included only four traditional maritime powers: Greece, Japan, Norway and China. Whereas in 1970 the percentage of flags of conven-

---

[19]Gunnar K. Sletmo and Susanne Holste, "Shipping and the Competitive Advantage of Nations: The Role of International Registers," *Maritime Policy and Management*, XX, No. 3 (1993), 243-255.

ience among the ten biggest fleets was 19.4 percent, by 2000 this had risen to seventy-seven percent.

While table 4 depicts fleets on the basis of the flag of registration, in terms of actual ownership the capacity of the fleets of the traditional maritime countries is significantly greater. A glance back at table 1, which includes the ten largest fleets in 2000 in terms of actual ownership, shows that in fact they comprised almost fifty-four percent of the world total. It is clear that in terms of actual ownership, Greek shipowners lead the field. The ten largest fleets include four European countries, the US and five East Asian nations. Together with Greece, which for virtually the entire postwar period had high growth rates, Japan, China, South Korea, Hong Kong and Taiwan comprise the most dynamic powers in shipping in the postwar period.

Business Networks

In the Greek case it is impossible to understand the development of shipping businesses without using tools derived from studies of human relations, networks and personal/familial capitalism.[20] The shipping business in Europe continues to retain a family character with international networking and a particular business culture at the core of which lie the concepts of trust and reputation. The expression "My word is my bond," which typified the way business was conducted on the Baltic Exchange in the mid-nineteenth century, carries the same weight today. Tramp shipping is a sector that is based exclusively on networks and personal relations.

The success of Greek shipping in international waters in competition with British, French, Austrian and other Western European vessels owed its strength in large measure to a Greek entrepreneurial network that began in Mediterranean seaborne trade in the nineteenth century and expanded globally in the twentieth. This transnational maritime and trading circuit was founded on two pillars: the Greek diaspora trading houses established in the main Black Sea and Western European ports and the Greek shipping companies based in the islands of the Ionian and Aegean seas. The collaboration of these two groups explains the size and the success of the Greek ocean-going fleet in the nineteenth century and its continuation in the twentieth.

Greek diaspora trading companies were principally network firms.[21] A network implies a particular type of relationship that links a specific group of people, and the study of this form of relationship is performed through net-

---

[20]Harlaftis, *History of Greek-owned Shipping*, 463-464.

[21]Geoffrey Jones, *Merchants to Multinationals: British Trading Companies in the Nineteenth and Twentieth Centuries* (Oxford, 2000), 160, introduces a typology of British trading companies and suggests three network-based organizational forms.

work analysis.[22] Mark Casson has defined a network as "a set of high-trust relations that either directly or indirectly link its members together into a social group."[23] Networks are based on the formation of an institutional framework that minimizes entrepreneurial risk and facilitates the flow of information. They allow the establishment of transnational connections based upon personal relations, bypassing official market mechanisms. In this way, networks can be viewed as governance structures for coordinating economic decisions.[24]

In the Greek case, networking produced a particular form of business culture that allowed members to react to opportunities in the same way and generated a willingness to emulate the organizational and managerial methods of the most successful companies. The business culture created a unified "front," enabling members to adopt the same methods for handling crises in a timely manner. The result was a strong business culture that enabled firms to survive over the long term.[25]

Processing information is the crux of this type of organization because information is more costly to trade than other resources. The Greek business network developed a system of information processing that was performed by family-based diaspora trading companies that internalized their activities in dispersed locations. "Processing of information and the processing of materials can both be analyzed in the same way. This insight is important because asso-

---

[22]Gelina Harlaftis, "Greek Maritime Business in the Nineteenth and Twentieth Centuries: A Paradigm for Comparative Studies on Family Capitalism and Diaspora Networks," in Ferry de Goey and Jan Willem Veluwenkamp (eds.), *Entrepreneurs and Institutions in Europe and Asia, 1500–2000* (Amsterdam, 2002).

[23]Mark Casson, "Entrepreneurial Networks: A Theoretical Perspective," in Michael Moss and Anthony Slaven (eds.), *Entrepreneurial Networks and Business Culture* (Madrid, 1998), 15.

[24]See also Gelina Harlaftis and John Theotokas, "European Family Firms in International Business: British and Greek Tramp-Shipping Firms," *Business History*, XLVI, No. 2 (2004), 219-255.

[25]Mark Casson, "Entrepreneurship and Business Culture," in Jonathan Brown and Mary B. Rose (eds.), *Entrepreneurship, Networks, and Modern Business* (Manchester, 1993), 44-45. See also Ioannis Theotokas, "Shipping and Entrepreneurship in Greece" (Unpublished paper presented to the Economic History Seminar, University of Athens, 2006); Theodore Syriopoulos and Ioannis Theotokas, "Corporate Governance and Takeovers in the Shipping Industry" (Unpublished paper presented to the Annual Conference of the Multinational Finance Society, Athens, 2005); and Ioannis Theotokas, "Organizational and Managerial Patterns of Greek-owned Shipping Companies and the Internationalization Process from the Postwar Period to 1990," in David J. Starkey and Gelina Harlaftis (eds.), *Global Markets: The Internationalization of the Sea Transport Industries since 1850* (St. John's, 1998), 303-318.

ciated with each production system is a system of control." By adopting the production-system approach, we can view an economic sector and its related disciplines within a wider framework.[26]

Remarkably, the production system of the Greek entrepreneurial network was transformed in the nineteenth century into an integrated economic sector based nationally in the new state. Its great strength grew out of the close relations that developed between the diaspora traders and the owners of sailing vessels on the Ionian and Aegean islands who specialized in long-distance shipping. In this way, the diaspora traders created a "production system" of closely-knit businesses of various sizes within a loosely organized network.[27] This commercial and maritime web operated on three different levels: local/regional, national/peripheral and international. It provided access to ports, agents and financial and human resources, providing its members with the strength to internalize many operations and to survive international competition. Its cohesion was derived from the business culture that the members developed, and through shipping they were able to survive economically in the international arena. The Greek diaspora entrepreneurial network, following the nineteenth-century European trend of colonial expansion, reached to the United States, India and Japan. By the twentieth century, it was embodied in the global maritime network of Greek shipowners. Greek shipping today represents the continuation of the diaspora Greek trading companies in the form of global ship-management firms.[28]

The earliest leaders of this network, like the Vagliano brothers who established the first Greek London shipping office in the 1860s, introduced a new form of organization and set the precedent for management in the tramp shipping sector. In a way, it was the predecessor of the modern ship-management company, which became the new organizational form in international shipping after the 1950s.[29] The office of Vagliano Brothers was in effect a channel to the world's maritime and economic centre and had multiple influ-

---

[26]Mark Casson, *Enterprise and Competitiveness: A Systems View of International Business* (Oxford, 1990), 7, 43 and 80-81.

[27]Gelina Harlaftis, "From Diaspora Traders to Shipping Tycoons: The Vagliano Bros.," *Business History Review,* LXXXI, No. 2 (2007), 237-268.

[28]Harlaftis, "Mapping the Greek Maritime Diaspora."

[29]Gunnar K. Sletmo, "Shipping's Fourth Wave: Ship Management and Vernon's Trade Cycles," *Maritime Policy and Management,* XVI, No. 4 (1989), 293-303.

ences on the Greek-owned fleet.[30] The Vaglianos developed a managing-agency system that ultimately separated ownership and management: Greek shipowners provided crews and ships from Greece, while Panagis Vagliano in London provided ship management on a global scale. The multinational dimension of these managing-agency operations made the London office the "national bureau," a conduit that enabled Greek shipowners to engage in international business. But more important was that Panagis Vagliano's London office provided a model of a modern ship-management firm that was imitated by his business associates. Twenty London Greek shipping offices had been established by the 1930s, and they became the driving force behind the globalization of Greek-owned shipping.[31]

Business Organization and Entrepreneurial Methods

Greek shipping enterprises were, and still are, family firms. At the beginning of the twentieth century there were about 200 families, all specializing in shipping, running 250 shipping firms, and at the end of the century about 700 families ran more than 1000 shipping firms. They formed an international maritime network that developed a certain business strategy and culture.[32] Table 5 shows the geographic expansion of Greek shipping firms and the tonnage shares managed by the various nodes of the network. Through the interwar period, Greek shipping companies were established in London, and the Piraeus-London axis was the focus of developments. In 1914 the London offices owned nine percent of total tonnage but represented and managed twenty-eight percent of the fleet; in 1938 they represented and managed forty-five percent.

After World War II Greek-owned offices were established in almost all the main ports of Europe, North and South America, Southeast Asia and South Africa. In the first two postwar decades, London and New York were home to the largest number, followed by Piraeus. From the 1960s onwards, however, the number of offices in Piraeus rose spectacularly to over 600 in 1975 and more than 800 in 1990. The largest number of shipping firms was always found in Piraeus because the port was home to all the small and single-ship companies. Table 5 also shows that in 1958, forty-five percent of the fleet was operated from London and thirty-five percent from New York. The adoption of flags of convenience, the rapid increase of tanker tonnage and the close relations of Greek shipowners to the US in the immediate postwar era

---

[30]On the Vaglianos, see Harlaftis, "From Diaspora Traders to Shipping Tycoons," 237-268.

[31]Harlaftis, *History of Greek-owned Shipping*, chapter 6.

[32]Theotokas and Harlaftis, *Leadership in World Shipping*, chapters 1-3.

made the American city the second most important operating centre after London. The volume of tonnage with headquarters in Piraeus dropped dramatically, from ninety-six percent in 1938 to eighteen percent twenty years later. From the mid-1960s onwards, Piraeus began slowly to resume its prewar importance as the main operational centre of the Greek-owned fleet; from eighteen percent in 1958, the tonnage operated from Piraeus rose to thirty-four percent in 1975 and sixty percent by 1990. In the last decade of the twentieth century the Greek-owned fleet had the same operational centres (Piraeus and London) as at its beginning.

Table 5
Main Headquarters of Greek-owned Shipping Firms, 1914-1990
(Percent of Total Tonnage)

Main Headquarters	1914	1938	1958	1975	1990
Piraeus	62%	96%	18%	34%	66%
London	9% (28%)	1% (45%)	45%	39%	22%
Istanbul	14%	-	-	-	-
New York	-	-	37%	18%	7%
Other	15%	3%	-	9%	5%

Note: Numbers in parentheses indicate the percentage actually managed in London before World War II.

Source: Harlaftis, *History of Greek-owned Shipping*, table 10.2.

Management, and all the branch offices of Greek shipping companies, continued to be in the hands of members of the same family or co-islanders. In this way kinship, local and ethnic ties ensured the cohesion of the international Greek maritime network. The unofficial but exclusive international "club" was extremely important for their economic survival. It provided access to all the necessary expertise connected to shipping: market information, chartering, sales and purchase, shipbuilding, repairing, scrapping, financing and insuring. It also provided consultancy services by older and more experienced men and information about the activities of the most successful members of the group. Imitation proved an extremely useful strategy. It is clear that the main strength of the Greeks has been the formation of an exclusive "Greek" transnational network of family enterprises that interacted with local, national and international shipping networks, organizations and financial institutions.[33]

The Greek shipping firms within this network developed particular entrepreneurial methods as part of their overall strategy. The first was to achieve access to the world's main maritime markets, London and New York.

---

[33]Harlaftis, *History of Greek-owned Shipping*, chapter 10.

The practice of establishing Greek shipowners in London was already 100 years old by the mid-twentieth century, and Greek membership in the world's biggest freight market, the Baltic Exchange, goes back to the 1850s. The Greeks also had long-standing connections to all the other facets of the British maritime infrastructure, including insurance companies, financial institutions and Protection and Indemnity (P&I) clubs. In fact, the establishment of Greek shipping companies in the City of London has provided such an important source of income for the British maritime infrastructure that any attempts to tax them have been always resisted.[34]

In the immediate post-1945 era New York aspired to surpass London as the world's main maritime market. Indeed, it had many advantages, including the fact that five of the major oil companies were established there and that American shipyards had launched such massive shipbuilding programmes in the 1940s that there was a large amount of tonnage available. Moreover, the postwar reconstruction of Europe made America the world's biggest exporter and purchaser of transport services. A significant number of European shipowners who fled to New York during the war stayed there and opened shipping offices. The Greeks, with the adoption of flags of convenience and entry into the tanker market, were able to borrow from American financial institutions for purchases of both second-hand and new vessels. Various conflicts with the American government in the 1950s, however, led many Greeks to move their operations back to Europe. The final blow to New York as a maritime centre was the American taxman; shipping companies based in the US were taxed according to a law promulgated in the early 1960s. New York never recovered its short-lived prominence in the maritime field.[35]

The second entrepreneurial method was the Greek specialization in tramp shipping and the carriage of bulk cargoes which has already been discussed. A related factor has been a systematic method of sales and purchases. This can be described simply as "buy when everybody sells, and sell when everybody buys." This has been described as the "counter-cyclical method of the Greek shipowners" who, following this golden rule, buy when freight rates and ship prices are low and sell when they are high.[36] This method, which started during the transition from sail to steam, became clearer during the 1930s when the Greek-owned fleet, unlike the merchant marines of other traditional maritime nations, enjoyed a positive rate of growth. The strategy continued after the Second World War when medium and small

---

[34]*Ibid.*

[35]See Harlaftis, *Greek Shipowners and Greece,* chapters 7-8.

[36]Helen Thanopoulou, *Greek and International Shipping* (Athens, 1994, in Greek).

shipowners imitated the methods of their bigger and more successful colleagues. In fact, many small shipowners use shipping much like the stock exchange, entering the market when prices of ships are low and leaving when they rise. The other side of this method involves the types of ships they buy. Greeks are known to be major purchasers of second-hand vessels which they keep in good repair and operate as long as possible. In fact, purchasing second-hand vessels has been the backbone for a large segment of Greek shipowners.[37]

The last – but by no means the least important – factor concerns the efficiency with which this second-hand tonnage is operated to keep fixed and variable costs low. This strategy focused largely on the structure and organization of Greek seamen and their relation to the shipowners and shipping offices ashore. Although this kind of relationship has gradually deteriorated and the "good old seamen" are disappearing, many Piraeus shipowners believe that "Greek seamen are the best in the world." This way of thinking, which is related closely to Greek seafaring traditions and has been passed down from generation to generation, has led to a productivity that cannot only be measured in numbers. As recently as 1980 almost forty percent of Greek seamen came from the islands, and two-thirds of the crew complement was comprised of Greeks. The 1980s crisis, however, struck a great blow to the use of Greek ratings. Most of the crews on Greek-owned ships today are foreigners, although the majority of the masters and officers are still Greeks.[38]

The Shipping Sector and the Greek Economy

The shipping sector has always been the most international branch of the Greek economy, and international factors have played a decisive role in its development. Indeed, this is also its "peculiar" future: it participates in international freight markets, generates its earnings and most of its costs outside of Greece and has little relation to the productive structures of the country.

The international activities of Greek shipping constituted a direct source of income in the economy of the newly-established Greek state in the nineteenth century. This influx of funds – profits of the shipping companies involved and the wages of the seamen – was essentially income from abroad and was invested in the Greek economy since the owners of sailing vessels still lived in the country with their families. Figure 4 indicates that the annual in-

---

[37]Harlaftis, *History of Greek-owned Shipping*, chapters 6 and 10.

[38]*Ibid*. See also Ioannis Theotokas, *et al.*, *Greek Shipping, Employment and Competitiveness: Strategies for Human Resource Management* (Athens, 2008, in Greek).

come from shipping for the period 1835-1914 was about thirty-four million *drachmas*, which was equivalent to one-fifth of the country's GDP.

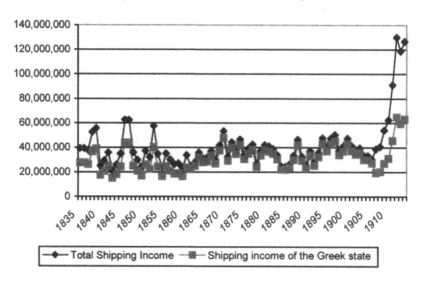

Figure 4: Shipping Income, 1835-1914

Source: Harlaftis and Kostelenos, "Tertiary Sector and Economic Development."

During this period shipping was the main non-agricultural sector, earning on average five times as much as industry and even more than the tertiary sector (see table 6). Beyond the profits of the shipping fleet earned abroad, shipping increased demand in the shipbuilding industry, thus providing an important stimulus to many local communities. In the economy as a whole, shipping income more than covered the balance-of-trade deficit. In short, the importance of shipping to the nineteenth-century Greek economy cannot be doubted.[39] During the interwar years Greek shipping companies were still centred in Greece, although about twenty major London offices were established. More than one-third of the balance-of-payments deficit was covered by shipping income.[40]

[39]*Ibid*.

[40]*Ibid*.

Table 6
Shipping Income as an Average of Greek GDP, 1835-1914

Year	Shipping Income in *drachmas* LMU (average)	Shipping as a Share of GDP (average)
1835-1845	27	36%
1846-1855	32	36%
1856-1865	26	16%
1866-1875	42	19%
1876-1885	35	11%
1886-1895	30	9%
1896-1905	30	6%
1906-1914	45	6%

Note: LMU denotes Latin Monetary Unit.

Source: See figure 4.

In the post-World War II period, the establishment of Greek shipowners in London and New York and the extensive use of flags of convenience alienated Greek shipowners from Greece but not from the Greek economy. The question of whether the Greek-owned fleet, which changes flag continuously depending on circumstances, can be considered part of the Greek economy still arouses debate? From one perspective, the activities of Greek shipowners have little to do with the domestic economy because the mercantile fleet owned and managed by Greeks is "international" and is involved mainly in the transit trade, meeting the marginal demand for transport services around the world; indeed, only about five percent of the Greek-owned fleet is continuously involved in the carriage of Greek cargoes.[41] And only a small percentage of shipping profits flow into Greece. In fact, in the period 1967-1974 only about eleven percent of all shipping profits were repatriated.[42]

The best-known way of transferring shipping capital to Greece from abroad is through shipping foreign exchange. Shipping foreign exchange covers the remittances of seamen and shipowners – both of which are declared to the Bank of Greece – and constitutes about one-third of the invisible resources of the economy. There is a common view in Greece that the influence of ship-

---

[41]See Harlaftis, *Greek Shipowners and Greece*, 63.

[42]*Ibid.*, table 4.2.

owners is linked solely to the import of shipping foreign exchange. Yet it is a fact is that shipowners have made investments in the Greek economy and have played an important role in some of its most important sectors.[43]

In the postwar years shipowners invested extensively in the secondary sector, particularly in five branches: petroleum refining and coal, metallurgy, transport, non-metallic minerals and the chemical and paper industries. It has been estimated that in 1975 shipowners owned nineteen percent of all the fixed industrial property in the country. They also invested in the tertiary sector, in banks, insurance companies, construction, real estate and other commercial enterprises. From the end of the Second World War to the early years of the restoration of democracy after 1974, shipowners were the biggest private bankers in Greece and were thus able to influence significantly investment decisions and the distribution of resources, a large part of which was directed to organizations and companies that they controlled.[44]

Shipowners also participated in developing tourism in Greece, with various investments in hotels, cruises and domestic airlines. They played such a dynamic role in tourism that in 1975 they owned about one-fifth of the fixed property in the hotel sector, and Onassis even owned the national air carrier, Olympic Airlines. They have invested extensively in real estate, although the overall value of their investments in this sector is impossible to calculate. Moreover, in the last fifteen years shipowners have invested in another particularly important sector, the mass media.[45]

Between the late 1960s and the 1990s, Piraeus became an important international shipping centre. Thousands of employees worked in the shipping companies or in ancillary services in the Piraeus "maritime cluster." The construction of new buildings, or the purchase of existing ones, was a primary concern of the companies which wanted to establish offices in Piraeus, while many shipowners set up their own construction companies in order to build their offices.[46]

As is easily observed, in contrast to the common view still promoted by the press, shipowners have played an important role in the development of postwar Greece, which has given them negotiating power in their dealings with the Greek state. Due to the enormous wealth of many shipowners and their international relationships, all Greek governments have sought their collaboration in the hope of attracting even bigger investments. In the course of these

---

[43]*Ibid.*

[44]*Ibid.*, chapters 4-6.

[45]*Ibid.*

[46]*Ibid.*

negotiations, and with the expectation of implementing the promised investments, shipowners enjoyed privileged treatment, although this has not always been to the benefit of the Greek economy.[47] Moreover, through their great negotiating power Greek shipowners have been able to influence the policies of all postwar governments and to secure the adoption of a shipping policy consistent with their interests.

Conclusions

Since the nineteenth century Greek shipping has been among the world's ten largest fleets, and in the last third of the twentieth century it became the world's biggest merchant marine. This essay has traced its development over the past 150 years, identified some of the reasons for its success and examined the impact of this international maritime industry on the Greek economy.

Greek shipowners involved in deep-sea trade between third countries became important international tramp operators able to exploit the opportunities presented by a tremendous rise in the circulation of bulk cargoes in world trade since the second half of the nineteenth century. From the 1850s to the 1940s they were engaged particularly in the carriage of grain from the Black Sea (Russia and Romania) or the South Atlantic (Argentina), with coal as the return cargo, whereas from the 1950s to the end of the century they were deeply involved in carrying oil and dry bulk cargoes on global routes. They adjusted in a timely fashion to the technological innovations of steam and diesel engines as well as to new types of ships, whether these were steamers, Liberty ships, tankers or bulk carriers. Their main strength has been the formation of an exclusive "Greek" transnational network of family enterprises that interacted with local, national and international shipping networks, organizations and financial institutions. They have developed their own entrepreneurial methods, business strategies and cultural, and have selected national and international maritime centres from which to operate.

The income generated by shipping appears to have comprised the most important invisible earning, until the First World War covering the country's total trade deficit. During the interwar and postwar periods more than one-third of the balance-of-payments deficit was covered by income from shipping. Indeed, in these periods the figures likely underestimate the overall importance of this activity in the context of the growth of the economy because the investments of Greek shipowners have not been calculated explicitly in the national statistics but rather have been regarded as foreign capital. What cannot be doubted, however, is that the shipping sector has contributed to a great

---

[47]For a preliminary assessment of the costs and benefits of investments by shipowners in the Greek economy between 1945 and 1975, see *ibid.*, chapters 4-6.

extent to the economic development of the country throughout the nineteenth and twentieth centuries.

A Guide to the Emergence of Japan's
Modern Shipping Industries

Peter N. Davies

To a large extent shipping is a service industry which reflects the circumstances under which it operates. This is certainly true in the case of Japan. The country consists of four main and numerous small islands which extend for over 2000 kilometres and thus includes considerable climatic differences. The total landmass is approximately fifty percent greater than the UK, but it is largely mountainous, and only a fifth of the land can be farmed. The limited amount of flat area has had the effect of concentrating the population into a coastal strip which runs from the Kanto Plain, around Tokyo and through to the Kansai Plain, which includes the major cities of Osaka, Kobe and Kyoto.[1] Since much of the food, mainly rice, needed to be moved to these expanding regions from elsewhere in Japan, a major coastal and inter-island trade gradually emerged, undertaken by small vessels which incorporated features of both the galley and the junk and which were well adapted to local conditions. By 1600 some of these *wasen* were reported to have reached a size of 700 tons and were sailing to Luzon, China and Siam, where small Japanese communities had already been established.[2]

Indeed, some authorities have suggested that had these trends continued, a Japanese conquest of the Philippines might have followed, and parts of Australia could have been settled. In reality, the Tokugawa government (which had recently united the country) decided to end Japan's tentative links with the outside world, and from 1638 an era of seclusion was established which prevented virtually all overseas contacts. The only exception to this rule was that one or two Dutch vessels were permitted to call at Deshima – an island close to Nagasaki – each year, and small numbers of Chinese merchants were allowed on the same site from time to time. These restrictions had a dramatic

---

[1]Janet E. Hunter, *The Emergence of Modern Japan: An Introductory History since 1853* (London, 1989), 1.

[2]Richard Storry, *A History of Modern Japan* (Harmondsworth, 1985), 65.

effect on Japanese ship construction, and this was made explicit by an edict which limited the *wasen* to a maximum of fifty tons.[3]

For the subsequent two hundred years Japan was effectively isolated, and the nation evolved free from major foreign influences. One consequence of this long period of peace was the growth of population, which by 1870 had risen to over thirty million, with a million living in Edo (later renamed Tokyo). Another was the development of indigenous banking, commercial and trading systems that strengthened the growing merchant class, which then began to pose a potential threat to the existing feudal structure. It was, however, changes in the international environment which eventually obliged Japan to open its borders and resume relations with the global community.[4]

The spread of European influence to India and East Asia, the development of colonialism and the overall growth in world trade were all important factors in this respect. More specifically, the rising number of American whaling vessels, advances in steam ship technology and increasing regional trade were particularly significant. The latter had already led to the establishment of trading centres in Singapore (1819), Hong Kong (1841) and at four ports in China, including Shanghai (1842). These activities brought into focus the need for convenient and secure supplies of water, food, repair facilities and (subsequently) coal. Better provision for the care and return of shipwrecked seamen was a further consideration, while the possibility of a valuable trade also prompted action.

At first, the most involved nation was Russia, which was interested in securing supplies to aid its expansion into Alaska and eastern Siberia, but all the overtures which began in 1805 were rejected by the Japanese. Britain also sought to establish diplomatic and commercial relations. These were unsuccessful, and although further effects would doubtless have followed, these were forestalled by the US, which in 1853 mounted a large-scale expedition under Commodore Perry. This landed at what was to become the port of Yokohama and eventually led to the Treaty of Kanagawa, which effectively resulted in Japan being opened to foreign trade. Many within the country were strongly opposed to this change in policy, and it was not until 1868 that the Meiji Restoration marked the end of the old Tokugawa administration.[5]

When the Meiji government came to power it faced the huge task of modernizing or reorganizing practically all the nation's commercial, industrial,

---

[3]Tomohei Chida and Peter N. Davies, *The Japanese Shipping and Shipbuilding Industries: A History of Their Modern Growth* (London, 1990), 2.

[4]Richard Bowring and Peter Kornick (eds.), *The Cambridge Encyclopedia of Japan* (Cambridge, 1993), provides a comprehensive guide to these events.

[5]Edwin O. Reischauer, *Japan: The Story of a Nation* (New York, 1970; 4th ed., New York, 1990), 114-116 and 118-121.

educational and communication sectors, as well as creating a new style of armed services. It was also necessary to absorb the former Samurai warriors, who formed six percent of the population, into the economy, for although they were unproductive they still needed to be paid. These policies meant fundamental changes to the central system of taxation and customs, the provision of banks and postal services and the establishment of suitable institutions to provide an educated workforce and arrange for the final termination of the feudal system.[6]

In spite of the immensity of these tasks, which required huge capital expenditures, the government was determined to avoid foreign loans. Instead, it hoped to finance most of its plans by overseas trade. Fortunately, it was able to enter the international silk market at a time when Mediterranean producers were being affected by pebrine disease and Chinese sericulture by the disruption of the Tai'ping War which ravaged the area around Shanghai. Exports of tea, especially to the US, provided a further long-term item, while for a few years Japanese cotton found a ready sale during the shortages caused by the American Civil War.[7]

Efforts to encourage these foreign trades led to attempts to improve communications, and modern ports were gradually developed at Yokohama, Kobe, Osaka and Nagasaki. Because these benefited the vessels of all nations, efforts to aid Japanese shipping were also given high priority. While this would certainly save foreign exchange, it also offered several other advantages. In the absence of a strong pro-maritime policy, many feared that the West would take over Japan's coastal routes as had happened elsewhere in Asia. As a result, in 1870 legislation was introduced which helped to promote viable services by local operators. Japanese policy was further strengthened in this area by the knowledge that tonnage under the national flag could be used for strategic purposes. This was emphasized when the government planned to invade Formosa in 1874 on the basis that its troops would be carried in chartered, foreign vessels. When this proposal was vetoed by the principal maritime powers, Japan decided to use domestic tonnage, and thirteen steamships were purchased for this purpose. These were entrusted to Mitsubishi, which managed them for the length of the campaign. When it had been successfully concluded, the state showed its gratitude by allowing Mitsubishi to retain the vessels for a nominal fee.[8]

---

[6]*Ibid.*, 124-127.

[7]Giovanni Federico, *An Economic History of the Silk Industry: 1830-1930* (Cambridge, 1997), 31; and Barry S. Hoyle and David Hilling (eds.), *Seaport Systems and Spatial Change: Technology, Industry, and Development Strategies* (Chichester, 1984), 113.

[8]Chida and Davies, *Japanese Shipping and Shipbuilding Industries*, 5-8.

This generosity was not without reason. The government appreciated that at this stage of Japan's economic development one strong line was preferable to a number of weak ones and so gave all its support to what it regarded as the most promising of the firms that previously operated only coastal services. This was further demonstrated when the state divested itself of all its remaining vessels, which were handed to Mitsubish, for a nominal charge. These events then encouraged the company, now reconstituted as the Yubin Kisen Mitsubishi Kaisha, to increase the range of its activities. It established its own marine training school so that a start could be made to replace expatriate deck officers with Japanese nationals. Then, with the aid of its additional capacity, it extended its coastal routes and commenced a new service between Yokohama and Shanghai. This brought it into conflict with the (American) Pacific Steamship Company, and this competition was ended only when Mitsubishi (with governmental aid) was able to buy the ships and shore facilities which their rivals had utilized on that route. Mitsubishi's strength was tested in 1876 when P&O attempted to secure a foothold in the trade. A six-month freight war followed before P&O was obliged to give up the fight.[9]

The outbreak of the Satsuma Rebellion in 1877 gave Mitsubishi a second opportunity to assist the state. With the exception of the vessels employed on the Shanghai route, all its tonnage was placed at the government's disposal. Once the revolt had ended, Mitsubishi was given further grants by the ruling Reform Party, which in turn led the opposition Liberal Party to demand funds for a second, subsidized line. This was finally agreed in 1882 when the government supplied half the capital to fund a new firm, Kyodo Unyu Kaisha (KHK), from a number of existing small companies. The KHK thus operated in opposition to Mitsubishi, but when this led to heavy losses by both lines, the government eventually ordered them to amalgamate; in 1885 this resulted in the establishment of the Nippon Yusen Kaisha (NYK) as the sole state-aided firm.[10]

To encourage this merger the government guaranteed an eight percent annual dividend on its capital. In return, it was agreed that the NYK's vessels would be used to provide fourteen specified services. These routes were mainly around Japan but also included short-sea services to China, Korea and Asiatic Russia. When it was first formed the NYK was a semi-official organization, but as a result of changes to its structure in 1892 it became an entirely private enterprise. In the same year it entered into deep-sea trade by commencing a service to carry cotton from Bombay to Kobe.[11]

---

[9]*Ibid.*, 8.

[10]*Ibid.*, 9.

[11]*Ibid.*, 20.

While the NYK was developing into Japan's major ship operator, other firms were also being attracted to the industry. The growth of the economy led to frequent fresh opportunities, and in the Osaka region many firms acquired small steam vessels. Indeed, by the early 1880s seventy companies were involved with over 100 steamers, but the uncoordinated growth of tonnage tended to make the business unprofitable. This situation persuaded a majority of the shipowners that they should join together to form a single body, and this decision resulted in the establishment of the Osaka Shosen Kaisha (OSK) in 1884. Unfortunately, the new line did not include all the Osaka owners, and those who chose to remain aloof continued to provide strenuous competition. This proved to be so damaging that the future of the OSK was in doubt until in 1887 the government decided to subsidize the firm for an initial eight-year period. In return, the OSK agreed to provide regular services to the west of Osaka; with the aid of state subventions these were gradually extended beyond the Inland Sea until they reached Korea. [12]

The establishment of the NYK and OSK provided Japan with two large shipping companies whose operations were very similar to those of many British firms. The vast majority of their ships were purchased in Britain until well into the twentieth century, and many British deck officers and engineers were employed. But a major difference was that while British lines frequently competed in the same trades, the two Japanese *shasen* (regular lines) were encouraged to operate on routes where they would not come into conflict. [13]

The policy of concentrating support on just the two *shasen* lines was further strengthened during the Sino-Japanese War (1894-1895). When this created large demands for additional capacity, the NYK purchased nine ships as soon as the war commenced, and the government subsequently bought a further fourteen which were then added to the company's fleet. Once the war was over the increased tonnage encouraged the line to find alternative outlets, and a service to Europe was begun in 1896. In the same year, the NYK opened a trans-Pacific line to Seattle where some of its additional ships found profitable employment, but an attempt to establish a service to Australia was frustrated when Orientals were restricted from entry to that continent. On the other hand, the potential of a service to San Francisco appeared to be so great that in 1896 the government founded a third *shasen* company – the Toyo Kisen Kaisha – to operate exclusively on this route. The Russo-Japanese War (1904-1905) provided further opportunities for expanding Japan's merchant fleet. Many additional ships had to be acquired quickly, although chartered vessels were used as much as possible to maintain existing services. Again, once hos-

---

[12]*Ibid.*, 9-10.

[13]Peter N. Davies, "The Rise of Japan's Modern Shipping Industry," *The Great Circle*, VII, No. 1 (1985), 48.

tilities were ended the extra capacity needed to be employed, so fresh routes were opened to Tacoma in North America and to Java and other ports in the South Seas.[14]

This account of the establishment and progress of the *shasen* lines covers only one aspect of the development of Japanese shipping. Many operators of *wasen* in the coastal trades gradually equipped their fleets with Western-style sailing vessels, a process accelerated by a government decision in 1885 to ban the construction of large *wasen*. This trend, however, was overtaken by another, for most owners became aware of the advantages enjoyed by steamships and acquired them as quickly as was practical. Their firms, known as the *shagaisen* (literally "outsiders"), were then given a significant boost by the activities of Mitsui Bussan (MB). This company, an associate of the Mitsui *Zaibatsu*, established itself as an ocean-going operator and utilized *shagaisen*-chartered vessels to supplement its own tonnage. This was originally to carry its own cargoes, but when it developed on a large scale it also hired out many of these vessels to both the *shasen* lines and foreign firms. Another twist in the somewhat complicated structure of the *shagaisen* came with a steady divorce between shipowning and ship operating. Over time some owners stopped operating their ships and merely provided the capital for vessels which were permanently hired out to firms which employed or re-chartered them as they saw fit. This division became to pronounced that in some cases operators, such as the Yamashita and Tatsuuma lines, which were entirely dependent upon chartered tonnage, emerged.[15]

While both the *shasen* and *shagaison* firms benefited considerably from war, the impact on coastal routes was not as great as on the near seas and long-distance services. The increase of tonnage prior to 1890 had been achieved with government assistance mainly by the *shasen* lines, but thereafter the unsubsidized *shagaisen* firms made the greatest progress. At the conclusion of the Russo-Japanese War both sides of the industry operated approximately the same levels of tonnage, but by 1911 the *shagaisen* had reached 750,000 gross tons compared with only 540,000 gross tons for the *shasen* firms. This difference can probably be attributed to the latter's entry into ocean-going liner services, for this brought them into direct competition with well-established foreign companies organized in shipping "rings" or conferences. The *shagaisen* faced a similar problem, but events were to prove that the liner market was much more difficult than that for tramp shipping. Nevertheless, at the end of each war both the *shasen* and the *shagaisen* were able to expand their tonnage and extend their service areas.

---

[14]*Ibid.*

[15]Chida and Davies, *Japanese Shipping and Shipbuilding Industries*, 10-11 and 24.

These advances continued with even larger opportunities for expansion during the Great War (1914-1918). While the three *shasen* companies worked at full capacity, since their freight rates were controlled by a government subsidy act they could not maximize their returns. But the shortages of tonnage previously provided by Western maritime nations on many routes enabled the *shasen* to take advantage of the resulting gaps, and they were able to extend their networks considerably. The *shagaisen*, on the other hand, were able to charge the market rate, and as freight charges (and vessel prices) rose to ten times the prewar levels, many owners made considerable fortunes, some of which were ploughed back into the industry, which also extended its activities to the long-distance oceanic routes.[16]

A further consequence concerned Japanese shipbuilding. Although the development of a modern industry was given a low priority by the state and was hindered by the lack of the necessary engineering complex, some progress was made, especially in the field of ship repairs. The Shipbuilding Promotion Law of 1896 encouraged the construction of iron and steel vessels of over 1000 tons, and soon thereafter the 6172-gross ton *Hitachi Maru* was constructed by Mitsubishi at its Nagasaki yard. Nonetheless, it was still cheaper to import vessels which were usually of a better standard, so the government brought in a Navigation Promotion Law in 1899 to provide larger operating subsidies for domestically-produced ships. This led to a rise in output so that by 1910 approximately half of Japan's merchant vessels and virtually all its naval ships were built at home. By then construction quality was approaching international standards, but the higher costs meant that there were no prospects for exports. The outbreak of war in 1914 changed all this, and Japanese output rose from 58,000 gross tons in that year to 226,000 gross tons in 1917 and to over 636,000 gross tons in 1919. It should be noted, however, that this was only possible with the aid of the Ship Steel Exchange Agreement concluded with the US in 1918, since Japan's domestic steel industry was still underdeveloped, and considerable quantities of plate needed to be imported even in peacetime.[17]

The postwar depression seriously affected all aspects of the Japanese economy, and the ship operating and shipbuilding sectors were forced to retrench. While the government continued to subsidize the *shasen* firms via the Distant Sea Liner Service Subsidy Law and the Specific Route Subsidy these were gradually reduced so that payment was increasingly linked to the carriage of mail. The economic slump and attempts by foreign companies to reclaim their former trades led the NYK to take over some of the routes of the Toya Kissen Kaisha, which ceased to be a *shasen*. It also forced the NYK and OSK

---

[16]*Ibid.*, 28-29.

[17]*Ibid.*, 33-35.

to compete against each other on some routes. But in 1931, when the depression was at its worst, an agreement to co-operate and rationalize their activities was finally reached. This tactic was strengthened by investment in high-quality ships with diesel engines for ocean-going vessels. The net effect of these policies was that the *shasen* lines were able to retain some of their wartime gains, and their fleets grew slowly for most of the interwar period.[18]

The division of the *shagaisen* firms into owners and operators, which was confirmed during the Great War, was further strengthened after 1918. This made more capital available for new tonnage built in Japan and for the acquisition of second-hand vessels from abroad at very low prices. Changes in the system employed by MB, together with a steady rise in the volume of Japan's overseas trade, meant that the *shagaisen* fleet increased more rapidly than did the *shasen*. The combination of these two sectors ensured that the size of the Japanese mercantile marine continued to grow throughout the 1920s and 1930s. This expansion included a substantial number of oil tankers, which after 1929 were operated by private firms. Prompted by the navy's decision to switch from coal to oil, these vessels proved profitable and replaced foreign tankers which had previously carried most of Japan's oil imports.[19]

The relative success of Japan's ship operating industry in the interwar period was not replicated by its shipbuilders. The output of steamships fell from a peak in 1919 to a low of only 48,000 gross tons in 1925. A slow recovery led to 423,000 gross tons being produced in 1938, but the poor returns prevented much investment in new facilities. By the 1930s Japanese yards could supply sound vessels, but they were still uneconomic in world terms. As a result, there are no records of any exports in this entire era, and domestic owners were extremely dependent upon low-interest loans from the Industrial Bank of Japan. This sorry tale would have been much worse but for the government's decision to make increasing use of the private yards for the construction of naval vessels. At the nadir of the slump in 1928-1931 this work represented forty-eight percent of all man-hours in these facilities, and a similar proportion was again achieved in the late 1930s as Japan prepared for war.[20]

When Japan entered the Second World War (known in Japan as the Pacific War) its merchant marine consisted of 1962 ships totalling 6,094,000 gross tons. A further three and a half million tons were constructed during the hostilities, but of this total of nearly ten million tons only about seventeen per-

---

[18]Davies, "Rise," 52.

[19]Tomohei Chida, "The Development of Japan's Post-war Shipping Policy," *Journal of Transport History*, 3rd ser., V, No. 1 (1984), 82-83; and Chida and Davies, *Japanese Shipping and Shipbuilding Industries*, 51-52.

[20]Chida and Davies, *Japanese Shipping and Shipbuilding Industries*, 45-46.

cent survived, and these were almost entirely comprised of obsolescent and damaged ships. Until the peace treaty was signed in 1952, the remaining tonnage was subject to varying degrees of control by the occupying powers. Even before this, however, the outbreak of war in Korea had already begun to revitalize both the Japanese ship repairing and ship operating industries. The shipbuilding sector was still in the doldrums, but the orders which had already been received from domestic and overseas owners were indications of significant future expansion. It is interesting to note that the first foreign orders came as early as 1948 when two whalers were built for Norwegian owners, and that by the following year sixteen ships totalling 62,000 gross tons had been contracted for by international buyers.[21]

At the end of the Pacific War some eighty-five percent of Japan's shipbuilding capacity remained undamaged, but builders were handicapped by shortages of materials, power and skilled manpower. Nevertheless, the chronic postwar shortages of tonnage and the long order books of the remaining European builders (the Americans required payment in dollars which were in short supply) enabled Japan to secure a number of commissions even though by international standards they were uncompetitive. Very little investment had been made in the yards since their creation in previous decades, and none of the innovations developed in the US for the mass production of "Liberty Ships" were adopted in Japan during the war. Thus, there was little use of welding, which had been discredited by the loss of the destroyers *Yugiri* and *Hatsuyuki* in 1935: almost no employment of large-scale standardization; and a failure to introduce any systems of "section" or "block" construction. The facilities which survived in 1945 essentially utilized the same methods as in 1939, and by world standards the entire industry was technically backward.[22]

While a transfer of new technology would have gradually occurred, the process was speeded by the activities of National Bulk Carriers (NBC). This American firm wished to build large iron ore carriers for the Venezuelan trade but found it difficult to find appropriate berths. It subsequently discovered that the Japanese naval yard Kure possessed an undamaged building dock with a 100-ton crane and a capacity for vessels of 150,000 deadweight tons (dwt). This yard had previously produced the 64,000-ton battleship *Yamato*, so it seemed ideal for NBC's purposes. The firm thus acquired the site on a ten-year lease for a "peppercorn rent" and over this period produced a series of high-quality vessels at very competitive prices (see table 1).

---

[21]Peter N. Davies, "Japanese Merchant Shipping and the Bridge over the River Kwai," in Clark G. Reynolds (ed.), *Global Crossroads and the American Seas* (Missoula, MT, 1988), 201-202; and Chida and Davies, *Japanese Shipping and Shipbuilding Industries*, 77-78 and 83.

[22]Chida and Davies, *Japanese Shipping and Shipbuilding Industries*, 91.

Table 1
Output of the Kure Shipyard, 1951-1961

	Number of Ships	Gross Tonnage
1951	1	23,500
1952	3	65,500
1953	4	91,400
1954	2	49,000
1955	11	288,400
1956	6	247,600
1957	9	364,410
1958	4	96,367
1959		
1960		
1961	3	112,370

Source:	Tomohei Chida and Peter N. Davies, *The Japanese Shipping and Shipbuilding Industries: A History of Their Modern Growth* (London, 1990), 201.

The success of the Kure yard enabled it to act as a prototype for the entire shipbuilding industry. Over the period of NBC operation, between four and five thousand engineers (mainly Japanese but also some Westerners and other Asians) visited the plant. This meant that the new technology was transferred and diffused much more quickly than would otherwise have been the case. The yard thus played a vital role in assisting the expansion of output, which grew at such a rapid rate that by 1956 Japan had become the world's largest producer of merchant vessels. As a result of these developments, total Japanese production rose from only 125,499 gross tons in 1947 to 2,355,854 gross tons a decade later. The downturn in demand in the 1960s then led to an amalgamation into larger units, and by 1971 the seventeen original firms in the early postwar years had been amalgamated into only seven new groups: Mitsubishi Jyukogyo (Mitsubishi Heavy Industries), Mitsui Jyukogyo (Mitsui Shipbuilding), Sumitomo Jykikai Kogyo (Sumitomo Heavy Machinery), Kawasaki Jyukogyo (Kawasaki Heavy Industries), Hitachi Zosen (Hitachi Shipbuilding) Ishikawajima Harima Jyukogyo (I.H. Heavy Industries) and Nippon Kokan (Japan Steel Pipe). These changes enabled output to rise still further, and by 1977 production had risen to 10,648,376 gross tons. By 2006 it had reached about 18,200,000 gross tons, which represented thirty-five percent of world construction, just marginally behind South Korea, which accounted for 35.8 percent of output. It should be noted that both are being increasingly challenged by China, which built approximately 7,500,000 gross tons in the same year.[23]

Table 2
New Structure of Japanese Merchant Shipping

Nucleus	Companies Merged	Ocean-going vessels (dwt)	Associate Companies (dwt)	Wholly Con-Trolled Com-Panies (dwt)	Total Tonnage (dwt)
Nippon Yusen Kaisha	NYK Mitsubishi Kaiun	1,052,084	1,012,000 (7)	223,616 (6)	2,287,696
Yamashita Shin Nihon Kisen Kaisha	Yamashita Kisen Shin Nihon Kisen	570,031	415,865 (4)	136,528 (9)	1,122,424
Showa Kaiun	Nippon Yusosen Nissan Kisen	609,727	355,787 (3)	57,049 (4)	1,022,563
Japan Line	Nitto Shosen Daido Kaiun	967,408	43,167 (1)	58,453 (2)	1,069,028
Kawasaki Kisen	Kawasaki Kisen Iino Kisen	933,130	390,266 (7)	220,452 (8)	1,543,848
Osaka Shosen Mitsui Senpaku (Mitsui-OSK Line)	Mitsui Senpaku OSK	1,237,230	307,572 (5)	773,533 (26)	2,318,355
Total					9,363,894

Note: Figures in parentheses represent the number of companies.

Sources: Japan, Ministry of Transport and Shipping, *The Current Situation of Japanese Shipping* (Tokyo, 1964); and Ryoichi Furuta and Yoshikazu Hirai, *A Short History of Japanese Merchant Shipping* (Tokyo, 1966), 162, as cited in Chida and Davies, *Japanese Shipping and Shipbuilding Industries*, 207-212 and appendix table J.

---

[23]Peter N. Davies, "The Role of International Bulk Carriers in the Advance of Shipbuilding Technology in Postwar Japan," *International Journal of Maritime History*, IV, No. 1 (1992), 131-142; Chida and Davies, *Japanese Shipping and Shipbuilding Industries*, 164-167 and 202; and Lloyds Register-Fairplay, *World Fleet Statistics 2006* (London, 2006), statistical notes, 16.

The progress of shipbuilding was paralleled by an enormous increase in Japan's merchant fleet, which rose from only 1.5 million gross tons in 1947 to nearly four million ten years later. Difficulties in the 1960s caused by the closure of the Suez Canal led to a need to reorganize the whole structure of the business, and this was accomplished with a minimum of delay and cost by 1964 (see table 2).

The restructuring of the ship operating side of the industry facilitated even further growth, so that by 1967 the fleet amounted to just over fifteen million gross tons and reached thirty-eight million gross tons by 1977. This expansion has continued in recent decades, and in 2006 Japan owned 99,750,854 gross tons. Only 12,798,237 gross tons of this total flew the national flag, which meant that Japan was the second largest owner, trailing Greece by a small margin.[24]

From the foregoing it is clear that after Japan reopened its borders to the West its ship operating industry rapidly adapted to the changed circumstances. This was essential if it was to avoid losing its routes to foreign companies, and it thus was given much support by the state. As the latest vessels could be readily imported, there was much less pressure to develop shipbuilding facilities apart from the need to conserve foreign exchange. Government assistance for construction was therefore much more limited, but even so by 1914 at least half of its merchant ships and all of its naval tonnage were being produced at home. This progress owed a great deal to a number of different subsidies. The two *shasen* lines were at first guaranteed a return on their capital and were beneficiaries of many vessels which had been acquired by the state for strategic purposes. They, but not the *shagaisen*, also received a number of subsidies for operating distant or specific services. These took the form of payments for route mileage – the level varied according to the quality of the ship being employed. This helped to ensure that the vessels were steadily improved, while the building of tonnage within Japan was aided by a higher rate for domestically produced ships.

The shipbuilding industry was supported directly by the government for the construction of larger or superior vessels with extra premiums being paid for features such as additional speed, refrigeration and communications facilities. Of even more significance was the provision of low-cost loans, which were provided by a range of state-supported bodies or through commercial institutions such as the Industrial Bank of Japan. Other financial aid was also given by the banking sector. This was particularly true for the *shasen* lines, for the NYK was closely associated with the Mitsubishi *Zaibatsu* and the OSK with the Mitsui *Zaibatsu*, and both these groups had their own banks at the centre of their activities. It is widely assumed that government funds were

---

[24]Chida and Davies, *Japanese Shipping and Shipbuilding Industries*, 206; and Lloyds Register-Fairplay, *World Fleet Statistics 2006*, statistical notes, 10-13.

made available to these bodies to encourage whatever policies were in vogue, while internal transfers between different sectors provided a great deal of flexibility. Thus, any profits within the system could be used to offset losses elsewhere or to invest in what appeared to be promising activities.

The Great War (1914-1918) had the effect of strengthening all aspects of the Japanese shipping industries. The high returns enabled many debts to be liquidated, and a substantial amount was used to invest in additional building capacity. Once hostilities had ceased and prices had fallen, the *shagaisen* purchased a large number of second-hand vessels from foreign owners. Although the subsequent slump produced desperate trading conditions, these operators were able to hold on to most of their wartime gains and gradually to increase their fleets. Their progress was partly due to skilled management and rising efficiency but was also aided considerably by the growing volume of Japan's overseas trade. This was almost guaranteed by the way in which the Japanese *sogoshohas* (General Trading Companies) organized imports and exports on behalf of the *Zaibatsu* firms they represented abroad.[25]

The *shasen* lines also experienced enormous difficulties after the wartime boom was over, and these intensified following Japan's financial crisis in 1927. Although the government was itself under huge pressure, it continued to provide significant subsidies to the remaining two regular lines until 1931. These were then gradually reduced so that on most routes only a postal subvention remained – while this was regretted by the firms, they welcomed the freedom from controls which this change ensured and were able to adopt more flexible policies. NYK's association with Mitsubishi and OSK's links with Mitsui meant that they could rely upon their parent groups for both cargoes and capital. As part of their strategy for survival, some of the latter was used to begin the process of equipping their fleets with modern motor vessels, and their tactics proved highly successful on many routes. A further aspect of this policy was that the NYK and OSK were obliged to cooperate and reorganized their services so that they did not compete with one another.

These developments in the operating sector had a major impact on Japanese shipbuilding. Output had remained low throughout the 1920s; but for naval work some yards would have closed permanently. The increasing demands for advanced vessels by both the *shasen* and *shagaisen* resulted in a rising level of production during the 1930s, and this expansion was further aided by the introduction of a Scrap and Build Scheme in 1932 which aimed to replace two tons of older shipping with one ton of new construction which had to be of at least 4000 tons and capable of speeds of thirteen knots. Although further schemes along the same lines were brought in during 1935 and 1936,

---

[25]Michael Y. Yoshino and Thomas B. Lifson, T*he Invisible Link: Japan's Sogo Shosa and the Organization of Trade* (Cambridge, MA, 1986).

many of the aged vessels were not scrapped but were placed in reserve and returned to service during the Pacific War.[26]

The net effect of these events was that both the Japanese merchant fleet and shipbuilding capacity were larger and more efficient than would otherwise have been the case. Although its defeat in the war left only a small amount of damaged tonnage, the country's shipbuilding facilities emerged mainly intact, and once the necessary fuel, material and labour were available production rapidly resumed. The yards at that stage remained basically unchanged from the 1920s, but the work of NBC in transferring the most modern technology enabled the entire industry to be reorganized so that it was able to respond to changes in demand as they occurred.

The closure of the Suez Canal, and the consequent need to build larger vessels which could handle the longer route around the Cape of Good Hope by taking advantage of economies of scale, rapidly increased the demand for this type of tonnage. Unfortunately, much of it came into service as the boom ended, and the depression which followed was worsened by the highly efficient ships which were produced. Much excess capacity ensued, but in Japan's case some could be employed to carry its growing overseas trade, as exports rose from US $2 billion in 1955 to US $6.6 billion in 1969, while imports increased from US $2.4 billion to US $7.9 billion over the same period. Since many of the imports consisted of bulk cargoes of iron ore and crude oil, the types of vessels used for these purposes formed a rising part of the Japanese fleet.

Although Japan was able to build larger tankers and bulk carriers, demand proved to be so great that many additional building docks and fitting-out berths were created. Thus, by 1973 the country possessed 124 facilities, of which thirteen could construct vessels of over 150,000 gross tons. An example of the speed with which these facilities were established was at Nagasaki, where Mitsubishi laid down its new Koyagi works and built its first ship within two years of beginning work.[27]

The net effect of these developments was that in 1964 the ship operators were amalgamated into a revised structure and that in 1971 seven major shipbuilders were established through a series of takeovers so that the entire industry was rationalized. With the aid of these fundamental changes, both Japanese shipping and shipbuilding became extremely efficient operators and constructors, but their achievements were based upon a much wider range of factors.

The new Meiji government, which in 1868 began the modernization of Japan, gave ship operating and later shipbuilding a high priority, both for

---

[26]Chida and Davies, *Japanese Shipping and Shipbuilding Industries*, 47-49.

[27]*Ibid.*, 159-160.

strategic reasons and either to save or earn foreign exchange. Thus, from its inception to the 1970s – when they were deemed to be no longer necessary – state support via subsidies, grants and cheap labour were always made available to both sides of the industry. These payments were concentrated on the *shasen* lines because the government rightly judged that this was a better tactic than spreading resources more thinly over a wider segment of the industry. The organization of Japanese ship operating and shipbuilding was also influenced by the creation of the *Zaibutsu* structure. These groups of companies emerged to maximize the use of scarce capital and skilled manpower during the early Meiji period. As they included both Mitsui and Mitsubishi, each of which developed *shasen* lines and became major constructors of shipping, their role was also of critical significance to their growth and success. At the centre of each of these conglomerates lay a bank which enabled government funds to be easily assimilated and distributed in accordance with the policy in place. At the same time, they were equally valuable in arranging loans or transfers which could be kept secret if necessary.

It should be appreciated that the structure of the *Zaibatsu* changed dramatically over time but was always linked in varying degrees by a series of cross shareholdings. Although the *Zaibatsu* were banned by the Allied powers in 1945, they subsequently reformed as six vertically-integrated groups known as *Keiretsu*. These competed vigorously and thereby gave the Japanese economy a strong competitive edge. Another advantage of this system was that it was comparatively easy to transfer employees from one firm to another as demand rose and fell in different sectors of the group. Thus, the problems experienced in the West when compulsory redundancies were necessary were largely avoided. This aspect of the labour market was further aided by the two-tier organization of the workforce. A proportion was permanent, and in the postwar era these people enjoyed jobs for life and many other benefits. A substantial number, however, which differed across the type of companies, were subcontracted from agents who supplied whatever was required on a daily basis. Some individuals therefore might work for (say) a Mitsui shipyard for their entire careers and yet remain casual labour, never achieving the permanent status they craved. As a result of this system, the reduction of shipbuilding sites by a third in 1978-1979 was completed in only eighteen months with few problems.[28]

Industrial relations were mainly good throughout the postwar era. This was partly due to the seniority system of wages which led to additional payments being made for age, experience and training. This meant that older employers who might have been expected to lead any opposition to manage-

---

[28]Johannes Hirschmeier and Tsunehiko Yui, *The Development of Japanese Business, 1600-1980* (London, 1975; 2nd ed., London, 1981), 206-208 and 332-336; and Chida and Davies, *Japanese Shipping and Shipbuilding Industries*, 181-182.

ment were too well paid and secure to take any serious action which might damage their welfare. In addition, the policy of recruiting supervisors from the existing staff led to a considerable understanding of shop-floor difficulties and aspirations.[29] In the immediate aftermath of the Pacific War, wage levels were initially very low but gradually rose so that today total remuneration is roughly double that of comparable British rates. But these increases were directly linked to productivity and were only paid after they had been achieved through the payment of twice-yearly bonuses. These arrangements between management and labour proved highly successful in generating a skilled and dedicated work force across a whole range of Japanese industries. These included the iron and steel producers whose products were critical to the shipbuilding sector.[30] Thus, although virtually all its raw materials and fuel were imported, Japan was able to remain competitive because its labour costs were lower than those of other nations (see table 3).

Table 3
Labour Costs per Hour in the Steel Industry (US$)

	1960	1970	1980
USA	4.12	6.05	20.17
EC	1.16	2.98	11.80
Japan	0.54	1.68	9.80

Source: International Iron and Steel Institute, "The Japanese Shipping Industry" (unpublished paper, 1995).

The original impetus given to the Japanese shipbuilding sector came when the government provided extra payments if the *shasen* lines utilized domestically-produced tonnage, and further assistance was supplied by the Scrap and Build Schemes during the 1930s. Recovery after the Pacific War was facilitated by the state totally ignoring environmental factors and allowing nothing to stand in the way of increased output. This was given a further boost by the demands of the Korean War, and production was subsequently placed on a permanently efficient and large-scale basis by the construction of modern capacity capable of building the biggest and most sophisticated vessels that were then required.

---

[29]Hirschmeier and Yui, *Development*, 209 and 360-364.

[30]For a full account of the background to the Japanese steel industry, see Etsuo Abe and Yoshitaka Suzuki (eds.), *Changing Patterns of International Rivalry: Some Lessons from the Steel Industry* (Tokyo, 1991); and Seiichiro Yonekura, *The Postwar Japanese Iron and Steel Industry: Continuity and Discontinuity* (New York, 1994), 193-241.

The progress of shipbuilding has enabled the Japanese merchant fleet to be equipped with the latest, most technically-advanced and efficient vessels. Unfortunately, these have also been made available to their international rivals who from the 1960s have increasingly purchased their requirements from Japan. Domestic firms had originally remained competitive in world markets because their low wage rates offset the more modern tonnage then employed by Western companies. This situation was reversed in the postwar period in order to keep the pay of Japanese seafarers in line with land-based industries. Compensation for what has become a high-cost operation in terms of their crews has come from the Japanese Seafarers Union. This body, which represents all grades (except Radio Officers) of engineering, deck and catering staff, gradually became aware of the potential threat that this posed for its members. As a result, it has reluctantly accepted the need for a reduction in crew numbers, and from 1987 a project began to "Modernize the Seafarers System." This was designed to unite the previous disparate jobs performed by the engine and deck departments with a view to economizing on personnel. Experiments were commenced with "Pioneerships" in which crews were at first limited to eighteen and then steadily fell to an eventual eleven for this class of vessel.[31]

The savings in costs which this trend promoted enabled Japanese-flagged vessels to remain competitive to some extent, but by 2006 only about thirteen percent of Japanese-owned tonnage was registered at home. A number of lengthy strikes in 1965 and 1972 encouraged other solutions so that more and more of the national fleet was organized on different lines. These included the use of flags of convenience and, most important, the development of the *Shikumisen* system. The latter has many legal technicalities but usually involved the sale of a Japanese-built and owned vessel to a company based elsewhere which was then permanently chartered back for the whole of its lifespan. This meant that what were Japanese ships carrying Japanese cargoes on Japanese routes could take full advantage of flag-of-convenience registry, including the employment of mixed or entirely foreign crews.[32] While these arrangements helped to solve many of Japan's problems, they created other tensions, some of which have still not been resolved.

The restructuring of Japanese ship operating in 1964 established six principal groups, all of which included a number of the smaller firms which became associates of the larger enterprises. This marked the beginning of the end of the division between the *shasen* and *shagaisen* and the start of a new era. The prosperity of the regular firms meant that they no longer needed to be subsidized and as a consequence were not bound by regulations which had

---

[31]Chida, "Development," 85; and Japan Shipowners Association, *Modernisation of the Seafarer's System* (Tokyo, 1988), 14.

[32]Chida and Davies, *Japanese Shipping and Shipbuilding Industries*, 151-152 and 177-179.

previously constrained their activities. Thus, as the liner trades began to decline or change their character Japanese operators were able to move into other areas. For example, the NYK purchased its first oil tanker in 1959, and both *shasen* subsequently entered the bulk, container and refrigerated businesses. The latter proved to be a particularly successful venture, with NYK holding a dominant position in the trade after acquiring the balance of Lauritzen A.B.'s shares in NYK Lauritzen Cool in July 2007.[33]

As a result of the diversification both the NYK and what has become Mitsui-OSK have continued to prosper and remain Japan's most important operators. The *shagaisen* have also transferred their roles quite successfully. Some entered the remaining liner routes, continued in traditional, chartered trades or redeployed their tonnage in a comprehensive range of activities which change according to market dictates. These changes to both of the former sections of the ship operating industry were greatly aided by the provisions of the *Saiken-seib: Ho* (the law relating to its reconstruction), which was revised in 1964.[34] This continued the Programmed Shipbuilding Scheme (introduced in 1947), which was advantageous to individual firms that could benefit from the accompanying Interest Subsidy Scheme if they agreed to its terms and conditions. It was also helpful to the state and the industry as a whole for it helped to ensure that the appropriate number of vessels of the necessary types and scale were constructed in accordance with national and international demands. In many ways this helped Japan to avoid the excesses which a totally free system might well have encouraged.

The enormous expansion of both Japanese ship operating and shipbuilding in the postwar years owed much to the growth of the entire Japanese economy. The country's success as one of the world's largest producers and exporters of sophisticated items, together with the need for it to import almost all of its energy and raw materials, has provided great opportunities for its shipping industries. From an early stage successive governments realized the significance of shipping, and their support laid the foundations for today's massive achievements. The future is, however, much less certain if gross domestic product, and hence exports, is the sole criterion. It is now estimated that by this measure Japan will fall behind many other producers (see tables 4 and 5).

---

[33]*Fresh Produce Journal*, 31 August 2007.

[34]Chida and Davies, *Japanese Shipping and Shipbuilding Industries*, 141-143.

Table 4
Gross Domestic Product and Its Projections, Various Nations, 2000-2050
(US$ trillion)

	2000	2005	2020	2030	2040	2050
Japan	3.27	3.47	4.24	4.71	4.99	4.99
China	4.96	7.73	17.33	25.16	30.42	33.39
South Korea	0.76	0.94	1.56	1.86	2.01	2.03
India	2.45	3.38	7.07	10.3	14.4	19.12
ASEAN	1.77	2.21	3.87	5.46	7.29	9.24
US	9.59	11.09	16.75	21.41	27.17	33.96
EU	10.26	11.16	14.52	16.31	18.11	19.89

Source: *Japan Echo* (Tokyo), August 2007.

Table 5
Gross Domestic Product, Average Annual Change, 2001-2050

	2001-2005	2006-2020	2021-2030	2031-2040	2041-2050
Japan	1.2	1.4	1	0.6	0
China	9.3	5.5	3.8	1.9	0.9
South Korea	4.4	3.4	1.7	0.8	0.1
India	6.6	5	3.8	3.4	2.9
ASEAN	4.5	3.8	3.5	2.9	2.4
US	2.9	2.8	2.5	2.4	2.3
EU	1.7	1.8	1.2	1.1	0.9

Source: See table 4.

This changing picture of Japan's future economic prospects, together with the rise of potential competitors, suggests that major difficulties lie ahead. The rapid growth of the Chinese economy appears to pose the most direct threat to Japan's shipping industries, for it is certain that more Chinese trade will be carried in domestically-built and operated vessels. While this aspect will not unduly concern Japanese operators, the cross-traders like Norway and Greece may well lose much of their current business. In this event the potential loss of demand for new tonnage from two of its principal customers would be of huge significance to Japanese (and South Korean) shipbuilders. Chinese ship construction is also expanding at an ever-increasing rate. It has the advantage of low (if rising) wages which, allied to its use of the latest technology, could easily offer a strong challenge to both of today's largest producers with their much higher labour costs.

To some extent these imbalances in overall efficiency might be offset by adjustments to Japan's rates of exchange, with the level of the *yen* against the US dollar being of special importance. But Japan's dependence upon imports for virtually all its fuel and raw material requirements – which should continue to provide substantial cargoes for its indigenous shipping firms – makes this a two-edged weapon which can only be used with the greatest discretion. Nevertheless, despite these very considerable imponderables, those who are familiar with Japanese economic development are convinced that the entrepreneurial skill and application which has served the nation so well in the past will continue to do so in the global market for many years to come.

British Shipping from the Late Nineteenth Century to the Present

Sarah Palmer

Introduction: The Long-Term Picture

The story of British shipping over the twentieth century is one of decline. As figure 1 shows, the tonnage of the UK-registered fleet recovered from the trade crisis of the 1930s and continued to grow until 1975 when it went into a free fall which was not reversed until the twenty-first century.

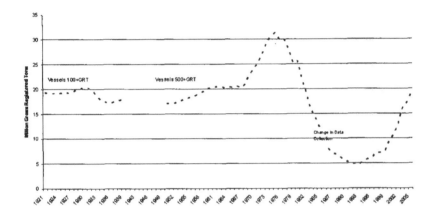

Figure 1: Size of the UK-Registered Fleet, 1921-2005.

Sources: Lloyds, *Register of Tonnage*, various years; and Great Britain, *Maritime Statistics* (London, 2006).

In relative terms, however, while Britain possessed the largest active world fleet until 1967, its position as the leading shipowning nation was eroded in the interwar years and thereafter receded rapidly. Contrasting the top ten fleets at the beginning of the century with those at its end (figures 2 and 3) makes the point.

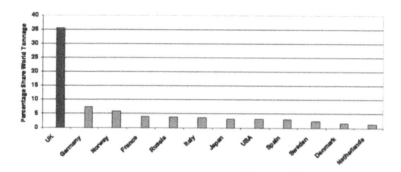

Figure 2: Leading National Fleets, 1900 (Flagged Net Tonnage)

Sources: See figure 1.

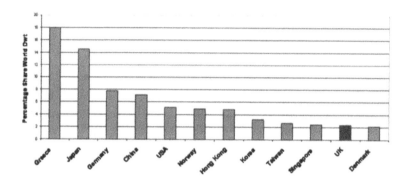

Figure 3: Leading National Fleets, 2006 (Beneficially-owned Deadweight Tonnage)

Sources: See figure 1.

Shipping and the British Economy

The contribution of shipping services to the British economy necessarily re-ceded as well, though the precise extent is difficult to determine. The size of the British economy as a whole before the mid-twentieth century is itself a matter of debate, since systematic collection of National Income statistics did not begin until that time. Moreover, commercial secrecy impeded the publica-tion of information on shipping costs, revenue and output.[1] Thanks to the reg-ister maintained since the nineteenth century by the Registrar General of Ship-

---

[1]Great Britain, Parliament, *Parliamentary Papers* (*BPP*), Committee of In-quiry into Shipping (Rochdale Committee), 1970 (Cmnd. 4337), para. 1564.

ping and Seamen, there is central source for data on shipping manpower, but again the statistics are not without their deficiencies.[2]

The contribution of shipping to the balance of payments through either export earnings or import savings was judged by both the government and the Chamber of Shipping during the twentieth century to be the most significant benefit to the nation, but figures are hard to obtain and even then are necessarily approximations.[3] At its zenith in 1975 British shipping was responsible for 5.7 percent of all "invisible" credits, but by 1985 this had fallen to 0.9 percent.[4] By 1997, when the British-owned fleet of 10.8 million deadweight tons (dwt) was a shadow of its former self, and UK-flagged vessels were carrying about eighteen percent of national trade by volume, the industry's turnover was approximately £9 billion a year, with half of this coming from the cross-trades.[5] A 1998 government report, *British Shipping: Charting A New Course*, described its importance to the economy as "the fourth or fifth biggest service-sector exporter for the UK – larger than telecommunications, films or television, or computer services."[6] Although interpreted by industry representatives as an accolade, these comparisons tell us something about the degree to which British shipping had lost its former standing as a major industry.

Britain's maritime services sector, which had developed in tandem with the nation's shipping interests, survived the decline. Though challenged in the late twentieth century by other maritime clusters, London retained its position as the leading maritime centre, providing services to the international shipping community. In consequence, while the direct contribution of shipping, as of shipbuilding, to British National Income diminished over the twentieth century, the maritime sector as a whole continued to make a significant contribution to the economy.[7]

---

[2]S.G. Sturmey, *British Shipping and World Competition* (London, 1962), 294-295; Rochdale Committee, 1970, para. 824-825; and James McConville, *et al.*, *UK Seafarers: An Analysis* (London, 1997).

[3]See Sturmey, *British Shipping*, 185-187 and 415-418; Rochdale Committee, paras. 1284-1356; and *BPP*, House of Commons, Environment, Transport and Regional Affairs Committee, Twelfth Report, "The Future of the UK Shipping Industry," 1998-1999, para. 153.

[4]Ronald Hope, *A New History of British Shipping* (London, 1990), 473.

[5]"Future of the UK Shipping Industry," para. 10.

[6]Great Britain, Department of the Environment, Transport and the Regions, *British Shipping: Charting a New Course* (London, 1998), para 1.

[7]See Mark Brownrigg, "The United Kingdom's Maritime Cluster," in Niko Wijnolst (ed.), *Dynamic European Maritime Clusters* (The Hague, 2006), 93-104; City

The continued economic significance of the wider maritime sector is one reason why alarm over Britain's diminished maritime status perennially surfaced in the second half of the century in the form of governmental and parliamentary investigations.[8] But these were not prompted solely by economic arguments. Defence considerations, oddly reminiscent of eighteenth- and early nineteenth-century justifications for the Navigation Acts, have also featured. Indeed, the Conservatives under Margaret Thatcher and John Major saw this as the only possible reason to support the industry – "Any case for assistance to the shipping industry must be strategic; it has no compelling economic basis."[9] A 1992 Commons committee concluded that a shortage of "ships or trained sailors at the disposal of HM Government may have a marked...and detrimental effect on the UK's ability to defend itself."[10] Alarm over the implications of the falling number of British seafarers employed in UK-registered ships (from 135,930 in 1952 to 96,000 in 1966, 73,400 in 1975 and 17,250 in 1995) and the small number of total British seafarers (29,610 in 1997) was one factor which prompted a "new course" in government policy in 2000.[11]

In view of the long-standing support for the Conservative Party by several leading shipowners, it ironically was a Labour government, spurred by the Deputy Prime Minister, John Prescott – a former seafarer and spokesman for maritime trade unions in Parliament – which responded to the shipping interest's long-term lobbying for government assistance. It introduced financial incentives in the form of a Tonnage Tax regime similar to that adopted by the Netherlands and other European nations, though it was unusual in requiring those who benefited to make a commitment to recruitment and training.[12]

Business Services, *Maritime Services* (London, 2003); and Fisher Associates, *The Future of London's Maritime Services Cluster: A Call for Action* (London, 2004).

[8]*BPP*, "Final Report of the Committee of Inquiry into Certain Matters Concerning the Shipping Industry" [Pearson Report], 1967 (Cmnd. 3211); Rochdale Committee; House of Commons, Transport Committee, *Report on the Decline in the UK Registered Merchant Fleet*, May 1988 (HC3031-11); "Future of the UK Shipping Industry;" and *British Shipping: Charting a New Course*.

[9]Department of Transport, 1988, quoted in Alan G. Jamieson, *Ebb Tide in the British Maritime Industries: Change and Adaptation 1918-1990* (Exeter, 2003), 49.

[10]House of Commons, Third Report of the Employment Committee, *The Future of Maritime Skills and Employment in the UK*, 1992-1993, para. 27.

[11]Rochdale Committee, table 13.1; and "Future of the UK Shipping Industry," tables 6 and 7.

[12]House of Commons, Second Report of the Transport Committee, *Tonnage Tax*, 2005 (HC 299), paras. 2-3.

The British Shipping Industry in 1900

At the beginning of the twentieth century British shipping dominated the world's sea routes. Over forty percent of the world's commercial tonnage was under the British flag and its nearest rival, Germany, had a fleet only a quarter of this size. A government committee in 1918 concluded that "at the outbreak of war, the British Mercantile Marine was the largest, the most up-to-date and the most efficient of all the merchant navies of the world."[13] In 1913 only fifteen percent of British-registered vessels were more than eighteen years old, and since the majority of British vessels were powered by steam, these accounted for almost half of world steam tonnage.

One distinctive feature of the British shipping industry at the start of the twentieth century was its commitment to both the liner and tramp sectors. Contrary perhaps to the impression given by the number of histories of British liner companies, vessels employed as tramps accounted for more than half the tonnage of the British deep-sea fleet. In 1910, for example, tramp tonnage amounted to 4.8 million net registered tons (nrt) compared with 3.8 million nrt employed as liners.[14]

A number of factors were responsible for Britain's leading position in shipping. As a strong industrial power and the world's leading trading nation, greater opportunities for cargo carrying were available to British vessels than was the case for most other national fleets. Britain was also the world's largest market for shipping services. Although history suggests that there is no necessary connection between trade success and a home-based fleet, given Britain's maritime traditions the interests of manufacturers, merchants and shipowners in this case coalesced. The extension of British commercial interests over the eighteenth and nineteenth centuries, mostly though not entirely associated with the Empire, impacted on the number of vessels and cargo space required. By the early twentieth century the UK had long been established as a global maritime power. A snapshot of where British-registered steam vessels were employed on a single day in the spring of 1911 showed that eighty-two percent were deployed outside Europe, thirteen percent in the Mediterranean and just five percent in the rest of Europe.[15] Not all these vessels, however, would have been trading directly with Britain. In 1913 British-registered ships carried ninety percent of UK/Empire Trade and fifty percent of UK/Foreign trade,

---

[13]*BPP*, "Report of the Departmental Committee on Shipping and Shipbuilding" (1918), XIII, 53.

[14]Gelina Harlaftis and John Theotakas, "European Family Firms in International Business: British and Greek Tramp-Shipping Firms," *Business History*, XLVI, No. 2 (2004), 220.

[15]*BPP*, "Report of the Departmental Committee" (1918), XIII, 80.

eighty percent of trade between Imperial territories and fifty percent of their foreign commerce.

As these figures demonstrate, much of Britain's share of international sea carriage was associated with the Empire. But it is worth remembering that since the abolition of the Navigation Acts in 1849 British vessels did not have any exclusive rights. This is not to say that political factors did not play a part, for companies like P&O and the Royal Mail Steamship Company were indeed "Flagships of Empire."[16] The boost given by government support in their formative years at mid-century, combined with the fundamental economics of the liner business, made them "favoured players" and in the long term difficult to oust from their established routes. Yet the fact that British-registered vessels also operated as third-party traders -- in 1913 they carried an estimated twenty-five percent of cargoes between foreign countries -- indicates that they did have a genuine competitive advantage as operators.

The 1918 government committee which reviewed the development of the UK's shipping industry over the previous half century identified three factors as particularly significant: Britain's industrial strength, its world-wide Empire and the coal export trade. We have touched on the first two of these, but what about the third -- the "Alpha and Omega of our trade," according to the economist William Stanley Jevons? In 1900 eighty-four percent of British coal exports went to European markets, with no more than half of this carried in British ships. In contrast, British-registered vessels dominated the oceanic long-haul coal trade which, because of the proportionately greater capacity required due to the distances involved, offered more employment to shipping.[17] How far the availability of this ballast cargo benefited British owners in particular by influencing the freight rate for return cargoes is a matter of some debate. What is not in doubt, however, is that the international coal export trade was a very important market for British tramp shipowners.

While these factors are not in themselves sufficient to explain Britain's late nineteenth-century maritime supremacy, we can dismiss the notion that British shipowners were uniquely advantaged by the development of the steamship in the 1860s since, with certain exceptions, the benefits of this innovation soon became accessible to foreigners, as the overseas sales of British shipyards testified. A similar kind of objection can be made to claims that the introduction of the international telegraph in the 1860s and 1870s gave British shipowners an informational advantage in seeking cargo, since again the bene-

---

[16]See Freda Harcourt, *The P&O Company and the Politics of Empire from Its Origins to 1867* (Manchester, 2006).

[17]Sarah Palmer, "The British Coal Export Trade, 1850-1913," in David Alexander and Rosemary Ommer (eds.), *Volumes Not Values: Canadian Sailing Ships and World Trades* (St. John's, 1979), 335.

fits were not restricted to owners resident in the UK.[18] A more convincing explanation, particularly in light of the history of the British shipping industry after 1918, is that the lack of a challenge from other fleets enabled British vessels to maintain their near-monopoly on many sea routes and trades.[19]

British Shipping, 1913-1939

The interwar years were difficult for all maritime nations.[20] Between 1881 and 1913 it has been estimated that the volume of trade grew by about forty percent every decade. In contrast, in the aftermath of the disruption caused by the First World War, world seaborne trade did not resume its 1913 levels until 1924. Growth continued until 1929, but demand for cargo space thereafter fell dramatically. Although there was some recovery in the later 1930s, by 1938 the volume of seaborne trade was no greater than it had been in 1929.[21]

Shipowners failed to adjust the available cargo space to these adverse trading conditions, expecting instead that as in traditional shipping cycles a decline in freight rates would lead eventually to a balance. Instead, the immediate postwar shipbuilding boom and government support for the expansion of national fleets meant that the world merchant fleet expanded from 58.8 million gross tons in 1921 to sixty-eight million gross tons in 1930.[22] Together with the impact of efficiency gains from the substitution of oil for coal as a fuel, this resulted in a chronic oversupply of tonnage which continued through the 1930s.

The general picture of depression, however, obscures the significance of interwar changes in the composition and direction of world trade which reduced opportunities in some cases but increased them in others. Since Britain, as the leading maritime nation, had the largest commitment to shipping, it was necessarily affected by the generally more competitive climate for cargo and

---

[18]On these issues, see C. Knick Harley, "Aspects of the Economics of Shipping, 1850-1913," and the following discussion, in Lewis R. Fischer and Gerald E. Panting (eds.), *Change and Adaptation in Maritime History: The North Atlantic Fleets in the Nineteenth Century* (St. John's, 1985), 167-192; and Daniel R. Headrick, *The Tools of Empire: Technology and European Imperialism in the Nineteenth Century* (New York, 1981).

[19]See Sarah Palmer, "The British Shipping Industry, 1850-1914," in Fischer and Panting (eds.), *Change and Adaptation*, 87-114.

[20]See Sturmey, *British Shipping*.

[21]See A.G. Kenwood and A.L. Lougheed, *The Growth of the International Economy, 1820-2000* (4th ed., New York, 1991); and Sturmey, *British Shipping*, 65.

[22]Jamieson, *Ebb Tide*, 12.

the increased challenge from other national fleets. The slump in coal exports and the reduction in international migration hit British shipowners particularly hard. The former was in part the context for the 1935 British Shipping (Assistance) Act, a temporary measure which gave tramp owners a subsidy if freight rates dropped below a prescribed standard. The latter was the context for the encouragement of tourist voyages, cruising and the Cunard "Queens," though such initiatives did not compensate for the loss of the migrant trade.

The maritime business environment differed in other respects from the prewar situation. The First World War loosened the hold of British shipping lines on their established routes and created openings for third-party operators. Interwar economic nationalism also had an impact on the prospects of certain fleets, which benefited from greater subsidies and protection than in the past. The political lesson of Britain's nineteenth-century maritime presence on the world's oceans had been taken to heart.[23]

For some commentators, the responsibility for British shipping's diminishing status was unfair competition:

> British shipowners fought, unaided by anything but their own
> efficiency and their own accumulated resources, an unnatural
> battle against the national treasuries of three Dominions
> [Canada, South Africa, Australia], the United States, and
> later of Japan, Italy, Germany and even Russia.[24]

This charge of "unfair" competition was examined in some detail by Stanley Sturmey in *British Shipping and World Competition* (1962). He concluded that while the policies of France, Germany, Italy, Japan and the United States did have some adverse consequences, the "direct damage to British shipping from their subsidy policies was not extensive."[25] In relation to foreign penetration of the UK import trade, he showed that over the period 1929-1937 British shipping's share fell from sixty-five to 55.8 percent but that *unsubsidized* foreign shipping accounted for two-thirds of this difference. Sturmey acknowledged that the American policy of supporting its mercantile marine had a serious impact. In 1913 over half of the entrances and clearances in American ports had been by British vessels, but in 1938 this had fallen to 27.5 percent. He pointed out that by the latter date the US share of its own trade (26.6 percent) was actually lower than the British and that those by the unsubsidized Norwegian fleet accounted for 12.5 percent. In the American trans-Pacific trades, British lines maintained their position on those routes where they had been active be-

---

[23]See Sturmey, *British Shipping*, 98-137.

[24]R.H. Thornton, *British Shipping* (Cambridge, 1959), 85.

[25]Sturmey, *British Shipping*, 136.

fore 1914, but they failed to exploit the new opportunities opened by the Panama Canal.

For Sturmey, this suggested that British owners, faced with subsidized competitors, were insufficiently enterprising. He came to much the same conclusion when he considered the issue of British tanker ownership. Looking at 1938, he contrasted Britain's puny 0.5 million tons of independent tanker ownership with Norway's 1.75 million tons. His explanation, however, was more quotable than convincing: "Underlying the objective factors, and of much greater importance, was that British shipowners scarcely thought of tankers, which they seem to have regarded as hardly being ships at all."[26] There were in fact perfectly rational considerations which deterred UK shipowners from investing in tankers.[27] The oil companies dominated the British tanker fleet: in 1939, sixty-six percent of tanker tonnage was owned by three oil companies and a further fifteen percent by associated firms. Independent tanker owners relied on the willingness of the oil companies to charter. Since such charters would be the first to be cancelled in a downturn, this was not a firm basis for investment in uncertain times. Moreover, the collapse of the tanker market in the 1930s favoured caution: by 1933, forty percent of the world independent tanker fleet was laid-up. The 1926 disposal of Anglo-Saxon Petroleum's old tankers with charter-back terms, though with hindsight very significant for Norway's development as a maritime power, was not such an obviously attractive opportunity at the time.

As further evidence of British conservatism in shipping, some observers have pointed to what they have alleged to be the relatively slow adoption of the motorship in comparison with the Scandinavians. In 1939 motorships comprised sixty-two of the Norwegian fleet, fifty-two percent of the Danish fleet and forty-six percent of the Swedish fleet, as against a quarter of the British fleet. This issue, touching as it does on wider debates about technological innovation, has aroused some scholarly debate.[28] But the choice of technology was more complex than some have suggested. In practice, the choice between coal- or oil-fired steamships and motorships was not clear cut, since each could deliver good results in certain trades. The motorship did not lack British advocates. Lord Kylsant of Royal Mail and the shipbuilders Harland and Wolff had

---

[26]*Ibid.*, 78.

[27]See Jamieson, *Ebb Tide*, 16-18.

[28]See Max E. Fletcher, "From Coal to Oil in British Shipping," *Journal of Transport History,* New ser., III, No. 1 (1975), 1-19; Graydon R. Henning and Keith Trace, "Britain and the Motorship: A Case of the Delayed Adoption of a New Technology," *Journal of Economic History*, XXXV, No. 2 (1975), 353-385; and Alex J. Robertson, "Backward British Businessmen and the Motorship, 1918-1939: The Critique Reviewed," *Journal of Transport History,* 3rd ser., IX, No. 2 (1988), 190-197.

identified the motorship as "a serious challenge to steam" as early as 1926.[29] Sir Frederick Lewis of Furness, Withy and Andrew Weir of the Bank Line were also enthusiasts for the technology. It is difficult as well to argue that British shipowners were particularly resistant to the technology considering that in 1939 Britain owned 1500 motor vessels, the largest such fleet on any register.[30] Even so, most UK tramp owners continued to favour the traditional nine- or ten-knot dry-cargo steamship.[31]

Table 1
National Fleets in 1913, 1920 and 1939 (Vessels of over 100 tons)

	1913 Million GRT	World	1920 Million GRT	% World	1939 Million GRT	% World
UK	18.3	44.9	18.1	35.1	17.9	27.3
US	2.0	4.9	12.4	24.0	8.9	13.6
Japan	1.5	3.7	3.0	5.8	5.6	8.5
Norway	1.9	4.7	2.0	3.9	4.8	7.3
Germany	4.7	11.5	0.4	0.8	4.5	6.9
Italy	1.3	3.2	2.1	4.1	3.4	5.2
France	1.8	4.4	3.0	5.8	2.9	4.4
Netherlands	1.3	3.2	1.8	3.5	3.0	4.6
Greece	0.7	1.7	0.5	1.0	1.8	2.7
Sweden	0.9	2.2	1.0	1.9	1.6	2.4
USSR	0.8	2.0	0.5	1.0	1.3	2.0
Denmark	0.7	1.7	0.7	1.4	1.2	1.8
All Others World	4.9	12.0	6.1	11.8	8.7	13.3
Total	40.8	100.0	51.6	100.0	65.6	100.0

Source: Calculated from Great Britain, Parliament, *Parliamentary Papers* (*BPP*), Committee of Inquiry into Shipping (Rochdale Committee), 1970 (Cmnd. 4337), table 2.1.

Comparing the situation of British shipping immediately before the Second World War to that in 1913 shows both an absolute and relative decline (see table 1). Its 1939 fleet of 17.9 million gross registered tons (grt) was smaller than it had been in 1913 and represented twenty-eight percent of the world's total as against thirty-five percent in 1913.

---

[29]*The Times* (London), 1926.

[30]Jamieson, *Ebb Tide*, 16.

[31]Rochdale Committee, para. 40.

To some extent this situation reflected Britain's smaller interwar share of world exports, particularly coal, and the decline in migrant traffic. Although Peter Davies has cautioned that "it is unlikely that British shipowners were any less enterprising after 1920 than they were before,"[32] given the growth of the world fleet between 1920 and 1939 by some fourteen million grt, it is hard not to endorse the conclusion of other commentators that opportunities were lost.

The difficult interwar business conditions especially affected the organization of the tramp sector. In the early twentieth century the British tramp sector was characterized by family-owned and family-run companies, with the largest number based in the North East, followed by London and Scotland; in the mid-1930s the single largest owner was Sir Robert Ropner's West Hartlepool firm with fifty vessels. Though operating their vessels as a fleet, most tramp owners registered them as single-ship companies. The decline in the international coal trade and the slump in freight rates led to the disappearance of many tramp firms, and there were few new entrants. In 1939 there were 189 companies as against 462 in 1910. Greek owners in particular benefited from the British retreat and seized opportunities to invest in the downturn.[33]

British Shipping, 1948-1973

The Second World War only minimally altered the UK's share of the world fleet. In 1948, when the volume of world seaborne trade had recovered its prewar level, this stood at twenty-seven percent, just one percent lower than in 1939. Financially, Sturmey has concluded, "the British Industry neither suffered heavily nor gained greatly [during the war and]...the shipping of other important maritime countries did not generally end up in relatively much more favourable positions."[34]

Benefiting from the growth in world trade during the long postwar boom, the UK fleet continued to grow from 1948 until 1975, after which it went into a precipitous free-fall. But the absolute rise in tonnage from eighteen million to 33.2 million grt over this period must be seen against a background of relative decline, as UK-registered tonnage fell from almost one-quarter of the world fleet in 1948 to under ten percent by the mid-1970s.[35]

---

[32]Peter N. Davies, "British Shipping and World Trade: Rise and Decline, 1820-1939," in Tsunehiko Yui and Keiichiro Nakagawa (eds.), *Business History of Shipping: Strategy and Structure* (Tokyo, 1985), 80.

[33]See Harlaftis and Theotakas, "European Family Firms," 227; and Jamieson, *Ebb Tide*, 20-21.

[34]Sturmey, *British Shipping*, 154.

[35]Hope, *New History of British Shipping*, 433.

After the Second World War tramp operators, mindful of the depression which followed the boom in orders after the previous conflict, postponed ordering new vessels until the mid-1950s. In contrast to the new bulk carriers being acquired by their competitors, most British tramp shipowners preferred general-purpose, medium-sized, dry-cargo vessels of traditional design. These came onto a market affected by the growing efficiency of the bulk carriers, leading the Rochdale Committee to comment in 1970 that "UK owners ordered many ships of the wrong type at the wrong time."[36] Movement in the 1960s into newer types of vessels did not much improve the profit position of the diminishing number of independent tramp companies, which now faced competition from liner companies seeking to solve *their* problems by diversifying into bulk carriage.[37] With the term "tramping" becoming an anachronism, older firms left shipping. As Alan Jamieson has pointed out, "in theory world tramp shipping was open to all, but British entrepreneurs had more attractive economic prospects on which to risk their capital in the post-war world."[38]

What were the factors behind the overall picture of slow relative growth in the British fleet during a time of economic boom? The Rochdale Committee identified six developments as having a "profound effect on the UK industry:" disruption caused by the two world wars, particularly the First World War; decolonization and its impact on the maritime aspirations of former colonies; slow growth in the types of trade in which British owners specialized; relatively slow growth of Britain's own trade; competition from the shipping of developing countries; and competition from air transport which affected the deep-sea passenger business. The committee made no fewer than 1697 recommendations about a wide range of topics, including research and development, education and training and government policy. While it shied away from directly blaming shipping companies for some of the industry's problems, the chapter dealing with management made it clear that it thought that there were serious failings. Here are two telling extracts from its report:

> Our study showed only 6 per cent of senior management staff, other than board members, with university degrees. We do not believe that the current intellectual demands of the shipping industry are any less exacting than for most other industries; indeed we are strongly of the opinion that, given the the complexity of international trade, the intense competition and the rapid technological change, effective management of shipping demands an acute awareness and under-

---

[36]Rochdale Committee, para. 501.

[37]*Ibid.*, para. 503-507.

[38]Jamieson, *Ebb Tide,* 30.

standing of word economic and trading conditions, normally supported by graduate education.

We have been left with the general feeling that, within the shipping industry at large and in the training of shore staff, the marketing function has not yet received sufficient attention...The selling of shipping services is still too often regarded as a function reserved to top management, and in particular to the chairman personally.[39]

In short, the conservatism of the British shipping industry, a charge also made earlier by Sturmey, seemed to the Rochdale Committee to be a serious impediment to success in the challenging conditions of the 1960s.[40]

If in the interwar period British owners had largely resisted involvement in tankers, in the far more attractive postwar circumstances the situation largely remained the same. As a result, they failed to benefit as much as they might have from the boom in demand for tankers between 1967 and 1973. Even so, the Rochdale Committee did see signs of a new dynamism in the liner sector and, as with the diversification into bulk carriers, a willingness to seize new opportunities, not least those offered by the British government's investment incentives. While American owners led the way into containerization, consortia of British companies followed swiftly. In 1971, of the 231 container-ships in the world, US interests owned seventy-five and the British fifty-one.[41]

The Rochdale Committee did not consider that competition from flags of convenience, which in 1968 were still mainly restricted to American and Greek interests, had any particular impact on British shipping and, despite the arguments it received to the contrary, specifically rejected flag discrimination and subsidies by other maritime powers as sufficient reasons for the UK's relative decline. It pointed out that "none of the unprotected Western European fleets had expanded as slowly as that of the UK."[42]

In fact, the size of the UK fleet was influenced by government assistance in the form of investment grants and loans for shipbuilding between 1967 and 1975. Eligibility was restricted to vessels destined to remain on the UK register for a minimum of five years, but since registration was open to "resident" shipping companies – an imprecise term – the effect was to attract for-

---

[39]Rochdale Committee, paras. 1212 and 1228-1229.

[40]See Sturmey, *British Shipping*, 394-402. Sturmey encountered much hostility from the shipping industry as a result of his criticisms. See S.G. Sturmey, "Blood on the Thames," in Sturmey, *Shipping Economics: Collected Papers* (London, 1975).

[41]Jamieson, *Ebb Tide*, 38.

[42]Rochdale Committee, para. 216.

eign owners to the UK flag. The fact that sterling was a cheap currency further encouraged the use of the British register as a flag of convenience.[43] In 1975, when the UK register reached its historic peak of thirty-three million grt, about a third of this tonnage was foreign owned. Indeed, as figure 4 shows, in the period 1950-1985 it is clear that foreign ownership masked the extent to which British interest in merchant shipping had already declined before the downward plunge after 1975. In an increasingly challenging business environment, with their flag obligations fulfilled and no further government incentives on offer, many "foreign" UK-registered vessels were sold or flagged-out.

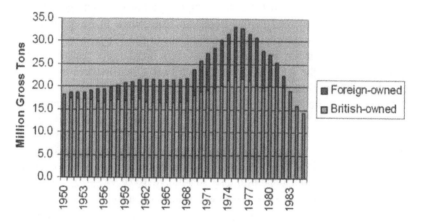

Figure 4: British and Foreign-owned Tonnage on UK Register, 1950-1985.

Source: Ronald Hope, *A New History of British Shipping* (London, 1990), 433-434.

British Shipping, 1973-2007

The 1973 oil-price crisis and the maritime depression which lasted until the early 1990s had a global impact on sea trade and threw the particular problems of British shipping into sharp relief. Now British shipowners, like their foreign counterparts, were increasingly attracted by the cost advantages of international registers. In 1987, only thirty-five percent of British-owned shipping was on the main UK register, though most was still within the orbit of the UK on the Isle of Man register. By 1990 only twenty-six percent of British owners opted for the UK register, and by 1998 the figure was twenty-four percent. Over this decade as well British owners increasingly flagged-out to registers with no Red Ensign connection. But it was not the case that the decline in UK-registered tonnage was simply a reflection of registration elsewhere. The re-

---

[43]Michael Davies, *Belief in the Sea: State Encouragement of British Merchant Shipping and Shipbuilding* (London, 1992), 209-211.

duction in UK-registered tonnage was accompanied by a "significant and continuing reduction in shipping tonnage owned by British companies."[44]

There were many factors contributing to this situation. A 1984 report produced by a private body, the British Maritime League, offered insights into the mindset of some of those in the maritime sector. It concluded that "the main underlying cause of the BMF's [British Merchant Fleet's] decline" was "the impracticability of trading fairly in a market which is no longer governed by economics alone." In support of this it cited a fairly detailed list of eighteen "international causes," followed by just five "national causes." The latter were higher crew costs than for flag-of-convenience ships; government policy or lack thereof; adverse exchange rates; management – "the Rochdale recommendations of 1970 have not been implemented;" and inadequate research. It would seem, in this instance at least, that in the 1980s a tendency remained among seemingly informed commentators to blame misfortune rather than the British shipping industry for its long-standing ills. [45]

This was far less the case twenty years later. In 2006 the Director-General of the Chamber of Shipping explained the downward trend from the 1970s as

> ...caused by the move of much of maritime manufacturing to the Far East, by the shaking-out of old fashioned attitudes spurred on initially by the after-shock of the first OPEC oil price rises in 1973, and then by the long and sometimes painful adjustments necessary to bring a very traditional sector into line with the requirements of the modern world and the new imperatives of globalisation.[46]

Over a much longer period, figures 5 and 6 reveal the changes in the composition and trading interests of the UK fleet from 1950 to 2005. There are signs that by the late 1960s some British owners were shaking off the traditionalism which had hindered progress in the past. Certainly the structures of the industry were adapting; for example, in 1968 P&O, the largest shipping company and one of the oldest, had interests in bulkers and tankers as well as

---

[44]*British Shipping: Charting a New Course*, para. 23.

[45]British Maritime League, "British Owned Merchant Shipping: An Examination of the Causes of the Decline of the British Merchant Fleet since 1975" (Unpublished research paper, September 1984).

[46]Brownrigg, "United Kingdom Maritime Cluster," 93. An indication of changing attitudes may be the fact that Brownrigg was the first chief executive of the UK Chamber of Shipping and its predecessor, the General Council of British Shipping, not to have a professional maritime sector background.

liners.[47] It may be significant, however, that growth was proceeding through shifts of specialization within the industry rather than a reaching out beyond these British-based interests.

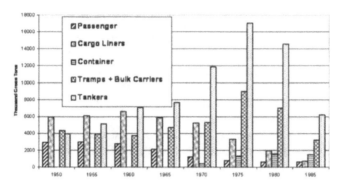

Figure 5: United Kingdom-Registered Trading Vessels, 1950-1985

Notes: 500 gross tons and over; includes Isle of Man and Channel Islands registries.

Source: Great Britain, *Maritime Statistics* (London, 2005).

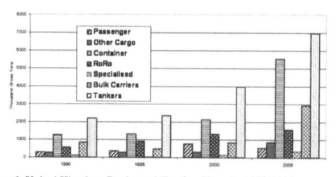

Figure 6: United Kingdom-Registered Trading Vessels, 1990-2005

Notes: See figure 5.

Source: See figure 5.

Even so, new dynamism was not sufficient to compensate for the weak performance and lost markets of the past. Nor was it sufficient to survive the competitive challenges associated first with the long shipping depression after 1973 and then with the globalized maritime economy of the later twentieth century. The early twenty-first century upturn in the size of the British-

---

[47]Jamieson, *Ebb Tide*, 40.

registered fleet in response to the introduction of the Tonnage Tax regime was impressive, but the United Nations Conference on Trade and Development statistics on the beneficial ownership of shipping, which in 2007 put the United Kingdom in tenth place with only 2.35 percent of world tonnage, suggest that it will require more than fiscal incentives to change Britain's now well-established position as the "once-greatest" maritime nation.[48]

---

[48]United Nations Conference on Trade and Development, *Review of Maritime Transport 2007* (Geneva, 2007), table 16.

North of England Shipowners and Their Business Connections in the Nineteenth Century

Graeme J. Milne

Long studied in isolation from other sectors, shipping is increasingly being recognized as an integral part of a vital and far-reaching economic complex. For a generation shipping historians have been producing a large body of work in areas such as shareowning, corporate finance, government subsidies, shipbuilding and cartels, all of which demonstrate that shipowners were embedded in networks of information and business connections. In turn, such studies have given shipping history new links with other branches of scholarship, such as the management theory of principal/agent relations and the economic geography of business districts. This essay continues that historiographic trend, examining relationships forged in the British shipping industry of the late nineteenth century and particularly in the great North of England maritime-industrial complex which rose to global significance in the production, consumption and service activities associated with textiles and heavy engineering.

Integrating shipping research with wider literatures brings business processes and practices together with economic and political institutions and structures. Here, the recent historiography focuses mainly on the manufacturing sector and its tendency to cluster into "industrial districts," often tracing its interpretive roots back to the work of Alfred Marshall and his quest to define the industrial "atmosphere" that characterized such places.[1] Maritime trade and shipping add another dimension given that interactions between firms were arguably even more important in commercial centres with large numbers of small firms, many working in brokering roles. Just as it provided crucial evidence for an earlier generation of business historians focusing on individual firms and corporate structure, the shipping industry and its associated sectors are again proving central to a number of new directions in the discipline.[2] One

---

[1]John F. Wilson and Andrew Popp (eds.), *Industrial Clusters and Regional Business Networks in England, 1750-1970* (Aldershot, 2003); Popp, *Business Structure, Business Culture and the Industrial District: The Potteries, c. 1850-1914* (Aldershot, 2001); and Alfred Marshall, *Industry and Trade* (London, 1919).

[2]Lewis Johnman and Hugh Murphy, "Maritime and Business History in Britain: Past, Present and Future?" *International Journal of Maritime History,* XIX, No. 1 (2007), 239-270.

of the most fundamental connections within the shipping complex – that between shipowners and shipbuilders – has been the subject of much recent work.[3] Relations between shipping and banking are less well known, although there is some pioneering literature upon which to build.[4] Negotiations and deals between shipping companies and government are once again becoming an important element in studies of imperial policy and intercontinental communications networks.[5]

This essay focuses on relationships among shipowners and between shipowners and merchants. It begins with a survey of the numerous, and often conflicting, pressures on shipowners as they sought to build their fleets and operations in an era of complex interactions with other businesses and a developing culture of associational collaboration in and around the conference system. It then offers a case study of some important business connections in the North of England around the opening of the Manchester Ship Canal in 1894, an unusual event that created a major new ocean port in direct competition to Liverpool, the existing regional giant. Important enough in itself, the opening of the Ship Canal is valuable here for its shock effect at the heart of regional business; few other events cast so much light on the role of northern shipping in this period or on the conflicting loyalties and motives of shipowners and their related businesses.

Contexts and Connections

The maritime-industrial complex of the late nineteenth century was a fragmented landscape of many competing interests, with a plethora of small firms and a balkanized array of local trade associations. As will be discussed throughout this essay, business culture often seemed individualistic and inca-

---

[3]Gordon Boyce, *Information, Mediation and Institutional Development: The Rise of Large-scale Enterprise in British Shipping, 1870-1919* (Manchester, 1995); Boyce, "Network Knowledge and Network Routines: Negotiating Activities between Shipowners and Shipbuilders," *Business History*, XLV, No. 2 (2003), 52-76; Ian Buxton, "*Mauretania* and Her Builders," *Mariner's Mirror*, LXXXII, No. 1 (1996), 55-73; and Graeme J. Milne, *North East England, 1850-1914: The Dynamics of a Maritime-Industrial Region* (Woodbridge, 2006), chapters 6 and 7.

[4]Philip Cottrell, "Britannia's Sovereign: Banks in the Finance of British Shipbuilding and Shipping, c. 1830-1894," in Leo M. Akveld, Frits R. Loomeijer and Morten Hahn-Pedersen (eds.), *Financing the Maritime Sector* (Esbjerg, 2002), 191-254.

[5]J. Forbes Munro, *Maritime Enterprise and Empire: Sir William Mackinnon and His Business Network, 1823-1893* (Woodbridge, 2003); and Freda Harcourt, *Flagships of Imperialism: The P&O Company and the Politics of Empire from Its Origins to 1867* (Manchester, 2006).

pable of setting aside short-term personal gain for the general good of a particular sector, let alone the economy as a whole. At the same time, it was common to assert, echoing Adam Smith, that any meeting between businessmen was likely to result in a conspiracy against the public. Shipping and its related sectors offer ample evidence for both viewpoints. In particular, relationships in and around shipping demonstrate problems of information and market power, with individuals, firms, trade associations and cartels struggling to achieve a balance between conceding their independence and gaining associational strength.

For most of the nineteenth century, shipowning remained steeped in a culture of personal capitalism, management and leadership that had grown out of mercantile business. Shipowners, brokers and merchants expected to work in a small partnership with one or two others who were often related by birth or marriage. Partners in such firms aspired to and often achieved a high degree of autonomy, independence and social cachet. At mid-century, the pioneering steamship operators were overwhelmingly men with existing involvement in the small-firm world of sailing vessels, merchanting and brokering.[6] Over time, members of shipowning or shipbroking partnerships often not only established limited shipping companies to run specific services but also kept their existing firms, pursuing their routine business and serving as managing agents for the new shipping "line." Families like the Holts, Booths and MacIvers in Liverpool, or North East owners like James Knott, James Westoll and Robert Ropner, built large shipping enterprises but retained old-fashioned partnership firms at their heart. Leading figures in the sector made a clear distinction between "true shipowners" who had grown up in the business and those who were just directors of joint-stock firms with no other involvement in the trade.[7] The popularity of business biography in the late nineteenth century, in the form of positive and sometimes hagiographical profiles and obituaries, ensured that these conventions of mercantile life were constantly reiterated in the public culture of industrial and commercial cities.[8]

For most businessmen, however, self-determination was counterbalanced and possibly eroded by associations attempting to regulate trade and traders alike. Business communities formed a large number of trade associations in the later decades of the century, trying to increase levels of security and certainty and to raise standards of business practice. One reporter listed

---

[6]Boyce, *Information, Mediation*, 37-41.

[7]Graeme J. Milne, *Trade and Traders in Mid-Victorian Liverpool* (Liverpool, 2000), 161-162.

[8]See, for example, detailed biographies of individuals and firms in G.J.S. Broomhall and John H. Hubback, *Corn Trade Memories, Recent and Remote* (Liverpool, 1930); and Thomas Ellison, *The Cotton Trade of Great Britain* (London, 1886).

fourteen Liverpool associations overseeing particular trades or commercial functions in 1887, concluding that "with such organisations in operation, there is no fear of anything creeping in...to the prejudice of commerce in general, and to that of Liverpool in particular."[9] Naturally, however, businessmen sometimes found it difficult to concede their autonomy to these associations, and the early histories of many trade bodies were marked by frequent disputes over the enforcement of regulations. In mercantile business, associations were able to address exchange processes, commodity standardization and simplification of documents but struggled to agree on disciplinary sanctions in grey areas. The widespread practice of clerks trading in their own name, which was in many cases condoned by senior traders as evidence of entrepreneurial flair, was a particular stumbling block.[10] In addition, organizations founded to clean up business were sometimes viewed from outside as a means of disguising scandals and sharp practices; not all commentators had the sanguine view of the Liverpool journalist just quoted.[11]

The diversity of the shipping industry was a challenge to associational cohesion. In Britain, the Chamber of Shipping always claimed to represent the industry as a whole but had to admit that its membership was an uneasy mix of tramp and liner owners. It survived by avoiding discussion of controversial issues, such as the rebate system associated with shipping conferences, which tramp owners saw as a restriction on their right to negotiate freights with merchants: "it would be one class against another, so to speak; so it could not be discussed in the Chamber."[12] In addition, the dividing line between tramps and liners often seemed unclear, and there was a growing middle ground in the long spectrum between obvious liners and obvious tramps. The distinction was often in operation rather than in ship design, and in tactics rather than strategy; it also shifted over time, both for the industry and for individual firms. Many mid-size steamships of the late nineteenth century served both functions at various times. Indeed, the oldest, slowest vessels in some liner fleets might be inferior to the newest tramp because the latter's operators demanded efficiency improvements from shipbuilders year after year.[13] Owners were pragmatic,

---

[9]*Liverpool Review,* 4 June 1887.

[10]Liverpool Record Office (LRO), 380 COT 6/3, 15 July and 30 September 1889.

[11]*Liverpool Citizen,* 5 November 1890.

[12]Great Britain, Parliament, *Parliamentary Papers (BPP),* Royal Commission on Shipping Rings, 1909, XLVII, Cd. 4670 (hereafter *BPP,* Shipping Rings), Fenwick Watts, q. 11,032.

[13]*Ibid.,* q. 11,063.

using their ships as opportunities presented with no preconceived idea that they were liner or tramp operators. Even the supposed benchmark of liner operations – sailing on a set date whether full or not – was often breached, or so competitors alleged, especially on routes where there were no passengers to complain.[14]

That said, divisions remained real enough. There were marked social distinctions within shipping by the end of the nineteenth century, and the pretensions of the elite attracted some ridicule. In Liverpool, a small minority had become "Steamship Kings," distanced from the "common people," while in Newcastle leading shipowners tried to assert their status by wearing top hats and tailcoats to the Quayside Exchange; irreverent colleagues asked them whose wedding they were attending.[15] At the top end of the industry, firms like Cunard and P&O negotiated government mail contracts and subsidies, vital elements in the maintenance of Britain's high global profile in both shipping and shipbuilding prior to the Great War. But as many scholars have pointed out, most shipowners, builders and merchants worked in a competitive environment, fighting constant battles over freight rates and struggling to develop the most cost-effective and cost-saving ships in the ordinary, unromantic cargo sector.[16] Apart from the giant passenger operators, the liner sector received little help from the state. Maurice Davies of Liverpool's Alfred Holt and Co. spoke for his peers in 1904 when he condemned Cunard's latest subsidy, the result, he argued, of a foolish scare over American competition.[17]

Conscious of its divisions, the shipping sector focused its associational structures on standardizing and formalizing contractual relationships among shipowners, brokers and merchants. The creation of model charter-party documents for particular commodities was intended to reduce disputes, although it often took many years of discussion between the various trade associations representing shipowners and merchants before clauses could be agreed. In addition, changes in the economic environment, shipping and cargo-handling

---

[14]*Ibid.*, J.P. Maclay, q. 9021.

[15]Graeme J. Milne, "Maritime Liverpool," in John Belchem (ed.), *Liverpool 800: Culture, Character and History* (Liverpool, 2006), 290; and *Fairplay,* 1 July 1897.

[16]Yrjö Kaukiainen, "Coal and Canvas: Aspects of the Competition between Steam and Sail, c. 1870-1914," *International Journal of Maritime History,* IV, No. 2 (1992), 175-191, reprinted in Lars U. Scholl and Merja-Liisa Hinkkanen (comps.), *Sail and Steam: Selected Maritime Writings of Yrjö Kaukiainen* (St. John's, 2004), 113-128; and Robin Craig, *British Tramp Shipping, 1750-1914* (St. John's, 2003).

[17]Maurice Davies, "Shipping Liners," in Harold Cox (ed.), *British Industries under Free trade: Essays by Experts* (London, 1904), 123. The "American competition" was principally J.P. Morgan's International Mercantile Marine Company.

technology required that these documents be revisited periodically as the balance of advantage shifted from one party to another. In 1919, the Baltic and White Sea Conference applauded the recent creation of a "Documentary Council" to standardize charter parties, but since that had been a core aim of the organization when it was founded in 1905, progress was evidently slow.[18]

The industry also developed insurance and certification institutions, which were self-regulating structures for monitoring the reputations of shipowners and for increasing the available quantity and quality of information about risk.[19] Ship-surveying and classification agencies created registers of seaworthiness, while average-adjusters working in individual ports maintained and disseminated detailed knowledge of the track records and reputations of shipowners. Even here, though, elite firms like Cunard sometimes refused to participate, arguing that their safety records and public profiles were such that they had no need for external certification.[20]

These associational structures helped smooth many procedural and administrative issues, but they were of little use in resolving serious conflicts between shipping companies over routes or markets and had no place in actual deal-making between shipowners and merchants. At the same time, many shipowners found that the late nineteenth-century trading environment was hardly conducive to striking individual deals with merchants. The shipping industry's transition from sail to steam had far-reaching effects on business relationships and on the interaction between port communities and their hinterland clients. Scheduled liner services altered the relationship between merchants and shipowners, raising expectations among overseas customers and effectively forcing all merchants in a given trade to use them. Supply chains moved toward a just-in-time pattern, locking merchants and shipowners together in mutual dependency. Manchester's textile exporters, for example, sold their goods in India with fixed delivery dates and thus needed to predict some time ahead which ship they would be using; waiting until they had enough material to charter a tramp ship was not an option.[21]

---

[18]*Newcastle Daily Journal*, 9 April 1919.

[19]Gelina Harlaftis and John Theotokas, "European Family Firms in International Business: British and Greek Tramp-Shipping Firms," *Business History*, XLVI, No. 2 (2004), 219-255.

[20]*BPP*, Royal Commission to Inquire into Alleged Unseaworthiness of British Registered Ships, 1874, XXXIV, Cd. 1027, John T. Danson, q. 17,663; and John Burns, q. 14,973.

[21]*Ibid.*, Select Committee on Steamship Subsidies, 1902, IX, 385, Elijah Helm, q. 3429.

Against all that, however, trade was notoriously prone to seasonal and cyclical fluctuations, and many trade routes had severe imbalances in the availability of cargo in either direction. The shipping industry faced escalating capital demands as leading firms built larger and more sophisticated steamers. Competitiveness in both the tramp and liner sectors required ever-larger vessels carrying full loads, but technological improvements and competition also led to a major decline in ocean freight rates from the early 1870s, reducing shipowners' revenues and encouraging them to seek artificial methods to increase their incomes or at least to make revenues more predictable. Liner shipowners therefore created another kind of associational grouping: the shipping conference. Fundamentally, conferences comprised groups of liner firms that agreed to operate certain routes at fixed freights, offering merchants delayed rebates if they remained loyal and did not charter non-conference shipping.

This conference system has not attracted much criticism from historians, although vehement controversy surrounded it at the time.[22] Scholars have concluded that conferences encouraged collaboration among shipowners and between shipowners and merchants, avoiding the booms and busts of relentless competition. Despite constant complaints, some merchant clusters, such as Manchester's exporters, did learn to combine their interests and negotiate with shipping conferences.[23] Merchants almost certainly paid higher freight rates than under a system of free competition but avoided a range of other costs. Negotiating each shipment separately would have been expensive and having some guarantee of delivery dates saved them storage costs and reduced litigation. In theory, the relative openness of the shipping industry was insurance against extortion – merchants who found their conference partners intolerable could seek independent shipping firms to carry their goods.[24] It is also evident that shipowners remained competitive with each other and jockeyed for position in advance of the periodic renegotiations that characterized the conference system. There was wide variation in the rigidity of conferences, suggesting that shipowners were unable to insulate themselves from outside pressures.[25]

---

[22]Francis E. Hyde, *Blue Funnel: A History of Alfred Holt and Company of Liverpool from 1865 to 1914* (Liverpool, 1956), xvi.

[23]Arthur Redford, *Manchester Merchants and Foreign Trade* (2 vols., Manchester, 1934-1956; reprint, Clifton, NJ, 1973), II, 170.

[24]Boyce, *Information, Mediation*, 160-174.

[25]Frank Broeze, "Albert Ballin, the Hamburg-Bremen Rivalry and the Dynamics of the Conference System," *International Journal of Maritime History*, III, No. 1 (1991), 1-32; and George Deltas, Konstantinos Serfes and Richard Sicotte, "American Shipping Cartels in the Pre-World War I Era," *Research in Economic History*, XIX (1999), 1-38.

At any given point, all this was true. The problem with restrictive business practices and the cultivation of favoured insiders was, however, the gradual erosion of competitiveness over time. Major merchants admitted that they did not mind what they paid as long as they all paid the same. Rather than striking the best possible deals among themselves, shipping conferences working from the major British ports and their local merchant houses passed on their costs to inland manufacturers and overseas buyers.[26] In most cases, overseas customers lacked good information and were often unaware of the rebate system, which suggests that merchants did not pass the rebate on to their customers. A new mercantile association was formed in 1897, for example, by traders who felt excluded from the existing South African Merchants Committee, which allegedly had a cosy relationship with the shipping conferences and major colonial institutions. The new association hoped that publicizing these connections would open the trade and encourage customers to ask awkward questions.[27]

The lines between merchanting, brokering and shipowning could also become blurred in some trades, creating moral hazards and distorting markets. One of the founding concerns of the Baltic and White Sea Conference in 1905 was that brokers and agents were increasing their market power relative to shipowners. Brokers were secretly purchasing cargoes and offering them to shipowners who believed that brokers were acting as honest middlemen when in fact they had a direct interest in keeping freight rates low. The names and activities of such brokers were published in circulars to discourage the practice.[28] In other cases, speculators would charter a large amount of shipping all at once, hoping to create the impression of high demand and a possible shortage of capacity on particular routes; they would then try to charge merchants a higher rate to guarantee cargo space on "scarce" ships. The speculators usually failed to attract sufficient cargo, but they were able to disrupt markets and undermine established relationships among shipowners, brokers and merchants. The shipping trade paper *Fairplay* suggested in 1891 that an annual conference of shipbrokers and shipowners to compare notes would reduce the problem.[29] Such calls for better information exchange were so frequent in this era, however, that it suggests that little progress was ever actually achieved.

If some brokers behaved like merchants, some shipowners took on brokering and other service functions that seemed to conflict with the interests of their shareholders. At the root of this was the realization that fees and

---

[26]*BPP*, Shipping Rings, q. 3624.

[27]Manchester Chamber of Commerce, *Monthly Record* (1897), 270.

[28]*BPP*, Shipping Rings, William Noble, qq. 21,590 and 21,623.

[29]*Fairplay*, 16 October 1891.

commissions from brokering, supplying ship's stores and directing joint-stock companies could far exceed the likely profits from operating a ship and, better yet, did not have to be distributed as dividends to investors. Shipping shareholders complained in the 1890s that their managing directors were running their vessels at a minimum profit in collaboration with other owners, brokers and suppliers while living on the fees and commissions earned for carrying out those functions.[30] Such practices were unsustainable in the long term, of course, but it remains unclear just how well informed ordinary shipping shareholders were in this era; major investor revolts certainly seem to have been unusual in the sector. In any case, where the directors were also the largest shareholders, as was the case with many shipping firms, there was little immediate danger to the wider investing public.

Important as all these structural issues were to shipowners, merchants and brokers, it is also vital to consider individual choices and entrepreneurial dynamism. Even within the same trade, some did better than others, and the reasons and attitudes expressed by contemporaries can be revealing. In tramp shipping, for example, Fenwick Watts, senior partner of Watts, Watts and Co. of London, Liverpool and Glasgow, believed that successful tramp operators (like himself) constantly had to investigate new markets. "Most of them, if they have any enterprise, look around," he argued, while acknowledging that "some of them get into a groove and stay there."[31] In 1891, *Fairplay* thought that "the beaten routes are crowded and profitless" and that the tramp sector needed the discovery of an entire new continent, keen to import coal and export wheat.[32] In the absence of such windfalls, entrepreneurial shipowners sought ways to break into and exploit existing markets. These efforts are the subject of the rest of this essay.

Breaking into the North West England Shipping Markets

The North West shipping market, and especially the port of Liverpool, was a magnet for would-be shipowners, brokers and merchants from the eighteenth century onward. The historiography of Liverpool's rise to maritime prominence is dominated by the activities of first-generation immigrants and by the (real enough) stereotype of ambitious young men from an extended hinterland moving to the port to make their fortunes.[33] We know more about successes

---

[30]*Ibid.*, 22 February 1895.

[31]*BPP*, Shipping Rings, Fenwick Watts, qq. 11,035-11,038.

[32]*Fairplay*, 30 October 1891.

[33]Francis E. Hyde, *Liverpool and the Mersey: An Economic History of a Port, 1700-1970* (Newton Abbot, 1971), 46-47; and Andrew Porter, *Victorian Shipping,*

than failures, however, and not all Liverpool entrepreneurs had an inexorable rise from immigrant office boy to chairman of a steamship firm. Even those who eventually became successful did not necessarily have a straight path to the top. Alfred Holt struggled in East Asia until he was able to form a working relationship with capable agents, Swire and Mansfield.[34] Given some very minor historical changes, the Holt story might have been one of a reckless young shipowner being mesmerized by his undoubted technological capabilities into neglecting the equally vital business infrastructure. Another Liverpool firm, Harrisons, tried to gain a share of the brandy trade from Charente to London in the early 1860s, buying new steamships suitable for the trade and recruiting agents in both ports. Crucially, though, the company failed to convince the major merchants that its service would be reliable enough to supplant that of the existing General Steam Navigation Company. Harrisons might have been cheaper in the short term, the merchants appear to have argued, but reliability of service and established business connections were worth paying for.[35]

In addition, the changing business environment was a crucial factor – most of the well-known case studies have focused on men who came to Liverpool before the middle of the nineteenth century. Those who tried to establish themselves late in the century, when the port's leading steamship lines were large, long-established and organized into powerful conferences, faced additional challenges. By that point not everyone who wanted to operate shipping from Liverpool intended to move to the city and become part of the local business community. Some were already active elsewhere, often in the coal ports from which they had grown initially, whether on the North East coast, the Bristol Channel or in London, the hub of the world's charter market. The process by which such shipowners tried to break into new markets was rather different than the picture of a newcomer working his way up through a port's trading hierarchy. In terms of the openness (or otherwise) of maritime business networks to outsiders, however, such cases have considerable value to the historian.

It is helpful to consider the regional dimension to this question. Although normally characterized simply as England's textile district, the North West had a diverse and broadly-based economy in the nineteenth century. Textiles were certainly crucial, but even within that sector there was considerable variety, and other activities, including agriculture, mining, engineering and

---

Business and Imperial Policy: Donald Currie, the Castle Line and Southern Africa (Woodbridge, 1986), 20-22.

[34]Hyde, *Blue Funnel*, 23-32.

[35]Francis E. Hyde, with John R. Harris and A. Michael Bourn, *Shipping Enterprise and Management, 1830-1939: Harrisons of Liverpool* (Liverpool, 1967), 13-14.

consumer goods and services, were far from being marginal. The trans-Pennine region had been building its industrial strength since the mid-eighteenth century, in particular by developing strategic road, canal and railway links that over time created a well-connected and integrated regional economy.[36] These districts also had great potential for entrepreneurs seeking investors: people in southern parts of Lancashire and in western Yorkshire paid taxes at well above the national average, suggesting a considerable amount of middle-class wealth to be tapped.[37]

Although Liverpool has dominated the maritime history of North West England, it was not the only port capable of serving the sprawling industrial zone of the trans-Pennine "near north." A number of other port authorities devoted considerable statistical ingenuity to claiming that their facilities served broad hinterlands and large populations. More important, some of them were also willing to invest in port infrastructure. By far the most significant such venture was the Manchester Ship Canal, opened in 1894, which was intended – in its promoters' optimistic moments – to move the centre of the cotton trade from Liverpool to Manchester.

Gordon Jackson has demonstrated that the hype and optimism surrounding such new ports was often badly misplaced; successful ports grew over decades, even centuries, and depended more on human capital than on the physical provision of docks and quays. Town councils, railway companies or property speculators who thought they could build a busy port from scratch were likely to be disappointed.[38] That said, in their enthusiasm to attract trade the owners of new ports were likely to offer inducements to shipowners and merchants. The first firms to use a port might gain a head start in a new market. In a business prone to periodic booms and busts as well as seafaring risks, maritime entrepreneurs were often happy to pursue short-term goals and could always redeploy their shipping elsewhere if a route failed to pay. As such, the willingness of various bodies to build new ports in the later nineteenth century offered relatively low-risk openings for enterprising shipowners.

Tyneside shipowner James Knott's approach to the North West market is revealing, and this section uses him as an extended case study. Knott started as a shipbroker in 1875, moving into the ownership and management of sailing vessels in the late 1870s. In 1881 he began a transition from sail to steam and sold the last of his sailing fleet in 1886. Knott developed a lasting

---

[36]Stephen Caunce, "Urban Systems, Identity and Development in Lancashire and Yorkshire: A Complex Question," in Neville Kirk (ed.), *Northern Identities: Historical Interpretations of the North and Northernness* (Aldershot, 2000), 47-70.

[37]Simon Gunn, *The Public Culture of the Victorian Middle Class: Ritual and Authority in the English Industrial City, 1840-1914* (Manchester, 2000), 20.

[38]Gordon Jackson, *The History and Archaeology of Ports* (Tadworth, 1983).

connection with Short Brothers, a Sunderland shipbuilder, and by the 1890s was Newcastle's largest shipowner by some margin. Knott identified the Mediterranean and Atlantic trades as offering greater scope for expansion than the traditional northern seas trades that dominated the traffic of North East England ports. He also sought to develop regular liner services rather than depend upon tramp shipping, and his Prince Line became a high-profile maritime brand.[39]

Fragmented references to Knott's activities appear in many places, but the best documented are his unsuccessful attempt to break into Liverpool's West African trade in 1890 and his subsequent success in running a service from Manchester. In the first case, he worked with existing Liverpool specialists in the field, the merchant John Holt and the shipping agent Henry Tyrer. These events were first revealed by Peter Davies' research and are a useful illustration of the problems facing a shipowner attempting to establish new business relationships beyond his home port as well as the tensions within Liverpool's business community. Some aspects of working a new trade were easier than others, and Knott was particularly confident that his ships would be well suited for the task. His relationships with North East shipbuilders, he believed, would enable him to build a technologically-advanced fleet, designed for the specific demands of the West Africa trade.[40]

Finding the cargoes to fill those ships, though, was more problematic. Here Knott was trying to break into existing networks dominated by Liverpool's Alfred Jones, who had established close links with the British government (the Crown Agents for the colonies effectively controlled the dispatch of cargoes to West Africa) and was also the main customer for the port facilities on the African coast. Knott's efforts to build alliances with Liverpool traders are a valuable reminder that business communities should not be seen as monolithic and that they were not necessarily better disposed toward insiders than outsiders. Liverpool had a number of ambitious traders who resented the dominance of men like Jones, and who were willing to bring in shipowners from outside the city to challenge his position. Henry Tyrer, who took the lead in encouraging Knott to get involved, had worked his way up from the bottom

---

[39]For Knott's career, see Norman L. Middlemiss, *Pride of the Princes: History of the Prince Line* (Newcastle, 1988).

[40]Peter N. Davies, *The Trade Makers: Elder Dempster in West Africa, 1852-1972, 1973-1989* (London, 1973; New ed., St. John's, 2000), 67-70; see also Davies, *Henry Tyrer: A Liverpool Shipping Agent and His Enterprise, 1879-1979* (London, 1979), 39-41. More generally, see Martin Lynn, "From Sail to Steam: The Impact of the Steamship Services on the British Palm Oil Trade with West Africa, 1850-1890," *Journal of African History*, XXX, No. 2 (1989), 227-245; and Robin Law (ed.), *From Slave Trade to "Legitimate" Commerce: The Commercial Transition in Nineteenth-Century West Africa* (Cambridge, 1995).

of Liverpool's competitive small-firm shipbroking sector and saw the agency of the Prince Line as a chance to take his business to a higher level.

Knott's other Liverpool ally, John Holt, struggled for years to undermine Alfred Jones' dominance of the Africa trades and their business associations. Holt had great difficulty organizing merchants to take the sort of united stand that might have given them greater negotiating strength against shipowners, let alone persuading them to invite new owners into the trade and thereby drive down freight rates. Recognizing that individual merchants were afraid to offend Jones, Holt also worked through mercantile associations. But when asked if he had tried to unite merchants through the Chamber of Commerce, he noted that the "Chamber of Commerce unfortunately is Sir Alfred Jones." Was there not a particular section devoted to the West Africa trades? "There again, it is Sir Alfred Jones." Only in Jones' absence, argued Holt, could any resolutions critical of the *status quo* be passed, and these were likely to be overturned later. In any case, even without Jones' formidable presence, getting more than a handful of merchants to agree on anything was always a problem. Holt also worked with the West Africa Trade Association, separate from the Chamber of Commerce, but rarely managed to engineer a common front: "I have, once in my life, united eight men, and it nearly killed me."[41]

Holt knew that shipowners relied on merchant disunity. He argued that there was no point in talking with shipping firms about freight rates unless merchants had agreed action among themselves: "the only way to speak with authority to any of these shipowners is to be in a position to act if they do not agree."[42] Holt, it should be stressed, did not see his problems in the West Africa trade as stemming from the conference system in particular but rather from the effective monopoly position enjoyed by Alfred Jones, and what he regarded as Jones's failure to devote his full attention to the shipping business, thus damaging the prospects of trading firms who might otherwise have been his allies.[43] A withering contempt for the business abilities of shipowners had long been an element in Holt's worldview. In a letter to Sir William McOnie of the British and African Steamship Co. in 1889, he complained that the firm was allowing German competitors to take an increasing proportion of trade and complacently renting out its ships for short-term profit rather than using them to build a better service in the African trades – shares were being "hawked about the market" when they could be sold at a premium, and "I assume that you and your colleagues sometimes think of these matters."[44]

---

[41]*BPP*, Shipping Rings, John Holt, qq. 5191-5195.

[42]LRO, 380 HOL I 4/8, Holt to G.L. Glasser, Hamburg, 18 November 1901.

[43]*BPP*, Shipping Rings, John Holt, qq. 5201-5202.

[44]LRO, 380 HOL I 4/5, Holt to William McOnie, 25 October 1889.

Holt often returned to the idea of running steamers of his own or in alliance with other merchants; this was a variation on the theme of encouraging existing shipowners from elsewhere to launch new services in competition. The short-term perspective of Holt's stance is clear, though. Running two ships on his own account in the West African trade would "be the most effective way of getting a reduction in our favour," argued Holt in 1901, but this was a tactic, not an intention to move seriously into shipowning. Incoming shipowners would have been well aware that Holt was interested in driving freight rates down, not in creating new shipping lines *per se*, and would have been rash to commit themselves too heavily on that basis.

James Knott duly launched a service to West Africa, but his experience in the trade in 1890 was frustrating. His vessels got low priority in the African ports and were often delayed. Henry Tyrer was unable to secure sufficient cargo and had to abandon the agency owing the Prince Line money, but Knott had no more success with a second firm and soon withdrew from the Africa trade. In part, this was evidence of the conspiracy against him by Jones and his local employees and allies, but it also suggests that shipping skills were not as easily transferable as Knott might have thought. John Holt agreed that "the detention is atrocious" on the coast but also complained that Knott's masters "do not work quick enough, your men being new to palm oil stowing and the general run of work there."[45]

Knott's difficulties with the practical side of ship stowage and with agents are reminders of the number of levels at which trading had to be managed. Success often depended on a few individuals with the knowledge and skills to do specialist jobs, and breaking into a new trade meant identifying and recruiting them. Practical knowledge was also important for establishing reputations, as potential customers were reassured by demonstrable competence. In addition, recruiting the right people might create a virtuous cycle. If Knott could sign up the chief clerk and the cashier from Elder Dempster, they would probably bring the best masters in the African trade with them, reckoned Holt.[46] At this level, shipping entrepreneurs faced some of their hardest tasks because they were trying to persuade salarymen to take real risks with their careers and incomes. Higher pay was not in itself much inducement because clerks and managers knew that once they had left the dominant firm in a particular trade, they would not be welcomed back if the new venture failed.

Reputation was also important at the boardroom level, although here direct experience in a particular trade was less important. Creating the board of a public company did not always involve the gathering of sycophants and ignoramuses, as satirized by Anthony Trollope, but neither was it likely to be a

---

[45]*Ibid.*, 380 HOL I 4/5, Holt to James Knott, 13 May 1891.

[46]*Ibid.*, Holt to Knott, 30 November 1891.

collection of real experts in the proposed activity. Shipping entrepreneurs did not necessarily want a board that was well-versed in maritime matters; that was, after all, the job of the shipowner himself and his staff. The board's role was to persuade outsiders of the gravitas and reliability of the venture, either directly or indirectly, and to provide the entrepreneur with a ready-made network of contacts in local business.

Knott considered creating a new company to re-launch his West Africa service in 1891 and sought John Holt's recommendations for possible directors.[47] Holt's suggestions are revealing, although there is no evidence that any of them were ever approached, nor is there any indication of how many Liverpool men for whom Knott was looking. Stephen Williamson, then the senior partner of the South American merchant house Balfour Williamson, would be "a good man," thought Holt. Williamson was a Member of Parliament and was delegating the firm's business to his son Archibald by the early 1890s.[48] Sir Andrew Barclay Walker was a prominent figure in Liverpool society, a long-term city councillor and alderman, and builder of the Walker Art Gallery.[49] Walker had made his fortune in the family brewing business and got richer still through strategic investment in coal mining; reasonably enough, Holt thought that Walker would be a good choice if Knott needed a major investor. It is unclear who Holt meant by "Percy Bates;" the man usually known by that name was a member of the third generation of the Bates shipowning family but was barely into his teens in 1891. Holt may have meant Edward Percy Bates, the son of the founder and an active shipowner in his forties.[50] Finally, the younger Ralph Brocklebank had been a partner in the shipowning firm T. and J. Brocklebank until 1886, when he and his father left its management to another branch of the family; he was still only in his early fifties when Holt suggested him.[51]

These four, Holt told Knott, were not directly connected with the management of shipping firms (which makes the Bates identification problematic) but were men whose "reputations stand high in our commercial world."

---

[47]*Ibid.*, 380 HOL I 4/5, Holt to Knott, 30 November 1891.

[48]Robert G. Greenhill, "Williamson, Archibald, First Baron Forres (1860-1931)," *Oxford Dictionary of National Biography* (Oxford, 2004).

[49]C.W. Sutton, "Walker, Sir Andrew Barclay, First Baronet (1824-1893)," *Oxford Dictionary of National Biography*.

[50]Philip Bates, *Bates of Bellefield, Gyrn Castle and Manydown* (Lymington, 1994).

[51]John F. Gibson, *Brocklebanks, 1770-1950* (2 vols., Liverpool, 1953), I, 167.

Holt ruled himself out as a director, arguing that he would do Knott more harm than good.[52] Holt's presence would certainly have focused Alfred Jones' hostility, but Jones was never going to be helpful to a new shipping competitor anyway, so this seems a little disingenuous. It seems more likely that it was a convenient excuse; Holt's irritation with Knott's apparent inefficiency on the African coast has already been noted.[53] While he undoubtedly wanted Knott to succeed and to increase the region's shipping capacity, this was not the same thing as seeking personal involvement in an uncertain enterprise.

Four years after these discussions in Liverpool, James Knott recruited a Manchester-centred board for his restructured Prince Line (1895) Ltd. The new Ship Canal offered another opportunity for Knott to gain a footing in the North West trades that involved less obstruction from an entrenched local business community. Indeed, Knott could expect a welcome in Manchester because the promoters of the new port feared correctly that it would be hard to persuade Liverpool shipowners to establish services using the Canal. What Manchester needed was a shipping fleet of its own, tied to the interests of the Manchester and district manufacturers, and this need coincided with the willingness of some North East shipowners to expand beyond their traditional short-sea and tramp markets.

Knott, along with other incoming shipowners, began operating from the Ship Canal even before it was finished: the short-lived port of Saltport was established for this purpose at the junction between the partly-dug canal and the River Weaver. His vessels carried Egyptian cotton from Alexandria and rapidly acquired a return trade in manufactured goods.[54] As had been his intention with the abortive West Africa services from Liverpool, Knott was determined to lock the North West business and investing community into the financial base of his operation. Shortly before its restructuring in 1895, Knott's firm (then called the Prince Steam Ship Co.) already got twenty-two percent of its capital from Lancashire and eleven percent from West Yorkshire; the combined shareholdings of Tyneside, North Yorkshire and County Durham – Knott's older connections, as it were – accounted for almost the same again (thirty-three percent).[55] Unfortunately, we do not know how Knott recruited his directors or whether someone in Manchester made the sort of recommendations that John Holt had made in Liverpool, but similar principles were evi-

---

[52]LRO, 380 HOL I 4/5, Holt to Knott, 30 November 1891.

[53]*Ibid.*, Holt to Knott, 13 May 1891.

[54]Douglas A. Farnie, *The Manchester Ship Canal and the Rise of the Port of Manchester, 1894-1975* (Manchester, 1980), 83.

[55]This, and other shareholding information in this section, is derived from *Turnbull's Shipping Register* (1895).

dently at work. The Prince Line's board included Charles Henry Scott, a leading Manchester tea merchant; James Dilworth Harrison, a Burnley cotton manufacturer; Walter Kay, from a Bingley wool combing firm; and John Unwin, a former mayor of Southport. John Donald of South Shields represented Knott's older networks in the North East.

Other North East entrepreneurs saw the new port of Manchester as an opportunity. The Pinkney family of Sunderland managed the Neptune Steam Navigation Co. which secured some of the first cargoes of American cotton to go directly to Manchester. Rather than trying to challenge the normal supply of American cotton that reached Manchester via Liverpool's brokers, Neptune carried shipments for sale direct to a few contracted spinners.[56] Like the Prince Line, Neptune tapped into the North West's investing hinterland. Just over thirty percent of the firm's shares were owned in Lancashire and another eight percent in West Yorkshire, with most of the remainder being owned in the Pinkneys' home port. West Hartlepool entrepreneurs were also quick to recognize the potential of the Manchester market. One of them, William Bacon, even became Chairman of the Ship Canal Company in 1916.[57] Bacon had spent ten years in the West Hartlepool shipbroking firm of Sivewright, Bacon and Co. before founding the Manchester and Bombay General Navigation Co. in 1894.

George Renwick, a Tyneside shipowner, operated coastal services from the Ship Canal and also chaired a dry dock company. He persuaded North East investors to subscribe most of the capital for Manchester's dry dock at Mode Wheel Locks before the Canal was even opened, having previously established a track record in dry-dock management at Wallsend-on-Tyne.[58] Renwick won the concession for the dry dock from the Ship Canal Company, which was promised ten percent of revenue in return: the more paranoid wing of the shipping press condemned this arrangement on the grounds that it gave the Canal Company an incentive to make the Ship Canal dangerous to navigate because it would profit from damage to ships.[59] Like Knott, Renwick moved quickly to establish a North West presence, operating from Saltport from 1892 and subsequently from Manchester itself. He deployed two of his twenty-two steamers on the route, labelling the service the Manchester and London Shipping Company.[60] Unlike other North East opera-

---

[56]Farnie, *Manchester Ship Canal*, 78.

[57]*Ibid.*, 22-24.

[58]*The Times* (London), 16 February 1894 and 20 June 1930.

[59]*Fairplay*, 30 October 1891.

[60]*The Times* (London), 6 December 1892.

tors, though, Renwick made no attempt to recruit Lancashire investors, and his shares continued to be owned predominantly in the North East and in London.

Christopher Furness is a useful final example. Furness' skills in building large joint-stock businesses in the iron-coal-shipping complex of the North East are well known, and his connections were vital to the creation of Manchester's most important shipping firm in 1898. Furness' Manchester Liners Ltd. was a major leap in scale for the new port's shipping and a high-profile demonstration that the Ship Canal could accommodate large vessels.[61] Such confidence-building events were vital to bringing in more investment and helping to consolidate the fledgling connection between trade and shipping in Manchester. Furness, like James Knott, had considered opening new African services from Liverpool and was approached in 1895 by John Holt and Henry Tyrer. In this case, Furness insisted that an investment network be in place before any service was attempted, but his prospective Liverpool collaborators failed to raise the capital for a new shipping company.[62] Furness, unusually for him, sold ordinary shares in Manchester Liners, seeking to lock local investors into the venture.[63] For Furness, Manchester was an opportunity to develop the facilitating role that became his key contribution to a series of mergers and agglomerations in the following decade and to consolidate his existing interests in the Atlantic trading combines.

Within a decade of the opening of the Ship Canal, the combination of North East and North West interests had established a dense network of overlapping and reinforcing links. These links tied the mobile part of the system (shipowners, brokers and new entrants in various trades) to the more static part (the Ship Canal Company itself, warehouse owners, established merchants and industrialists). Networks of interlocking directorships, a common feature of industrial districts, were quickly built up: William Henry Bailey, for example, became over time the owner of a Salford engineering works, a leading investor in the Canal Company and a member of its board, a director of Trafford Park Estates and a director of James Knott's Prince Line.[64]

Liverpool's shipping community did not reject Manchester entirely, but only a few firms attempted to run services from the new port. Lamport and Holt began a triangular New York-Manchester-Brazil service when the Ship Canal opened in 1894 and expanded its operations to include cattle imports in 1903. It carried Sea Island cotton from Florida via New York and also lamp oil from Standard Oil in the US to its UK subsidiary. The Larrinaga family

---

[61]Farnie, *Manchester Ship Canal*, 36.

[62]Davies, *Henry Tyrer*, 42-43.

[63]Boyce, *Information, Mediation*, 86-87.

[64]Farnie, *Manchester Ship Canal*, 122.

firm began importing cotton from Galveston to Manchester in 1897.[65] These ventures succeeded, but at least one Liverpool attempt to exploit the new Manchester opportunity was more problematic. William Tapscott, a shipbroker, launched a new shipping company called Manchester Traders Co. in 1894 and ran a single ship from Manchester to London for two years. It emerged at his subsequent bankruptcy hearing that Tapscott had spent years juggling the finances of a number of firms under his management and that the Manchester service was just another opportunistic addition to his fleet.[66]

Thus, Manchester was able to attract shipowners looking for new opportunities, but only in a limited sense. Those outside shipowners who did well in Manchester – Knott, Furness, and Lamport and Holt, most notably – found trades that were outside the established networks built over the decades by Liverpool firms, rather than in direct competition. The biggest Liverpool operators saw no need to start Manchester operations, while at the other extreme the new port gained speculative shipowners like Tapscott. Overall, the Canal Company's fears about a lack of shipping were well founded, albeit partly refuted by a few entrepreneurial firms.

What the Canal Company failed to anticipate was the conservatism of Manchester's own merchants and industrialists and the extent to which they were locked into Liverpool's markets and processes. Most of the cotton complex continued to use the port of Liverpool, and this remained the fundamental gap in the Canal Company's income stream. Whether this was primarily the result of the shipping conference system as it worked in Liverpool is unclear. Edward Langdon, President of the Manchester Chamber of Commerce, told the Royal Commission on Shipping Rings in 1907 that the conferences were at the root of the problem. Exporting merchants could not use Manchester services if they also wanted to use ships sailing from Liverpool at other times (as they almost always needed to do); this naturally discouraged independent shipowners from starting services from Manchester because they feared low demand. Any conference shipowner that wanted to run a Manchester service was either threatened by his fellow operators or forced by them to charge the same freight as from Liverpool, when Manchester should have been able to charge less.[67]

Langdon was in a difficult position because his own members in the Chamber of Commerce had been criticized by the Ship Canal Company for their failure to support services from Manchester; blaming the conference system was a tempting distraction. On the other hand, he had to work with conference shipowners in his own business, and later in his evidence he distanced

---

[65]*Ibid.*, 35, 80 and 143.

[66]*Fairplay,* 8 July 1897.

[67]*BPP*, Shipping Rings, Edward Langdon, q. 619.

himself from the idea that conferences were boycotting the Ship Canal; the fact that three out of four liner firms loading from Manchester were outside the conference system (and the fourth was limited in what it could carry by conference rules) was just "chance," he argued.[68]

The railway companies, the Mersey Docks and Harbour Board and various Liverpool shipping companies all slashed their rates and charges when the Ship Canal opened. On some routes, rates were cut in half, such as the drop from forty shillings to twenty shillings per ton on freight from Liverpool to the Persian Gulf, although most savings were less dramatic.[69] By 1905, one manufacturer reckoned that the Ship Canal was saving the cotton industry £500,000 a year in transport costs for raw cotton alone.[70] It did so mainly by driving down railway rates, however, and Manchester merchants saw little need to abandon their established networks and actually use shipping services via the Ship Canal. Indeed, they went further, using the new rates to pursue yet more individualistic hard bargaining. Some traders, the Canal Company claimed, were adopting "a policy of squeeze" and were trying to drive rates even lower: this undermined the efforts of the Canal Company to persuade shipowners to operate services to Manchester.[71]

Merchants gambled that the Canal Company would keep the Canal open regardless of the volume of traffic and that actual closure was unlikely. Indeed, many noted that it was possible for the Ship Canal to have a thriving import trade in food and provisions, as well as servicing the engineering works at the new Trafford Park industrial estate, without having much impact on the textile sector.[72] The mere existence of the Canal as a real or potential competitor was the crucial thing – costs would fluctuate over time, depending on the exact scale of competition between shipowners and railways, but the overall trend would be downward. While the Canal Company argued that Manchester's long-term prosperity depended upon increasing the volume of shipping using the canal, merchants believed that it was more dependent on the success of the business community in general and that it was just another element in a complicated picture. Canal Company officials complained that some traders treated them "as if we were canvassing for some private business concern of

---

[68]*Ibid.*, Edward Langdon, q. 905.

[69]Manchester Ship Canal Company, *Report of the Ordinary General Meeting* (hereafter Ship Canal Co., *Report*), 28 August 1894.

[70]Great Britain, *Report of the Tariff Commission* (2 vols., London, 1904-1905), II, part 1, Charles Eckersley, para. 368.

[71]Ship Canal Co., *Report,* 28 August 1894.

[72]*BPP*, Shipping Rings, Edward Langdon, q. 889.

our own...these fossilised individuals do not grasp the fact that this is a great national undertaking working practically for the public good."[73] The "fossils" had a different view: "damn sentiment when you come to business."[74]

If textile exporters remained committed to Liverpool, the other major gap in the Ship Canal's traffic was imported raw cotton, and again it is hard to argue that this was the fault of the conference system. Since the mid-nineteenth century, Lancashire cotton spinners had travelled by rail weekly to Liverpool to meet the cotton brokers, study samples and buy cotton. By the 1880s the Liverpool market had become a sophisticated exchange in which real transactions in cotton were supported by a closely integrated market in futures which served to make prices more predictable and secured traders against major swings and fluctuations. Direct imports of cotton to Manchester, therefore, could only be part of this system if they were given eligibility by the Liverpool Cotton Association; without that, spinners were effectively abandoning half a century of improvements in exchange procedures. Indeed, most cotton manufacturers were happy for Liverpool to control the raw cotton market and simply wanted the freedom to bring some cotton direct to Manchester. Spinners petitioned the Liverpool Cotton Association in August 1894 to recognize cotton stored in Manchester for the purposes of futures contracts.[75] This was rejected on the ground of "impracticability" by a full meeting of the Association the following month, and Manchester duly created its own Cotton Association in November to build an independent raw cotton market.[76] But this was slow to develop anything like the scale, scope and security of the Liverpool market.

Failing to make the economic case, the Ship Canal Company tried to encourage a sense of local patriotism, adding another layer to the pressures and tensions at work in the shipping complex. Officials began deriding as "unpatriotic" those merchants who continued to use Liverpool and refused to commit to the new route.[77] The Canal Company urged Mancunians to raise capital for new shipping firms because "the honour of the city is at stake," and "a great port is not merely a source of wealth but conveys honour and dignity on a city."[78] Such appeals became a cliché that was turned against Manchester

---

[73]Ship Canal Co., *Report*, 17 February 1903.

[74]*Ibid.*, 25 February 1915.

[75]LRO, 380 COT 5/2, 13 August 1894.

[76]*Ibid.*, 380 COT 6/3, 24 September 1894; and Farnie, *Manchester Ship Canal*, 78.

[77]Manchester Chamber of Commerce, *Monthly Record* (1894), 82.

[78]Ship Canal Co., *Report*, 17 February 1898.

by the disgruntled and disappointed. The manager of the General Steam Navigation Co., after two years of running unprofitable services to West Africa and Rotterdam, was quoted as saying that he had "had enough of Manchester; your patriotism is all froth."[79]

Only in the most extreme cases, therefore, would merchants risk the sort of disruption to their businesses that would result from abandoning long-established Liverpool trading relationships and market processes, and shipping conferences were only one aspect of a much more complicated web of connections. Manchester had to accept that the costs of building home-port networks were far greater than just the cost of buying or chartering ships, and the early years of the Ship Canal demonstrate the rigidity of the maritime-industrial complex when confronted with challenges and opportunities. Nonetheless, they also reveal that entrepreneurial shipowners could develop new lines, even in difficult and restricted trading environments, and that they were able to find local allies to do so.

Conclusion

This essay has demonstrated some of the ways in which shipowners and shipping firms connected with the wider economy of the North of England in the late nineteenth century. It also raises questions about the relationship between entrepreneurship and associationalism in maritime business. Much of the evidence offered here supports aspects of Mark Casson's conceptualization of business culture, in particular his thinking on the need for entrepreneurs to sacrifice some of their autonomy in order to achieve broader success.[80]

It has long been argued that the conference system provides evidence for the willingness of shipowners to compromise with other shipowners, for the extent to which merchants could achieve some unity within their ranks and for the balance of market power between the two camps. This essay has tried to demonstrate that those questions also need to be studied outside the conferences by exploring other dynamics at work in regional business systems and hinterland industrial districts. While not denying the oddities and exceptionalism of the shipping industry, the article also suggests that much light can be cast on shipping by studying its interconnections with the wider economy and by seeking evidence for the tensions between associational cohesion and entrepreneurialism in related sectors which were at once comparative with and connected to research into shipowning itself.

---

[79]*Ibid.*, 24 August 1897.

[80]Mark Casson, "Entrepreneurship and Business Culture," in Jonathan Brown and Mary B. Rose (eds.), *Entrepreneurship, Networks and Modern Business* (Manchester, 1993), 30-54.

Network Structures, Processes and Dynamics: Inter-firm Cooperative Frameworks in the Shipping Industry

Gordon Boyce

Shipping has always been a "networked" industry, and its history therefore has much to offer in terms of insights into the structure, processes and dynamics of this organizational form. Maritime historians are well placed to contribute to the further development of network theory and analysis. We have rich empirical data that can support longitudinal investigations aimed at exploring the causes of change as network-based marine enterprises adapted to new environmental conditions. Detailed reports and correspondence among shipowners and their business partners expose the processes of networking and their social/cultural underpinnings. Corporate records and share registers enable us to explore the structure of maritime networks and their constituent vertical, horizontal and diversified links. Highly developed skills conducting biographical studies, which influenced the writing of many early company histories, provide a platform to examine the social and cultural links that shaped the networks employed by maritime businessmen who represented a group recognized for their considerable upward mobility. Finally, as an international industry, whose members interacted with a variety of government agencies at home and abroad, shipping offers a wonderful opportunity to explore networks in action on the global stage.

This essay examines recent network theory in order to highlight questions that maritime historians can explore using the rich resources and well-developed skills at their disposal. The first section considers networks as a distinctive framework that operates within and alongside of other structures, such as hierarchies and markets. The second part of the article examines network structures and the various links that might sustain them. Next, we probe the contents of these supporting ties, exploring in particular their knowledge and information-handling functions. The final section describes computer software that supports the study of networks.

Networks as Cooperative Structures

A network may be defined as an informal web of participants who band together to mobilize resources needed to carry out some form of mutually rewarding endeavour. Members contribute capital, physical assets, information and/or reputation to support transactions that individuals would not be able to undertake independently given the limitations of the resources at their disposal or the degree of risk involved. Among their collective and personal attributes, reputation is of salient importance to participants because it mitigates the uncertainty surrounding exchanges, especially those involving information and knowledge.[1] Trust, cooperation, reciprocity and interpersonal knowledge are vital supporting elements. Networks serve a wide variety of purposes; they can stimulate growth, promote collusion and distribute risk. They are important in business, social and intellectual endeavours.

Sociologists and economists have been the principal agents for developing theories regarding networks. The former are interested in exploring the types of bonds that link social actors and the behavioural norms that condition their interaction. Economists are attracted to networks as a distinctive coordinating framework that harnesses resources for productive purposes (and to a lesser extent as collusive devices). The perspectives of sociologists and economists provide valuable directions for business analysis. The sociological approach focuses attention on processes, while the economists' outlook highlights the efficiency properties of these frameworks. The combination of these two approaches is particularly appropriate because it makes it possible to examine business activity within a broader social and cultural context.

Articulating the main thrust of the sociological approach in his classic article, Mark Granovetter stressed the importance of what he called "embeddedness," that is the need to examine institutional development within a specific context of social relations.[2] Pursuing this idea, Walter Powell suggested that the "relationship" ought to be the central unit of analysis.[3] He intended this focus to contrast with the transaction-cost economists, principal among them Oliver Williamson, whose work concentrated on the "transaction"

---

[1] In an important work, Kenneth J. Arrow, *The Limits of Organization* (New York, 1974), used the concept of "the Paradox of Knowledge" to highlight the difficulty of arranging transactions involving knowledge. Market failure is likely because the buyer cannot assign a value to knowledge without first knowing what it is, and the seller cannot divulge the knowledge in advance of payment because to do so would in effect mean giving it away.

[2] Mark Granovetter, "Economic Action and Social Structure: The Problem of Embeddedness," *American Journal of Sociology*, XCI, No. 3 (1985), 481-510.

[3] Walter W. Powell, "Neither Market nor Hierarchy: Network Forms of Organization," *Research in Organizational Behaviour*, XII, No. 3 (1990), 295-336.

as the key element.[4] These distinctions highlight a link between exchange and interpersonal relations that demands exploration by network analysts.

George B. Richardson conceived of networks as one institutional arrangement within a spectrum of alternatives.[5] In his schema, markets resided at one pole and price mechanisms served to coordinate transactions. At the opposite pole, hierarchies relied upon managerial authority to provide coordination. Between these points, Richardson observed a series of intermediate modes (including long-term contracting arrangements, licensing agreements, joint ventures, strategic alliances, cartels and networks) that mobilize trust and cooperation to shape exchange.

Walter Powell challenged Richardson's depiction of an institutional spectrum by suggesting that individual frameworks do not necessarily function as alternatives. Powell's purpose was to draw attention to the ubiquity of networks. He argued that they are found within markets and inside hierarchies. This is obviously true; every hierarchy is laced with informal networks upon which people rely for information and expeditious action outside of the normal chain of command. Markets are also permeated by preferred channels that streamline purchasing and selling. (One could also suggest that markets have hierarchical features, for example, embodied in tiers of sub-markets and that hierarchies have internal markets.)[6] Powell's insight is valuable, for it highlights the importance and ubiquity of networks and sets up a useful contrast between formal and informal mechanisms that provides greater depth to organizational study. Nevertheless, empirical observation confirms that networks also constitute a distinctive organizational framework in their own right.

These insights invite us to consider the efficiency properties of the three main frameworks. Markets are characterized as self-organizing systems that automatically accommodate change and deliver economically "optimal" outcomes among participants who are completely "autonomous" and "anonymous." Hierarchies achieve superior efficiency when small numbers of bar-

---

[4]Oliver E. Williamson, *Markets and Hierarchies: Analysis and Antitust Implications* (New York, 1975). See also Williamson, *The Economic Institutions of Capitalism: Firms, Markets, Relational Contracting* (New York, 1986).

[5]George B. Richardson, "The Organisation of Industry," *Economic Journal*, LXXXII, No. 3 (1972), 883-896.

[6]For sub-markets within the London Stock Exchange, for example, see Bernard Attard, "Making a Market: The Jobbers of the London Stock Exchange, 1800-1986," *Financial History Review*, VII, No. 1 (2000), 5-24. Some intermediate structures have hierarchical features, such as the tiers within Japanese supply and distribution chains. See Susan Helper, "Comparative Supplier Relations in the US and Japanese Auto Industry: An Exit/Voice Approach," *Business and Economic History*, 2nd ser., XIX (1990), 153-162. Internal markets are explored in Williamson, *Markets and Hierarchies*.

gainers conduct exchanges that depend upon dedicated assets or transaction-specific investments. U-form structures – that is, organizations that integrate the operations of functionally related departments, such as purchasing, production and sales – win economies of scale, and M-form organizations, which consist of separate divisions, each of which are constituted along the same lines as U-form entities, secure economies of scope as well as scale advantages. Both types of hierarchy employ systems to provide the information needed for coordination, and they mobilize authority structures to direct the necessary decision-making processes. Networks depend upon cooperation and trust to effect "coordination." Network members have varying degrees of influence over each other depending upon the size of their ownership stakes, the extent of their commercial relations and the strength of their interpersonal ties. These investment, business and personal links all convey information. For example, investment furnishes financial data and, if large enough, access to Board-level intelligence gained through representation. Commercial ties convey information about the efficiency and quality of a network ally's operation. Finally, interpersonal links provide an impression of personality, character and cognitive patterns.

In contrast to markets, where "perfect" information (that is "public" information free to all participants) supports transactions, and hierarchies, where formally constituted systemic links provide "inside" (or "private") data needed to integrate functions and internalize markets, networks circulate preferential information that is of higher quality than public intelligence and less intimate than inside knowledge.[7] This form of information enables networks to mediate market transactions. It makes it possible for network affiliates to have more influence than would be the case in an arm's-length market context but less than those at the apex of a hierarchy can exert. The result is not administrative imprecision but rather quasi-autonomy that enables members to use their initiative to exploit their specialized knowledge base and other intangible assets (brands, goodwill and established business contacts). At the same time, they can lever their assets by effecting mediated transactions with their network partners.

---

[7]Agents play an important role in mobilizing preferential information regarding trading opportunities based on analyses of commodity flows, contacts with shippers and local intelligence. See Lewis R. Fischer and Anders M. Fon, "The Making of a Maritime Firm: The Rise of Fearnley and Eger, 1859-1917," in Fischer (ed.), *From Wheel House to Counting House: Essays in Maritime Business History in Honour of Professor Peter Neville Davies* (St. John's, 1992), 303-322; and Gordon H. Boyce, "Agency Agreements in International Business: Communicating, Transferring Knowledge and Learning across the Corporate Frontier," in Boyce, *Co-operative Structures in Global Business: A New Approach to Networks, Technology Transfer Agreements, Strategic Alliances and Agency Relationships* (London, 2000), 14-34.

Networks are also considered to be more flexible than hierarchies but less so perhaps than markets.[8] Networks are also thought to be superior to hierarchies in coping with turbulence arising from a business environment. Finally, they tend to be more supportive of innovation primarily because they possess multi-directional communication channels in contrast to the vertical conduits that typify hierarchies (see below).

The types of incentives underpinning these communicating structures differ. In hierarchies, formal rewards or monetary payments encourage members to submit to authority relations. Informal inducements, such as culturally-based norms, and recognition from peers or superiors also motivate participants. Within networks, informal incentives are perhaps of greater significance. While pecuniary gains are vital, members also attach particular importance to reputation, especially achieving renown as a dependable cooperator. Such an attribute represents a major investment over a considerable time and is subject to precipitous debasement in the event that one behaves in a way deemed to be opportunistic. As such, reputation acts as a guarantee upon which a member depends to gain access to a larger stream of contracting opportunities in the future. Norms of reciprocity provide ways to signal goodwill and cooperative intent, especially when asymmetry is evident (one gives up more than one gains in a particular situation, thereby signalling trust and observance of a long-term view of relations). Cooperation may also give rise to psychic rewards. All of these considerations encourage members to collaborate in pooling diverse sets of resources that one person acting on his own could not mobilize in order to take advantage of a particular productive opportunity. Various forms of economic efficiency, as well as risk-spreading, stem from such assembly.

Achieving these gains and advantages depends on how well related costs are managed. Chief among these expenses are those associated with communication and information handling. One of the advantages of hierarchy lies in the efficiency with which decisions are implemented. Formal incentives and authority structures are the key. (In contrast, the gathering of information needed to inform decisions may be more constrained given the primacy of vertically-aligned channels within hierarchies.) Since networks rely on cooperation, however, more extensive and prolonged discussion is required. (One of the great strengths of networks lies in their ability to muster diverse sets of information and knowledge for decision making, but see below.) Both Oliver Williamson and Susan Helper draw attention to the importance of "communicating economies" in mitigating expenses and ensuring the efficiency of cooperative frameworks such as networks. But their reluctance to explore this theme or delineate the mechanisms used to streamline information exchange

---

[8]See Helper, "Comparative Supplier Relations;" and Williamson, *Economic Institutions*.

leaves clear an important field of investigation, and historians of maritime networks are well placed to explore it.

One device that could be employed to contain these expenses is an informal communication infrastructure consisting of forums in which prospective bargainers can make contacts, deliberately configured communication conduits, conventions that governed discussion and personal qualities that distinguish deal makers. The role of social and cultural forces in reducing communication costs is another area for investigation. What roles were played by behavioural norms, conventions and accepted etiquette? Were industry-specific behavioural patterns or more pervasive ones such as those associated with "gentlemanly capitalism" important? When examining cultural influences it is important to consider both cognitive and value-based dimensions. The roles played by language, routines, symbols and rituals await attention. All these instruments shaped the efficiency of networks in their manifold forms.

Network Links and Typologies

Mats Alvesson and Lars Lindkvist provide a general typology consisting of the blood kinship network based on extended family, the social integrative form that shapes member behaviour and the economic cooperative type that reflects purely economic or business relations.[9] These forms often overlap or intermingle. Network members may be related by social and cultural ties that serve to reinforce business relations by mobilizing common values, cognitive frameworks and behavioural norms. The pervasiveness of family, religious, ethnic, educational and political links has been documented extensively. These intertwined ties play important roles in binding participants operating across the globe.

Links within business networks and hierarchies exhibit similarities and differences. These ties are based upon investment stakes, commercial relationships, personal/social bonds and information flows. In terms of ownership patterns, networks do not always consist solely of wholly-owned units as do hierarchies. Instead, partial ownership stakes give networks greater flexibility, especially in making divestments which can often be undertaken without issuing overt signals to the market. Risk reduction can be an important consideration. Moreover, cross holdings are common and serve to safeguard control from outside predators. Regarding operating links, networks may consist of vertical links similar to those of U-form organizations; they may have horizontal ties like merged multi-unit structures; or they may have diversified bonds typical of M-form or conglomerate hierarchies. Social and personal ties are more pervasive and play a more important role in networks than they usually

---

[9]Mats Alvesson and Lars Lindkvist, "Transaction Costs, Clans, and Corporate Culture," *Journal of Management Studies*, XXX, No. 3 (1993), 427-452.

do in hierarchies. In particular, this type of bond supports multi-directional communication and reduces cost transactions. Indeed, hierarchies consist largely of vertically-aligned information flows. While matrix structures provide horizontal conduits, these may be temporary in nature and are usually more constrained than the wide-ranging links that bind network members.

More internationally comparative investigations of vertical, horizontal and diversified maritime networks are needed. In the British case, vertical links appeared early and were initially based upon personal and commercial ties, although investment bonds also arose, particularly between shipowners and shipbuilders.[10] In this regard, many shipowners had ties with several shipbuilders in order to gain improved access to yards that specialized in various types of vessels. Apart from tapping into different knowledge sets possessed by various builders, shipowners also sought to gain competitive prices. In addition, network links between shipowners and builders provided a secure platform to support technical innovation. Lyle and Lithgow jointly financed an experiment with a diesel-powered vessel; Scott, Holt and Swire cooperated in the commercial application of a series of new vessel and engine designs; and Furness and his shipbuilding allies built experimental turbine and motor ships. Innovation also permeated Furness' extensive vertical channels; his firms commercialized new steelmaking technology, standardized marine engines and developed a range of advanced machinery.[11] Indeed, Lord Furness was one of the earliest shipowners to build a large, vertically-aligned corporate network, and he did so by using his purchasing power to lever open ownership positions in shipbuilding, steelmaking, marine engineering, coal mining and other related businesses.

At the turn of the twentieth century, but on a much greater scale during and immediately following World War I, vertical links became more extensive and appeared within most of the major British shipping groups. This development occurred as a result of internal shocks and external threats. The passing of company founders exposed their business allies to uncertainty which was mitigated by the purchase of an ownership stake to safeguard established information and commercial links. Wartime losses, buoyant profits, excess-profit duties and difficulties securing tonnage induced shipowners to acquire yards. Shortages of vital components caused the wave of vertical acquisition to spill over into a number of allied industries, especially steelmaking. As the first generation of the pioneering steamship owners passed away, these vertical

---

[10]Gordon H. Boyce, *Information, Mediation, and Institutional Development: The Rise of Large-scale Enterprise in British Shipping, 1870-1919* (Manchester, 1995), 176-197.

[11]John Orbel, Edwin Green and Michael Moss, *From Cape to Cape: The History of Lyle Shipping Company* (Edinburgh, 1978), 74; and Boyce, *Co-operative Structures*, 35-53.

ties came to assume the form of an inter-organizational network, usually based upon the holding company structure. Managerial and financial crises, respectively, caused the dissolution of the vertical structures built by Furness and Lord Kylsant during the interwar period.[12] Further dissolutions occurred after World War II as a result of adverse tax legislation, company laws that undermined the viability of private family firms and nationalization programmes introduced by Labour governments.

Horizontal ties between shipowners appeared in the early days of steam. Jointly-run services were developed to spread risk and reduce competition. A few formal mergers, principally to eliminate rivalries, also took place, one of the most famous being Union-Castle. Other horizontal acquisitions, in which the purchased entity retained a separate identity, occurred for the same reason, but the form employed was designed to obscure the purpose. The purchase of China Mutual by Holts, and Booth's acquisition of Singlehursts, are examples. The form of the International Mercantile Marine Company was somewhat similar, but the intent of its formation was obvious.[13] In this case, and in many other acquisitions that followed between 1902 and 1919, the desire to retain goodwill, brand power, trading contacts, conference memberships and intangible assets also explained the tendency to retain the separate identity of wholly-acquired subsidiaries. Conferences were a supra-corporate form of horizontal network. They were designed to restrain price and some aspects of service competition, but they also provided a framework for shaping relations between shipowners and merchants.

Many of the major British shipping groups that appeared in the early twentieth century became broadly diversified entities. In addition to their vertical links, some of the "Big Five" expanded into "support" industries, such as insurance, investment and banking, as well as into some businesses unrelated to shipping.[14] Furness Withy held many small investments in mining firms, car manufacturers, newspapers, taxi operators and chemical companies to name a few, most of which were conveyed from its founder and his personal allies. These transfers were intended to release liquidity in personal portfolios, and some of the investments were subsequently sold to other units within the group for the same purpose, indicating that the holding company framework operated

---

[12]*Ibid.*, 260; Peter N. Davies and A.M. Bourn, "Lord Kylsant and the Royal Mail," *Business History*, XIV, No. 2 (1972), 103-123; and Edwin Green and Michael S. Moss, *A Business of National Importance: The Royal Mail Shipping Group, 1902-1937* (London, 1982).

[13]Boyce, *Information, Mediation*, 97-104.

[14]As a result of acquisitions during the prewar boom, P&O, Royal Mail Steam Packet Co., Ellerman Lines, Cunard Steamships and Furness Withy and Co. emerged as Britain's largest liner firms.

as a quasi-internalized capital market. Some smaller firms developed broadly diversified interests – Bowring, Swire and Booth in particular – by levering operating information to tap new business opportunities. Just before and after World War II, over a dozen shipping firms entered or tried to enter the airline business. In this instance, their links with government departments were of major importance.[15]

Shipowners were well known for their public service and their ties with government officials and departments. Furness was a Member of Parliament for fifteen years, Lord Runciman was President of the Board of Trade and Lord Inchcape served on numerous high-level government committees. Lord Inverclyde forged what Francis Hyde called "a virtual partnership" between Cunard Steamship and the government which his successor, Sir Percy Bates, strengthened.[16] Sir Alfred Jones was on close terms with the Colonial Office, and Sir William Mackinnon had wide-ranging ties with colonial and imperial governments.[17] These links arose because shipping was a strategic industry for the empire. Apart from contracting to provide mail services, shipowners secured agreements to carry troops, indentured labour, government stores and personnel. Premier passenger lines, including Cunard, White Star, P&O and Union-Castle, entered into Admiralty subvention agreements wherein they agreed to make their fast vessels available to the government in times of national emergency in return for an annual payment.[18] Britain's major liner operators provided the transport and communication channels needed to bind the official empire (and much of the informal empire as well). During the world wars, ties between shipowners and government departments drew even closer. When decolonization took place following the second global conflict, these ties proved disadvantageous when former colonies fostered the growth of their own shipping industries at the expense of British operators. New Zealand and Nigeria nationalized airlines formed by British shipping firms.

Nevertheless, in forming these valuable channels with official circles, shipowners were assisted by their dramatic social and economic mobility. Indeed, William Rubinstein found that of all occupational groups, shipowners

---

[15]Gordon H. Boyce, "Strategic Diversification: British Ship Owners Entering the Airline Business, 1920-80," forthcoming.

[16]Francis E. Hyde, *Cunard and the North Atlantic, 1840-1973: A History of Shipping and Financial Management* (London, 1975), 147.

[17]Peter N. Davies, *The Trade Makers: Elder Dempster in West Africa, 1852-1972, 1973-1989* (Liverpool, 1973; New ed., St. John's, 2000); and J. Forbes Munro, *Maritime Enterprise and Empire: Sir William Mackinnon and His Business Empire, 1823-1893* (Woodbridge, 2003).

[18]Boyce, *Information, Mediation*, 114-117.

achieved the greatest wealth and the most titles.[19] Their notable rise helped them gain access to high-level sources of information which expanded their business opportunities. Many shipowners rose to the peerage and adopted aristocratic lifestyles, in the process gaining public renown and enhanced reputations. Their growing stature enabled them to open up a wider range of financial facilities, including bank loans, stock flotations and private lines of credit. Many shipowners, including Furness, Inchcape, Bates and Ellerman to name but a few, joined the boards of major British banks, insurance firms, railways and other important public companies.[20] As they did so their sources of information widened, their networks expanded and their reputations grew further. Social and economic mobility were interlinked and mutually reinforcing.

One salient advantage that rising in society and business conferred upon shipowners was enhanced intermediary capabilities. Early steam shipping enterprise depended upon such brokering capabilities, but shipowners who achieved considerable business success, public renown and growing acceptance by political and social elites could operate on a grander scale in arranging deals between parties who knew the intermediary but lacked direct knowledge of each other and therefore had no basis of trust to facilitate a transaction.[21] In terms of formal network theory, such men achieved greater "centrality" within their networks and came to occupy positions as "nodes" within the mesh of communication channels. For example, the second Lord Inverclyde and Sir Percy Bates were adept brokers, and Sir John Ellerman was a noteworthy intermediary who exploited opportunities in such unrelated businesses as real estate and brewing.[22] Although they lacked the public profiles of the aforementioned businessmen, several leaders of John Swire and Sons brokered a series of new ventures in unrelated fields, including sugar refining, paint manufacturing and airlines. These intermediary operations created new communication channels and played a key role in mobilizing specialized commercial, procedural and technical knowledge that was vital to the success of projects in businesses that lay beyond their core shipping expertise.

---

[19]William D. Rubenstein, *Men of Property: The Very Wealthy in Britain since the Industrial Revolution* (London, 1981; 2nd rev. ed., London, 2006), 62-65.

[20]Boyce, *Information, Mediation*, 291-311.

[21]Mark C. Casson, *Information and Organization: A New Perspective on the Theory of the Firm* (Oxford, 1997).

[22]James Taylor, *Ellerman's: A Wealth of Shipping* (London, 1972); and Hyde, *Cunard and the North Atlantic*.

Network Structure

Recent theoretical work on networks has explored the knowledge-handling capabilities and internal dynamics of these cooperative frameworks. The foundation for much of this inquiry was laid in a highly influential essay by Mark Granovetter, who distinguished between two types of network links.[23] "Strong ties" are based upon high levels of trust derived from interpersonal knowledge, shared values, similar patterns of cognition and common procedural tendencies and routines. By contrast, "weak ties" do not exhibit the same degree of interpersonal, cultural or cognitive intimacy.

Reflecting these characteristics, strong and weak ties convey different quantities and types of information and knowledge.[24] What Robert Burt called the "bandwidth effects" refers to the greater volume of transmissions among those who have strong ties because close social/psychological affiliation generates more exchanges than weak ties.[25] Further, more "redundant intelligence" (familiar facts) circulates between those with strong ties. People joined by weak ties communicate less frequently, but in comparison with those linked by strong ties, their exchanges contain relatively large amounts of "novel information" derived from different social, cultural or business backgrounds that generate distinctive knowledge sets.

Within networks consisting mainly of strong ties, "conventions of etiquette" and "echo effects" tend to promote a common outlook and, in extreme cases, "group think." Thus, conventions of etiquette, which reflect a desire for inclusion, induce members of the same group, who know each others' predispositions, to agree with one another, thereby reinforcing existing predispositions. In contrast, members bound by weak links are less aware of each other's predispositions and are more likely to transmit novel information or insights

---

[23]Granovetter, "Economic Action."

[24]Information and knowledge may be distinguished as follows. Information is a "flux" of impressions concerning the world. Knowledge consists of information that is "pinned down" by being organized and attached to a context shaped by existing knowledge and wider social/cultural forces. Knowledge constantly generates both new information and new knowledge as new impressions are received. Bernard Ancori, Antoine Bureth and Patrick Cohendet, "The Economics of Knowledge: The Debate about Codification and Tacit Knowledge," *Industrial and Corporate Change*, IX, No. 2 (2000), 255-288; and Robin Cowan and Dominique Foray, "The Economics of Codification and the Diffusion of Knowledge," *Industrial and Corporate Change*, VI, No. 3 (1997), 595-622.

[25]Ronald S. Burt, "Bandwidth and Echo: Trust, Information and Gossip in Social Networks," in James E. Rauch and Alessandra Casella (eds.), *Networks and Markets: Contributions from Economics and Sociology* (New York, 2001), 30-75.

derived from a different perspective that may challenge preconceptions and generate learning.

Similarly, new ideas arise when "structural holes," or gaps between network nodes, are bridged.[26] Nodes consist of people or firms who occupy central positions within networks characterized by numerous dyadic links which may be strong or weak. When nodal figures in different networks bridge structural holes, very novel information is transmitted. This highly novel information is more stimulating than that conveyed by weak ties, since it is derived from the knowledge base of another entire network rather than just an individual member. Although some filtering of information occurs as nodal members "translate" novel information into terms understandable to members of the receiving network, the impact is likely to be significant.

Weak ties, and more importantly bridged structural holes, may generate ideas that "initiate" innovative proposals.[27] In contrast, the strong ties that typically link members of the receiving network are likely to facilitate the "execution" of an innovative strategy. Thus, after novel information enters a network and is translated for members, their bonds of trust and shared cognitive patterns tend to promote commitment, resource mobilization and coordination.

The preceding discussion suggests a number of themes for examination. First, recent theoretical work does not consider how strong ties arise in the first place. Some initial investigation has exposed how inter-generational socialization occurred and the efficiency properties of common cognitive frames that arose between maritime entrepreneurs bound by strong ties, but bandwidth effects and conventions of etiquette await examination.[28] Second, the literature does not clearly distinguish between the different types of information and knowledge flowing through the various network ties. Although

---

[26]Ronald S. Burt, *Structural Holes: The Social Structure of Competition* (Cambridge, MA, 1992); and Burt, "Structural Holes and Good Ideas," *American Journal of Sociology*, CX, No. 2 (2004), 349-399.

[27]Samuel MacAulay, "Tuning Biotechnology Landscapes to Enhance Innovation Performance: The Case of Network Structure, Information Density and Innovation Performance with the Brisbane Biotechnology Industry" (Unpublished Honours thesis, Queensland University of Technology, 2005).

[28]Socialization processes that unfolded across different generations of the Bates family are examined in Gordon H. Boyce, "Language, Family, Diversions, and Socially Constructed Reality in the Merchant-Shipowning Community: The Bates of Liverpool, 1870-1945" (paper presented to the Business History Conference, Cleveland, Ohio, 2007). For a consideration of routines that conditioned negotiations between shipowners and shipbuilders who were members of the same networks, see Boyce, "Network Knowledge and Network Routines: Negotiating Activities between Shipowners and Shipbuilders," *Business History*, XLV, No. 2 (2003), 52-76.

some preliminary work has been done, particularly in assessing information quality, the rich empirical data available to shipping historians may be used to delineate more clearly the boundary between novel and redundant information.[29] Third, dynamics may be important; thus, network ties may change over time, for example weak ties may become strong ones. Again, the sources we use may show how "outsiders" become socialized to emerge as "inside" network members. Correspondence may support an assessment of the extent to which transmissions of novel information abate as a result. Fourth, are there any counterparts to etiquette or echo effects for weak ties? What conventions influence brokering activities? Finally, broker-induced translating and filtering need further exposition, and the widespread intermediation used within the shipping industry may yield insights. These concerns are important in showing how network activities changed and how diversification occurred within the shipping industry, since they address the issue of how growth occurs when specific types of knowledge cross social, cognitive or organizational boundaries.[30]

New Tools

In the last ten years, a number of powerful software programmes have been developed specifically to assist with network analysis. To mention one system, "Inflow" is adept at measurement and graphic representation. Scholars can use it to depict different types of ties, to identify nodes and to map the overall structure of a network as a preliminary to comparison. The software can also measure the centrality of individual nodes based upon the extent of their connections with other members. It supports the analysis of clusters and can be used to measure the ratio of insiders to outsiders.

"NVIVO" is particularly useful in analyzing qualitative data such as correspondence and reports. The researcher enters the text and then codes passages according to different themes or topics. While coding is time consuming, the software can be used to organize text in ways that generate more powerful insights than is possible by "manual" handling. NVIVO can organize themes hierarchically and has powerful search capabilities that facilitate comparisons and contrasts. It is especially valuable in exposing unexpected connections between concepts.

---

[29]Gordon Boyce and Larry J. Lepper, "Assessing Information Quality Theories: The USSCo Joint Venture with William Holyman and Sons and Huddart Parker Ltd., 1904-35," *Business History*, XLIV, No. 4 (2002), 85-120.

[30]For an exploration of some of these concerns, see Boyce, "Networks, Tacit Knowledge and Innovation," in Jacques-Marie Aurifeille, Serge Svizzero and Clement A. Tisdell (eds.), *Globalization and Business Partnerships: Features of Business Alliances and International Cooperation* (Paris, 2006), 47-59.

NVIVO can be used for straightforward content analysis (counting the number of references to a particular topic) and for gauging the relative importance of specific themes (by measuring the percentage of the entire text devoted to an individual subject). The software can be used to develop correspondence "maps," genealogical tables and organizational charts. It is especially helpful in analyzing longitudinal change, for example in showing how concepts evolve over time. Finally, the software has a range of drawing capabilities. All these properties make it particularly valuable in supporting analyses of network culture, social forces and cognitive frames.

Conclusion

This paper has provided a brief overview of recent developments in network theory and measurement in the hope of sharpening future analysis of organizations in the maritime sector. The aim is to suggest a way for scholars of shipping to attract a wider audience among historians of business and especially service sector industries, as well as management scientists. This endeavour can be furthered not only by considering contexts in which cooperative frameworks thrived but also more challenging circumstances, such as those prevailing in the interwar period, when adverse demand conditions and debt-induced gridlocks tested the adaptability of these structures. Similarly, explaining why network organizations collapsed and brought down related industrial complexes will enhance our understanding of their vulnerabilities.

With rich empirical data and new computing capabilities at their disposal, shipping historians are well positioned to extend network theory and to develop new insights firmly grounded in a specific social and business context. As a group, we can develop international comparisons of business practices and structures as well as social/cultural contexts. Our subject matter is a valuable resource for examining the operation of formal and informal structures in a global arena.

Printed and bound by CPI Group (UK) Ltd, Croydon, CR0 4YY

16/04/2025

14658578-0002